IMAGES
of America

ANDREW COUNTY
A RURAL WAY OF LIFE

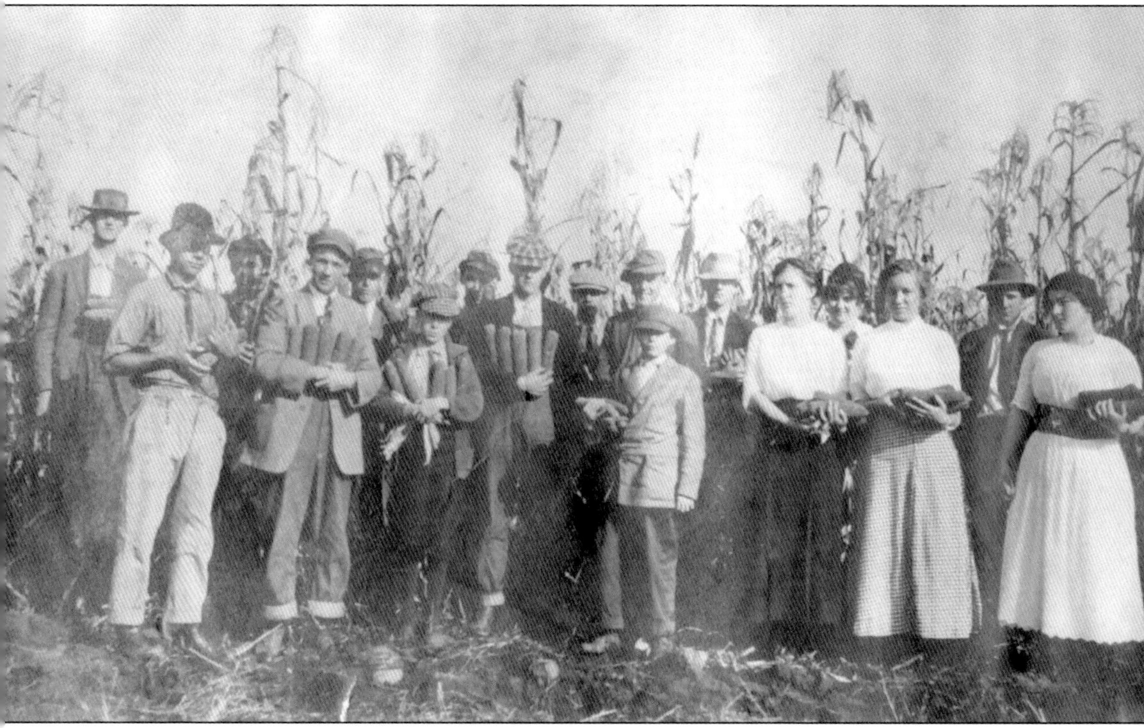

In this c. 1915 image, students in the agricultural class at Fillmore High School display their harvested corn. (Courtesy of the Andrew County Museum and Historical Society.)

On the Cover: In 1915, a professional photographer created this image of the Andrew County Courthouse in Savannah, Missouri. The courthouse was the most elaborate local landmark in this county seat. (Courtesy of the Andrew County Museum and Historical Society.)

IMAGES
of America

Andrew County
A Rural Way of Life

Andrew County Museum and Historical Society

ARCADIA
PUBLISHING

ISBN 978-0-7385-9115-5

Published by Arcadia Publishing
Charleston, South Carolina

Printed in the United States of America

Library of Congress Control Number: 2011937612

For all general information, please contact Arcadia Publishing:
Telephone 843-853-2070
Fax 843-853-0044
E-mail sales@arcadiapublishing.com
For customer service and orders:
Toll-Free 1-888-313-2665

Visit us on the Internet at www.arcadiapublishing.com

For the people of Andrew County, whose generous contributions to their museum's collections made this publication possible.

Contents

Acknowledgments

In *Main Street on the Middle Border* (1954), Missouri historian Lewis Atherton explored the history of Midwestern small towns and the farm families they served. Among Atherton's conclusions, he determined that rural people viewed the world through the prism of the "cult of the useful and practical." They evaluated social and business activities based on the practical good for a town and the contributions to the larger community's financial health.

Nevertheless, Atherton stressed that cultural aspirations were not entirely discouraged on the "Middle Border." Local libraries, for example, were widely supported as symbols of culture, providing an interface with the outside world of ideas.

In 2009, the citizens of Andrew County demonstrated that rural people were active participants in the exchange of ideas about the evolution of American history and culture. With the opening of the 4,000-square-foot exhibit "A Rural Way of Life: Andrew County, Missouri," these citizens made it evident that the outside world had much to learn from the history of Midwestern towns and farms.

Andrew Countians contributed to the creation of *A Rural Way of Life* and continue to support their county museum's operation. Equally importantly, they donated the artifacts and images needed to make the exhibit a reality. The extraordinary collection of photographs in this publication testifies to the commitment of rural Andrew Countians to preserving their heritage.

The rural life exhibit resulted from the dedication and hard work of dozens of museum volunteers, staff, and board members. For advice, support, and preparing images for this publication, special thanks go to curator Jess Rezac and collections volunteer Carole Johnson. Appreciation is also extended to Kathy Ridge and Danny Sybert. The guidance of Elizabeth Bray, our editor at Arcadia Publishing, through the production process is also most gratefully appreciated.

The images in this volume appear courtesy of the Andrew County Museum and Historical Society.

INTRODUCTION

In his book, *It's A Small Town If . . .* (2005), Sam Breck wrote, "They're writing obituaries for small towns. The nation's heavy thinkers—the sociologists, psychologists, and assorted other –ologists—are doom saying, predicting that the American small town is a goner. We'd better act soon, they imply, and use some government money to preserve our towns in museums."

It is remarkable how often scholars observe that the majority of Americans think of small towns as "museum pieces." Lacking both economies of scale and the cultural sophistication found in cities, so the argument goes, these communities appear destined for a place on an extinct species list. They simply cannot adjust to the changes that began with America's shift toward becoming an urban-industrial nation. Small-town values and perceptions appear antiquated in the 21st-century era of globalization.

The "heavy thinkers" Breck took issue with embraced the viewpoint of novelists like Sinclair Lewis who engaged in a "revolt from the village" in the 1920s. Admittedly, there is a countervailing opinion called the "myth of the small town." Compared to cities, small-town people lived life on a human scale, neighbors looked out for neighbors, and communities remained connected to the countryside, which was dotted with family farms.

The aim of this publication is to present images that reflect the history of rural life "on the farm" and "in town" from the 1840s into the 21st century. Both "myths" and "revolts" play a part in that story, but neither term alone adequately describes rural life.

Over time, rural people have proved to be resilient and adaptable when faced with change. In Andrew County, for example, farmers transitioned from subsistence to diversified agriculture, eventually specializing in just a few row crops; changes largely resulted from evolving agricultural technology. In Andrew County, the era of plowing with horses or mules and threshing with steam-traction engines was supplanted by the use of gasoline-powered tractors and massive combines. The size of family farms dramatically increased over the course of a century, as larger tracts of land were required to justify investments in modern farm technology.

In rural areas, however, technological advances sometimes produced surprising results. In Andrew County, power companies heralded the benefits of rural electrification, especially for farm wives. The following pages contain images of Ida Eisiminger, who was presented with a wide range of "laborsaving" electrical appliances, ranging from a waffle iron to an electric range. Power companies sought to affect the lives of rural women, transforming them into homemakers just like their big-city sisters.

However, in *Entitled to Power: Farm Women and Technology, 1913–1963* (1993), historian Katherine Jellison notes that rural women demurred from accepting the role of solely being a housewife. In the Midwest, there was a long tradition of women working on the farm. In addition to tending a kitchen and garden and raising chickens, women worked in the fields when needed; their roles expanded with the evolution of farm technology. The Andrew County Museum collections contain several images of women on tractors. This publication also includes a photograph of

Lorena and Everett Schindler on a combine, with their son Curtis behind the wheel of a tractor. Such images serve as evidence to support Jellison's conclusion that rural women sought to remain "farm producers" regardless of the direction their duties as homemakers might evolve.

For both farm families and townspeople, the 20th century brought technological innovations credited with breaking down rural isolation, including radio, motion pictures, and television. In Andrew County, rural people embraced these new communications technologies. In the 1930s and 1940s, most radio programs were produced and broadcast from major cities, and historians credit radio with introducing rural people to urban-based popular culture.

The same has been argued about the movies. The Globe Theatre, Savannah's first motion picture house, opened in 1914. Almost immediately, the Globe began to advertise a "Matinee for Country People." Above this headline, an illustration featuring stereotypical country folk showed them marching toward the theater entrance. Grandpa urged his spouse to "hurry on ma," with her replying, "I'm coming." (See page 119 for a peek at the illustration.) The Globe's proprietor noted that, for the convenience of those living in the country, a "continuous moving picture show" would be offered every Saturday afternoon. For farm families, Saturday was typically the day to come to town to shop and socialize. Local merchants quickly realized that motion pictures provided a draw for potential customers, so they began to sponsor free Saturday matinees.

In 1938, the New Globe Theatre opened. It was designed by a Kansas City architect who specialized in movie houses. The theater was promoted as "modernistic," with many features found in urban picture palaces. It is worth noting, however, that a recurrent theme in movies shown at Savannah theaters in the 1920s and 1930s centered on the triumph of wholesome small-town values over big-city wickedness. The major studios recognized that rural people constituted part of the "mass" in American mass culture, and country people sitting in theaters like the Globe influenced the content of screenplays and the world of ideas.

Over the last 50 years, many small towns have had a rough time. Automobile ownership expanded the range of shopping and entertainment opportunities for rural residents, resulting in the decline of many downtowns. Local businessmen, imbued with an unadulterated booster spirit, once formed the leadership group in any town. As early as 1934, in the pages of his *American Mercury* magazine, H.L. Mencken noted a changing mood. In an article that posed the question, "Are Small Towns Doomed?" he concluded, "Where once a healthy activity could be noted one now observes a dull lethargy. There are few people on the streets; the store fronts look discouraged and uninviting. Upon the faces of merchants and business men has settled a dull apathy to replace the once bright eagerness. The old confidence, the old expectancy have vanished."

In 2005, Breck answered Mencken's question differently in *It's A Small Town If . . .* (originally subtitled *A Field Guide for Midwesterners and Those Who'd Like to be One*) when he insisted, "The small town is as alive as anyplace. It simply lacks the exhaust, the noise, and the squeeze-and-shove lifestyles that are epidemic in larger places." Ironically, some urbanites seeking escape from those lifestyles find country life increasingly attractive. In a 1983 *Time* magazine essay titled "Welcome to Ruburbia," J.D. Reed wrote about the impact of expatriate urbanites on their new environment, asking, "Where is this curious landscape of clashing images, this zone of hay and Harvard graduates, of pigs and Porsches, of pancake breakfasts and imported cheeses? This is ruburbia, a geographical mezzanine between the rural and the suburban."

Breck encouraged his readers to park their cars on a main street, then walk around and learn about a small town. For current and past residents of Andrew County or potential future "ruburbanites," this book offers an invitation to get out and learn about the history of rural life in town and on the farm. Some of the people one will meet qualify as great storytellers full of surprising tales.

One

Farm Is Family

Family farming has been the mainstay of Andrew County agriculture from the 1840s into the 21st century; however, the size of farm families changed. Families with as many as 12 children were common in the 1800s and early 1900s, when youngsters were needed to work a farm. Boys usually assisted their fathers in the fields and with the livestock. Girls helped their mothers gather eggs and churn butter. Both girls and boys milked cows and tended the garden. Until the 1940s, children often missed school because they needed to help with farm chores. Some children—most often boys—had to quit school because of farm workloads. In 1988, Clyde Bowlin remembered, "Our father, born in 1868, was removed from school at the third-grade level. He was needed to help with the farm work."

Tractors and other innovations lessened the need for children's work on the farm. As a result, family sizes were reduced and the total number of farm families declined. The families that remained frequently passed their farms from one generation to another, adding additional acreage purchased from those who had left for jobs in larger towns or cities. Average farm size increased from 117 acres in 1880 to 274 in 1992, with 46 of Andrew County's 830 farms topping 1,000 acres and another 119 farms measuring 500 acres or more. These highly mechanized operations focused on one or two agricultural products such as corn and soybeans. In 1991, Crystal Schweizer Adkins, who grew up on an Andrew County farm, observed that families once raised cattle, sheep, hogs, chickens, turkeys, ducks, geese, corn, hay, wheat, and oats. By the 1960s, this diversified form of agriculture was coming to an end.

Changes in the nature of farm production affected the work patterns of farm families. By 1950, children still did chores, but school became their first priority. Many women also shifted focus and began taking jobs in town to contribute to the family income. Most men continued to work the land, but if extra income was needed, they also took on nonfarm work.

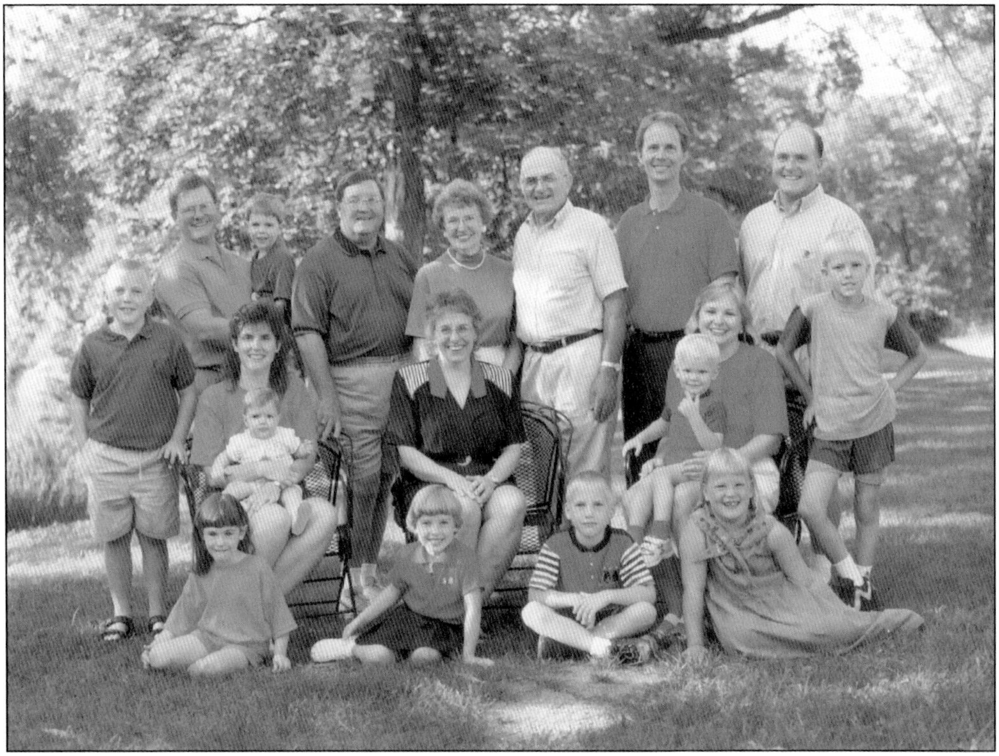

The Hegeman family has farmed in Andrew County since the 1840s. In 1996, Joan and Don Hegeman (third row, center) posed with their children and grandchildren. In 1976, the Hegemans were one of 97 families whose agricultural roots extended back at least 100 years and who worked on a Missouri-certified "Centennial Farm."

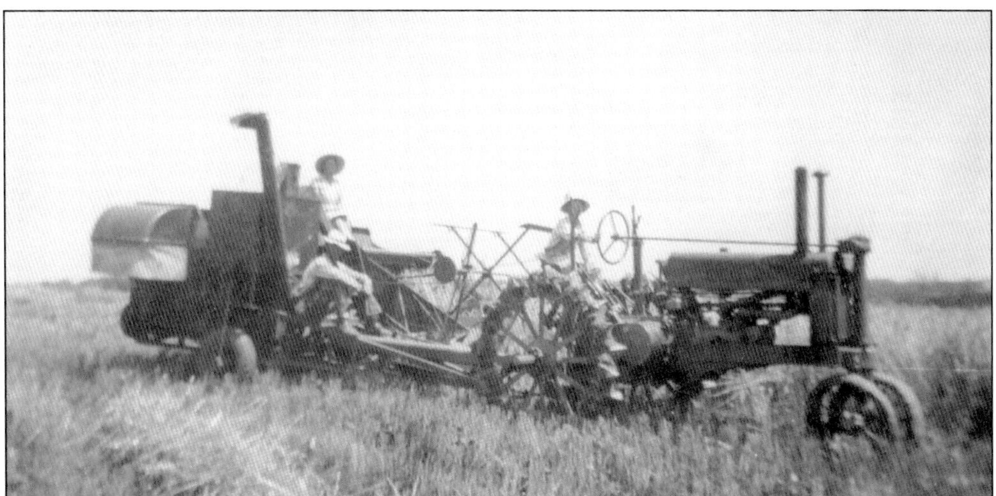

In 1941, Lorena and Everett Schindler and their son Curtis harvested wheat using a combine and tractor. At harvest time, every able-bodied family member worked the fields. In 1980, Marceline Simerly observed that her farm was also a family operation, "with the men in the field and the women either with them, running errands for them, or on the road with the trucks hauling the grain to market."

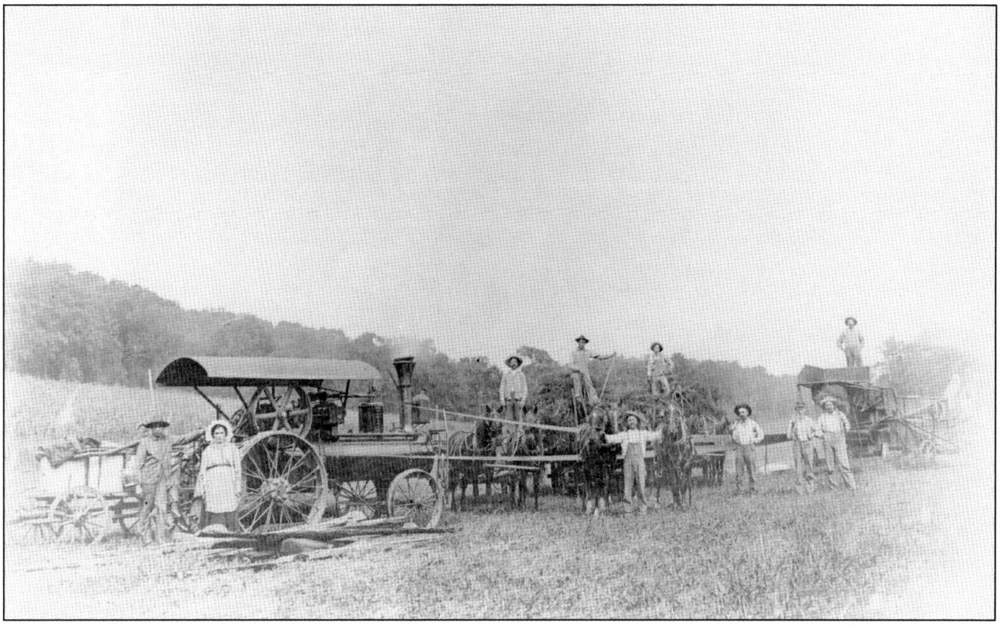

Like many farm women, Pearl Tipton White went out to the fields when an extra hand was needed. In this c. 1915 photograph, she stands next to a traction steam engine providing power to a threshing machine. The members of the threshing crew are, from left to right, Cleat Tipton, Pearl Tipton White, Bill Hatcher, Grover Davis, Ike Todd, Arva Davis, Tom Tipton, W.P. Davis, Jessie Walker, and Marion Clorer Huller.

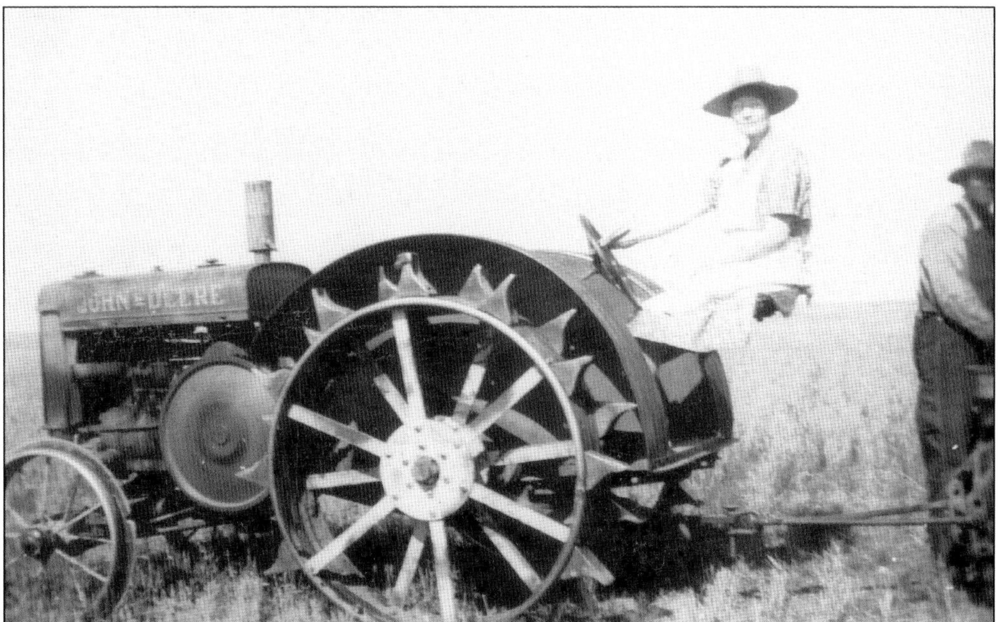

This photograph of an unidentified woman on a John Deere tractor likely dates from the 1930s. She is wearing a light-colored dress, white apron, and wide-brimmed hat. The mechanization of agriculture greatly enhanced the ability of women to be farm producers, a role they valued and sought to maintain.

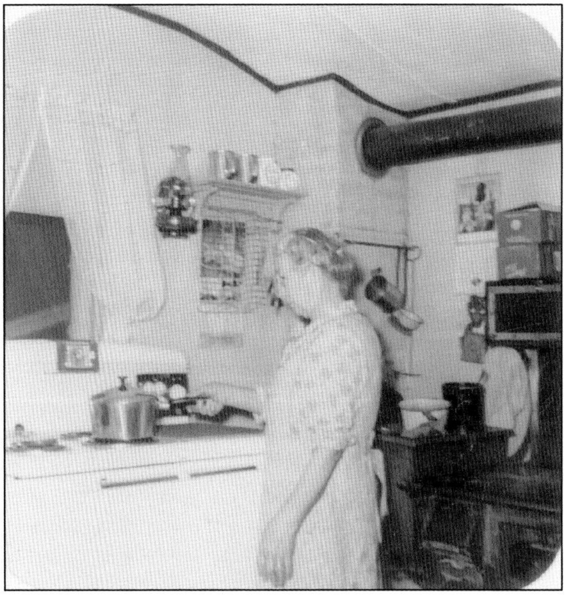

Rural electric service finally reached the home of Ida Eisiminger around 1950. The Rural Electric Administration, along with most power companies, actively promoted the benefits of bringing electric service to country people, especially farm wives. Probably as part of a promotional effort, Eisiminger's home was filled with modern laborsaving devices, both large and small. She is pictured at left cooking on her new electric stove, although it was reported that Eisiminger much preferred her old coal- or wood-burning Majestic stove. A number of other, smaller electrical appliances in her kitchen are pictured below, including an iron, a fan, a waffle iron, a heater, and a toaster.

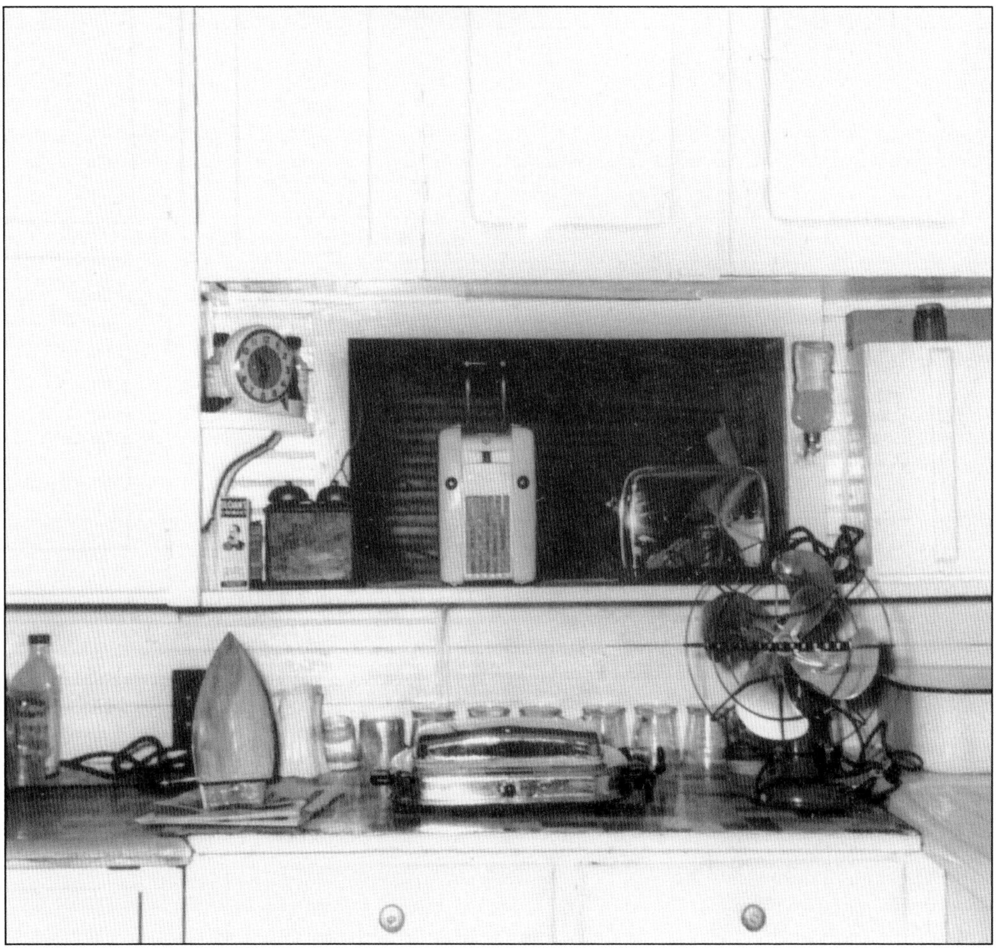

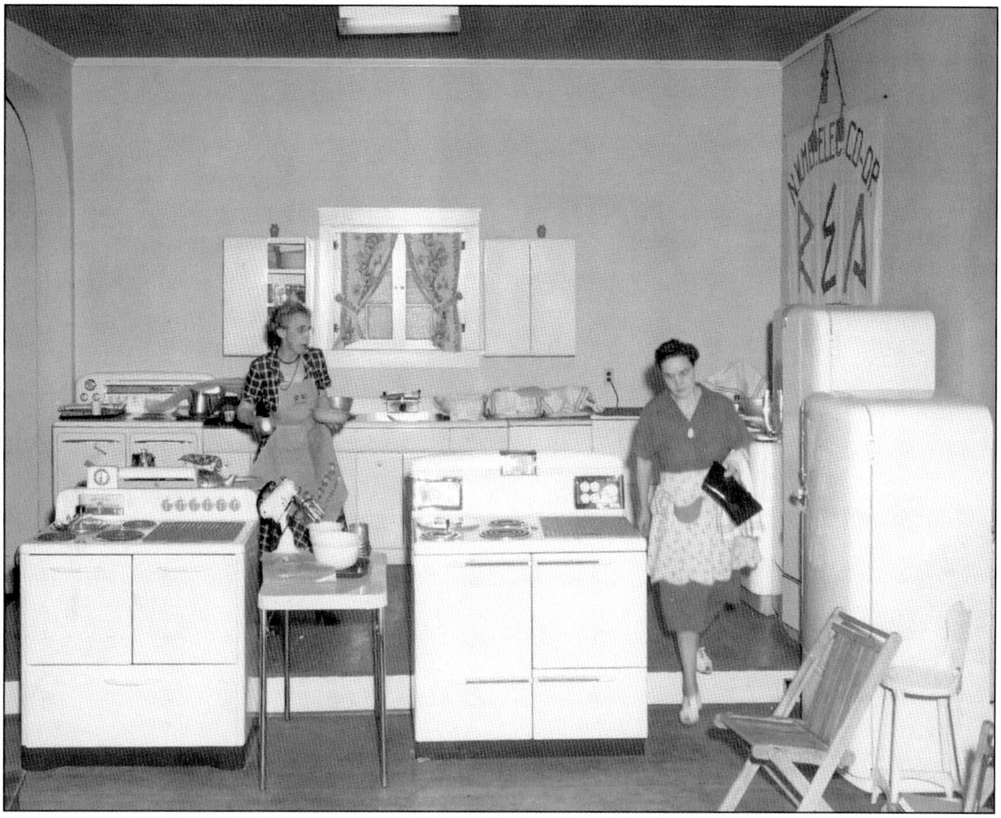

Many local residents learned about electrically powered consumer goods at programs and meetings of the Northwest Missouri Electric Cooperative. These two images probably date from the 1950s. In the electric kitchen display shown above, two women demonstrate three electric stoves and two refrigerators. A veritable carousel of progress, featuring small appliances including an electric coffeepot, Dutch oven, mixer, and electric knife, dominates the foreground of the photograph at right. An appeal is also made to the abiding affection for power tools among the men in the audience, with an electric drill and power saw placed on the carousel alongside the kitchen appliances.

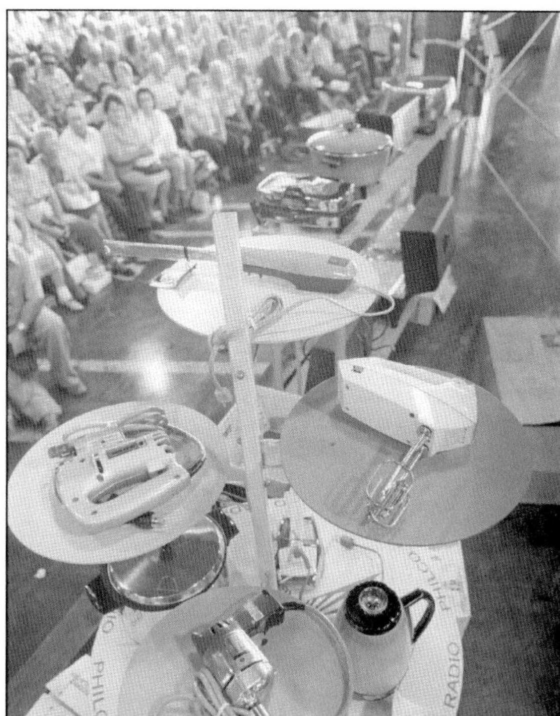

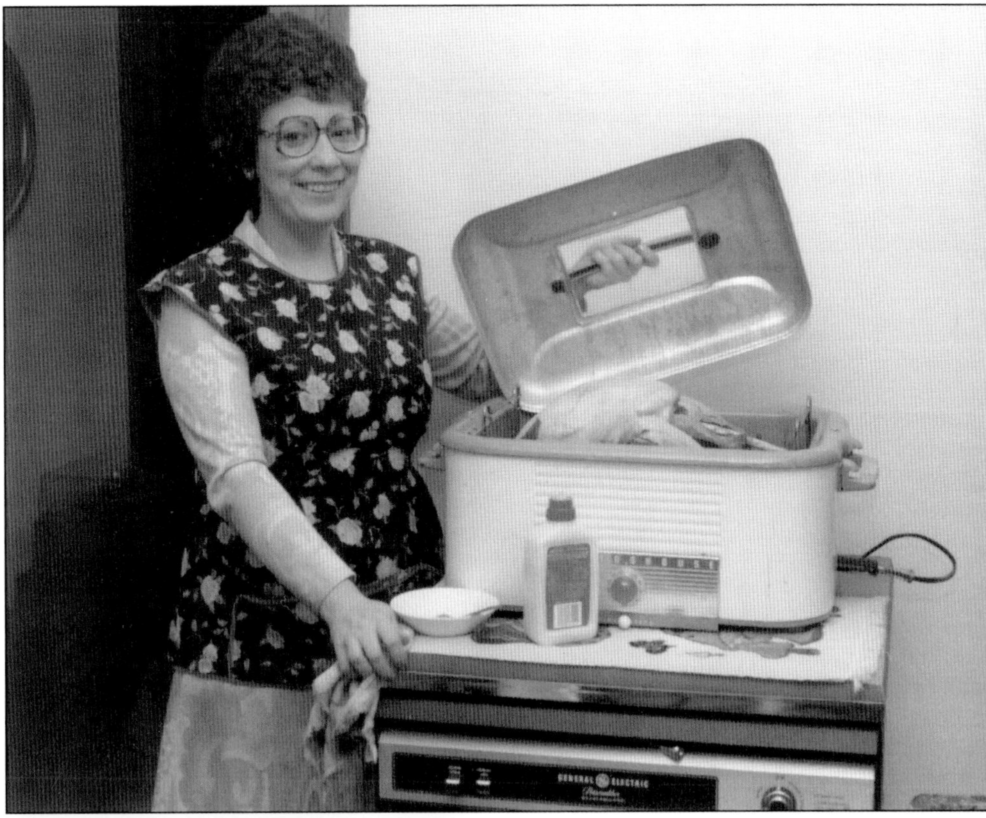

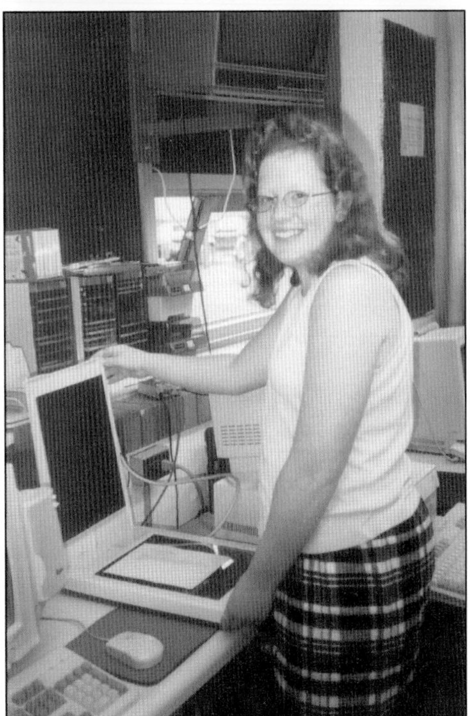

These late-20th-century images illustrate the impact of changing technology on women's work both at home and in the office. In the above image, Bonnie Rudolf holds the lid of an electric roaster sitting atop a portable dishwasher. The image at left depicts Christy Hendrix in an office setting that includes computers and a scanner. For many women, the workweek has increased with work outside the home. Ironically, despite dubbing modern appliances as "laborsaving," historians have discovered that the amount of time women spend on domestic chores has not decreased over several generations. Roasters and other appliances encouraged women to spend more time in the kitchen as recipe choices expanded, while electric dishwashers and washing machines resulted in increasingly frequent chores.

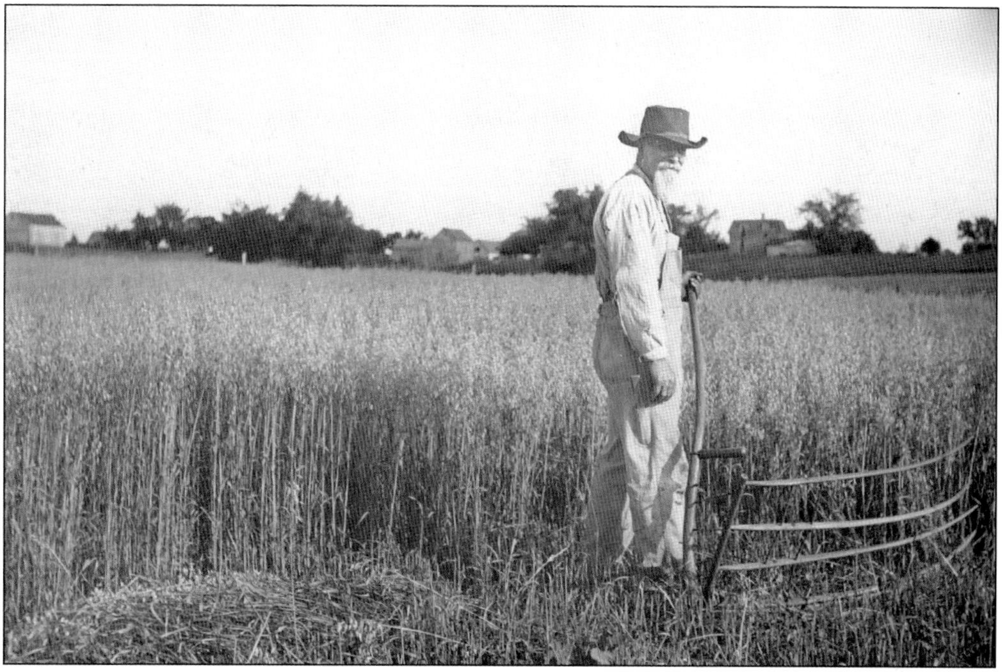

These images illustrate the dramatic changes in farm technology over the course of the 20th century. James Harvey Goforth was born in 1849 and died in 1935. He came to Bolckow, Missouri, in 1881 and operated a flour mill. From 1910 to 1935, Goforth had a truck and dairy farm; in the 1915 photograph above, he is in his mid-60s, holding a cradle scythe used to harvest grain. By then, most farmers had shifted to mechanized agriculture. In contrast to Goforth, Nelson Kapp is pictured below in the 1940s, cultivating corn with his Allis-Chalmers tractor.

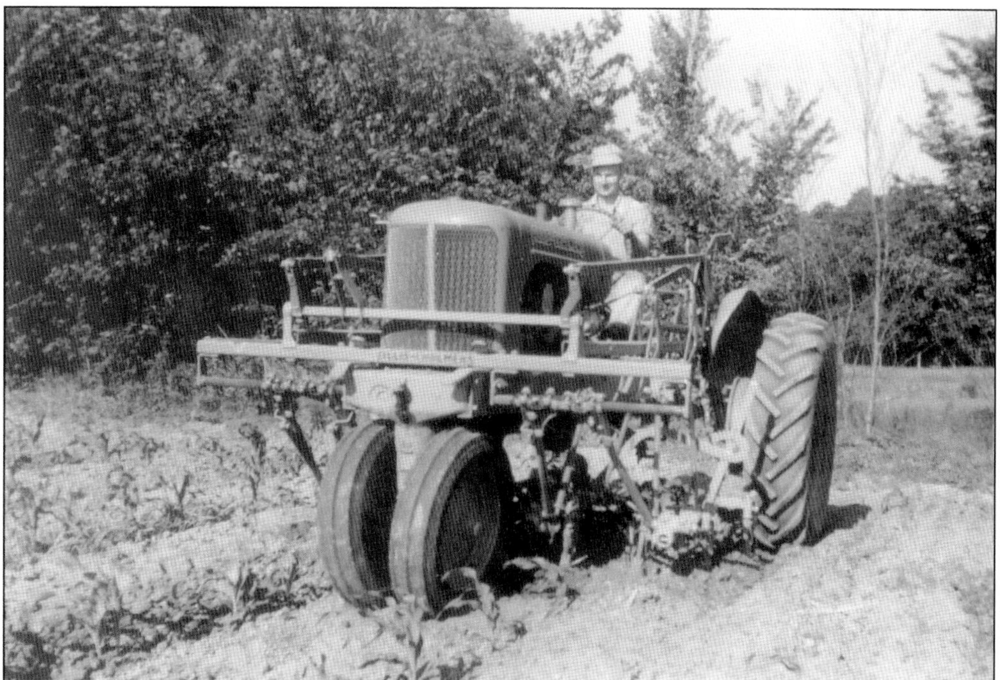

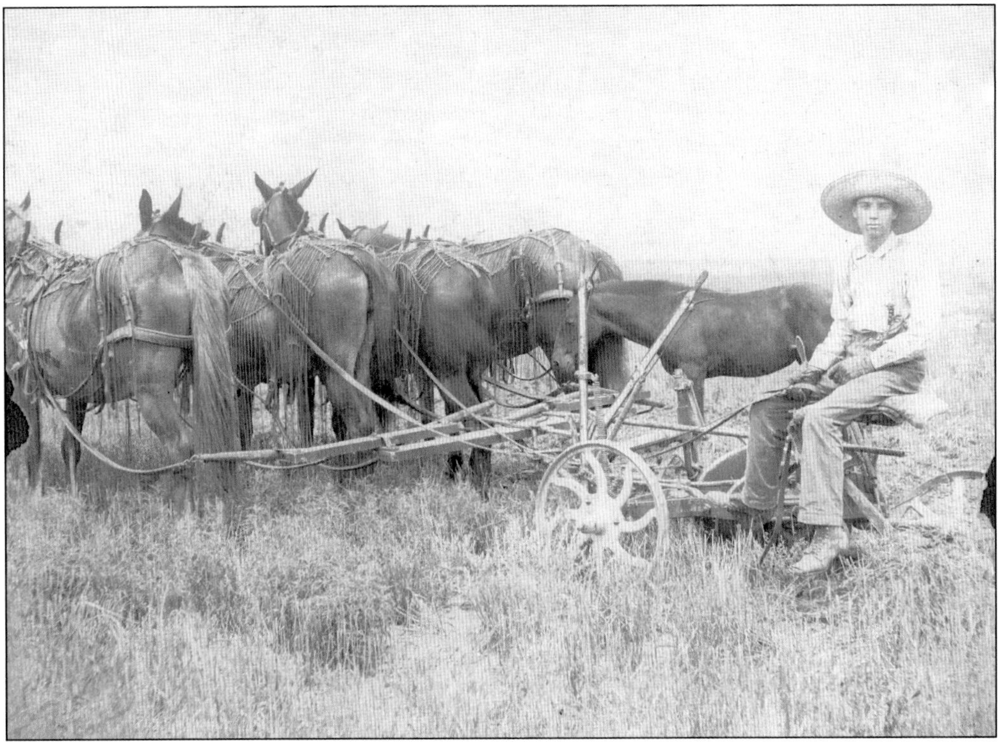

In the late 19th and early 20th centuries, mule- and horsepower largely drove Andrew County agriculture. In the photograph above, young Edd Tice sits on a mule-drawn plow. In the 1936 image below, Carl M. Eisiminger plows with a team of four horses. During the Great Depression, the shift to gasoline-powered tractors could be halting and slow in Andrew County and other rural areas. Robert A. Townsend remembered that horse-powered fieldwork proved "a tedious chore" involving plowing, a one-row drill, a walking cultivator to pull weeds, and a binder to harvest the grain.

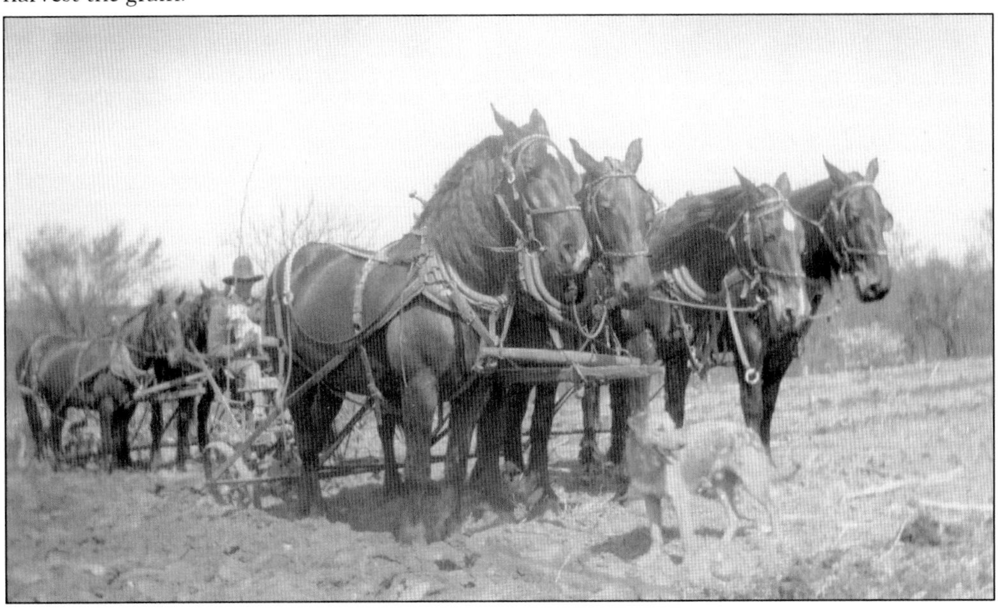

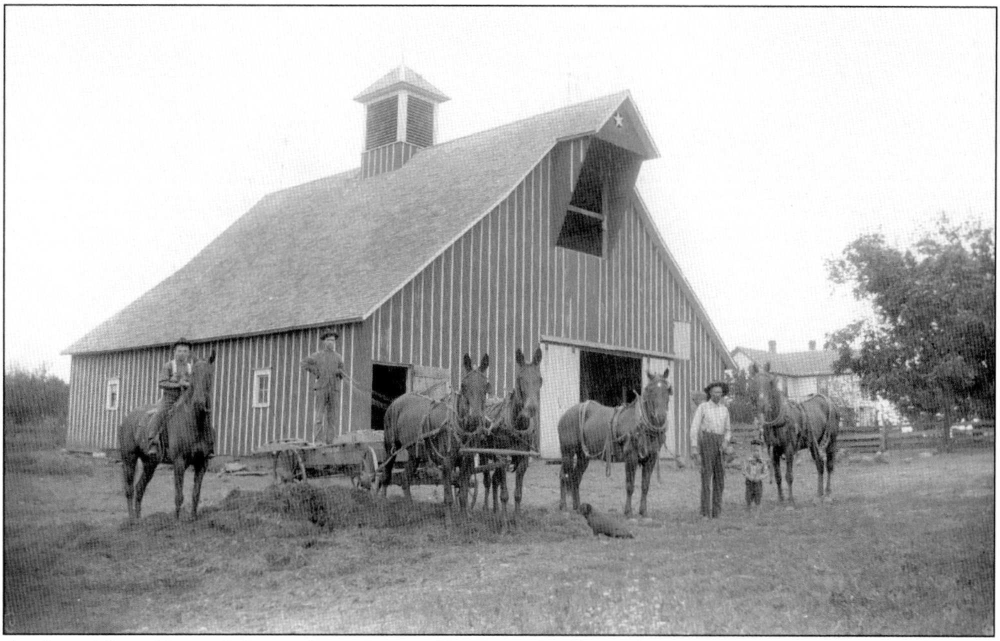

Andrew Blair (far right) stands in front of his barn holding the reins of two horses with his son by his side in this c. 1900 image. At left, an unidentified man holds the reins of a team of mules pulling a wagon, while another unidentified individual sits on a horse.

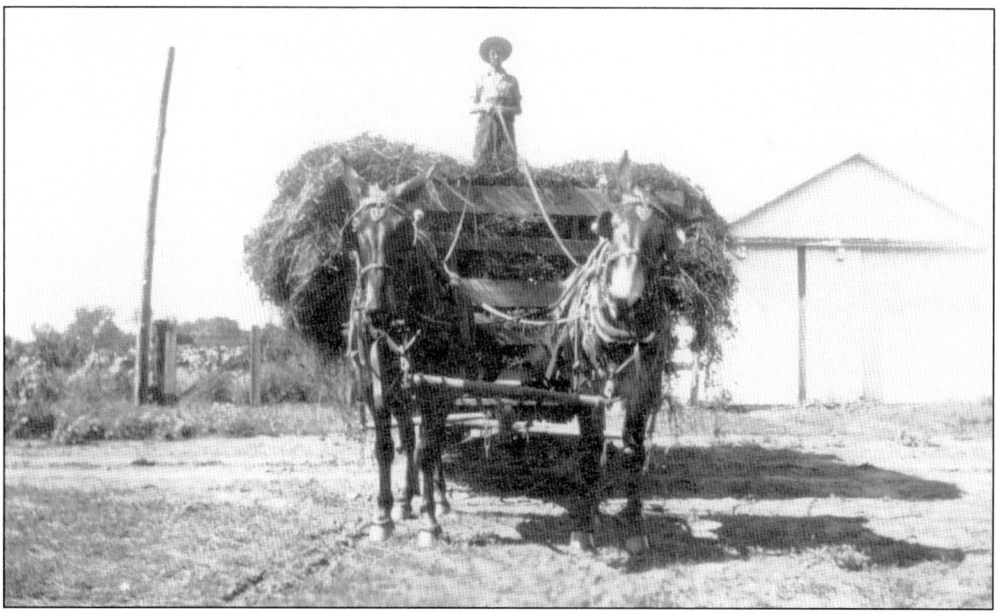

In this 1930s photograph, Glen Duffy stands on top of a hay-laden, horse-drawn wagon. The Duffy farm was located near Fillmore. Hay wagons became less common in Andrew County within a few decades after this photograph was taken. Automatic balers produce the rectangular or round bales that now dot the countryside during haying season.

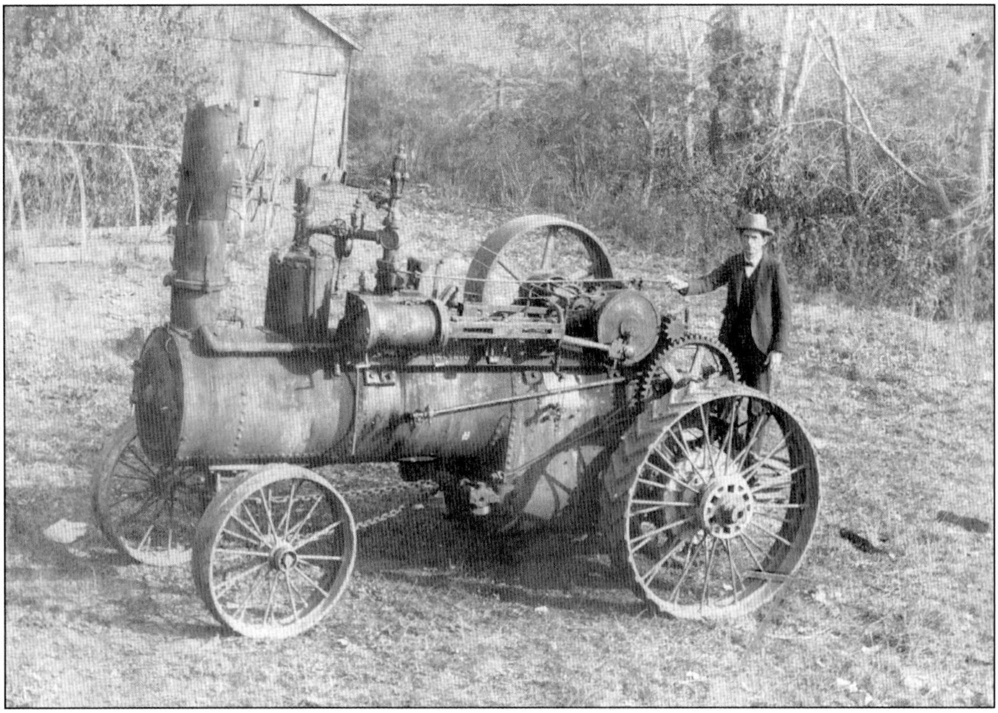

By the late 19th century, agricultural production in rural America was fueled by steam-traction engines. Modern youngsters often gape at these smoke-belching machines rumbling over the landscape; they look like locomotives that have somehow gone off the tracks. The c. 1900 image above shows a relatively small traction engine, while the photograph below captures the J.L. Martin threshing crew at work on the D.A. Hardin farm on August 3, 1916. As with modern farm machinery, outfitting a threshing operation involved considerable expense, and crews moved from farm to farm in late summer and early fall to earn their keep. Many of the extremely durable traction engines remained in use into the 1930s.

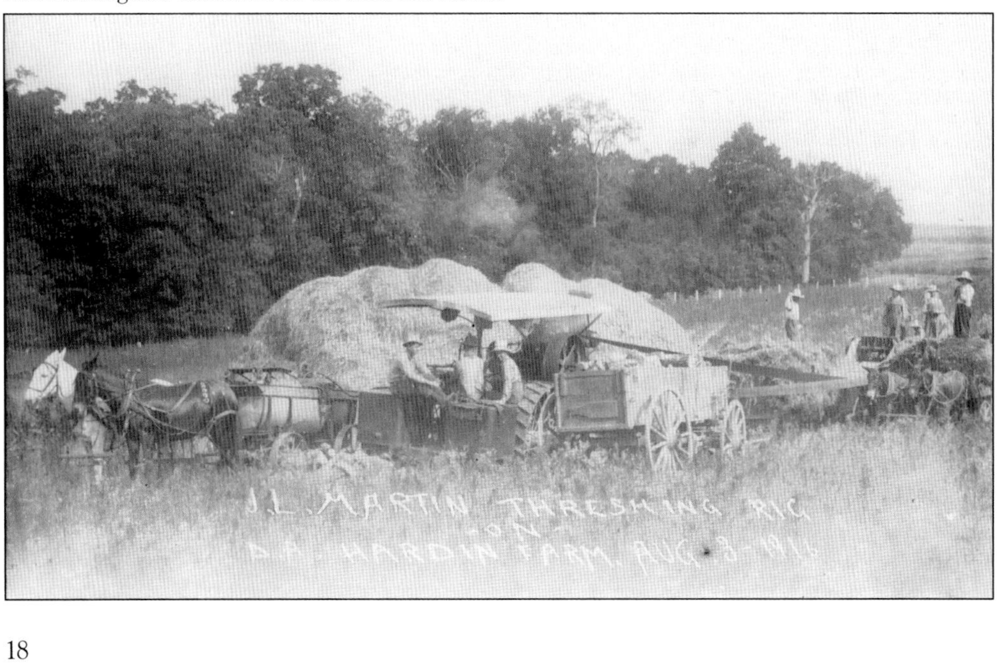

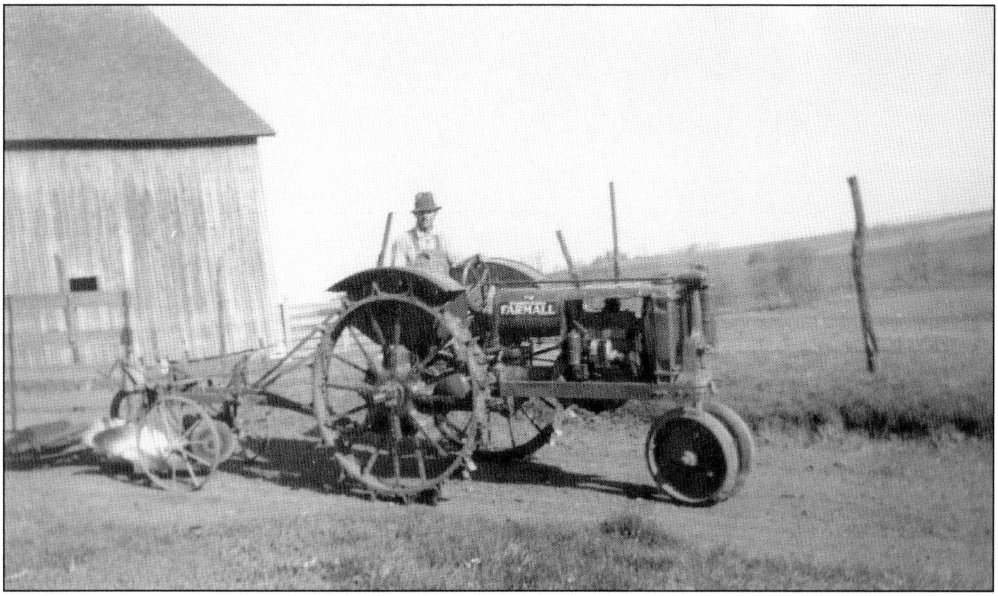

Donald Faires sits on his Farmall tractor in this 1930 photograph. In 1900, it took a farmer roughly 108 minutes to plow an acre with a horse. By 1938, the amount of time had been reduced to 30 minutes with a tractor. In the 1990s, remembering his 1936 John Deere, J.W. Stanton recalled, "I thought I could whip the world with that little tractor, and I did."

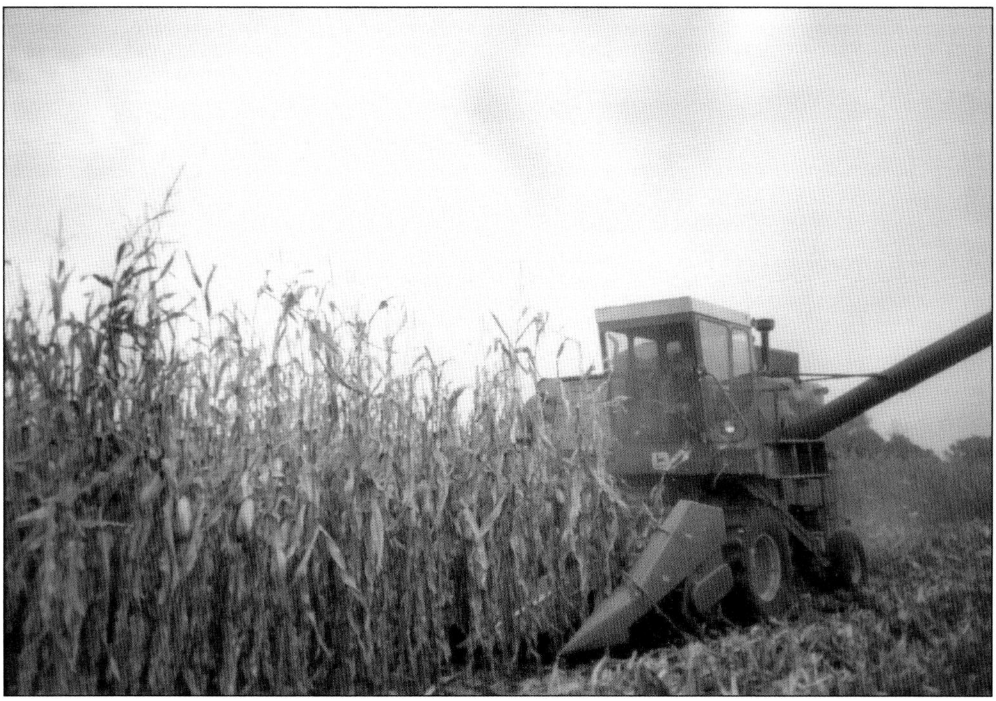

In this 2003 image, John Maag uses his green-and-yellow combine in a cornfield. The cost of such a machine is considerable and can only be offset by working increasingly larger farms. In 1997, Lester Fothergill remarked that a modern tractor is the price of what a whole farm used to cost.

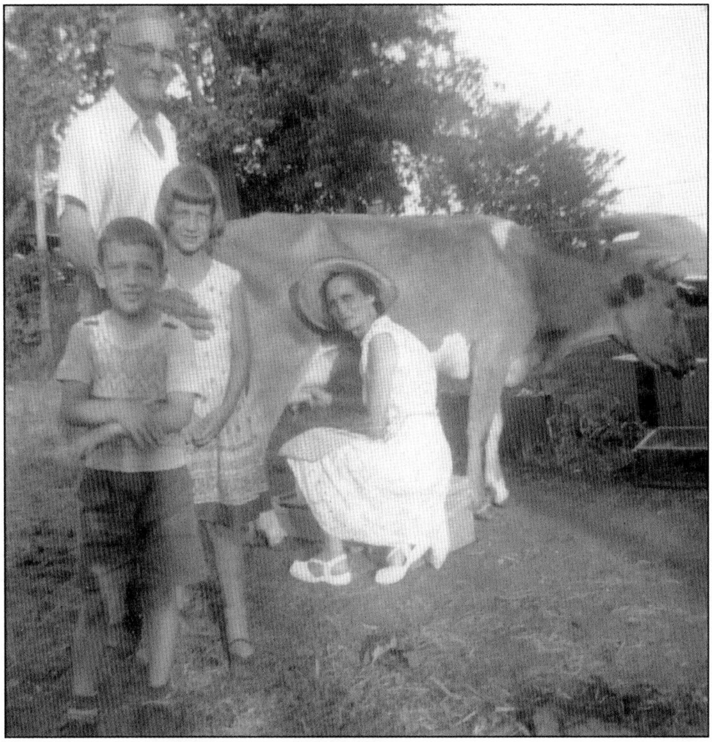

Dairying was an important part of Andrew County farming until the 1950s. Milking by hand was a tiresome, time-consuming chore that had to be done every morning and every night. Processing cream and churning butter took additional time—usually women's time. The image at left shows Clara Poage milking a cow as her husband and his grandchildren stand nearby. She is dressed up, and a picnic basket rests beside her. The 1920s image below shows Lawrence Davis squirting milk at the barn cat while milking his Holstein.

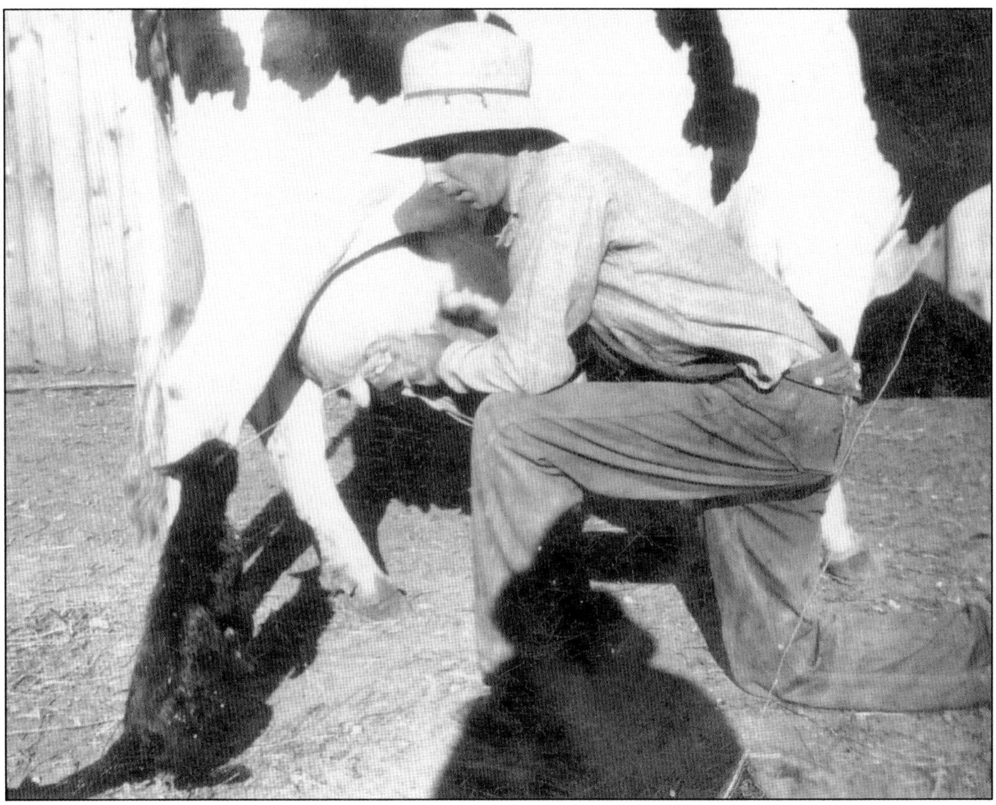

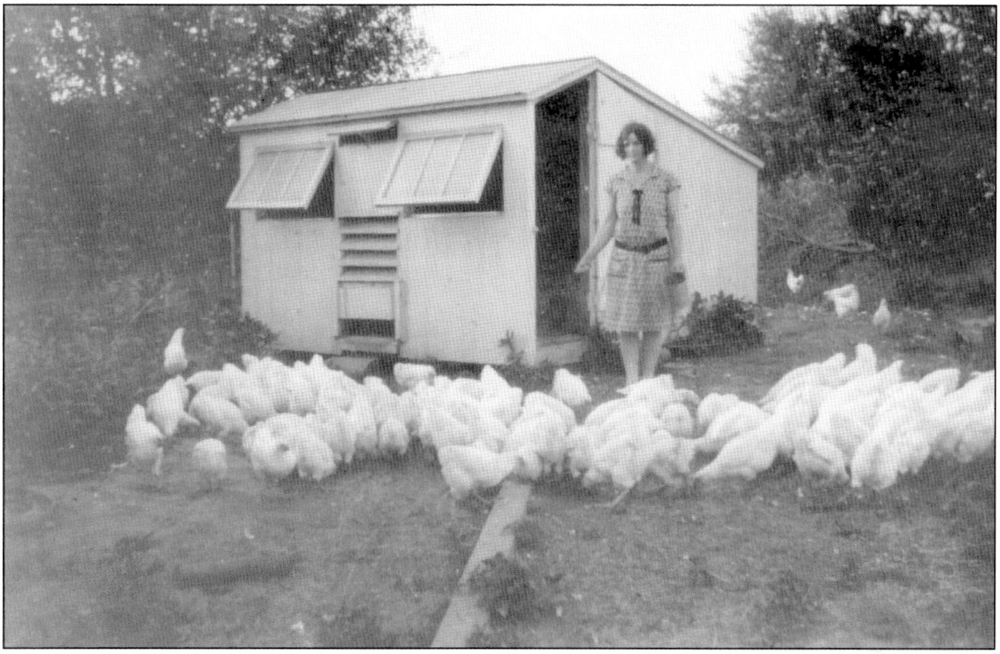

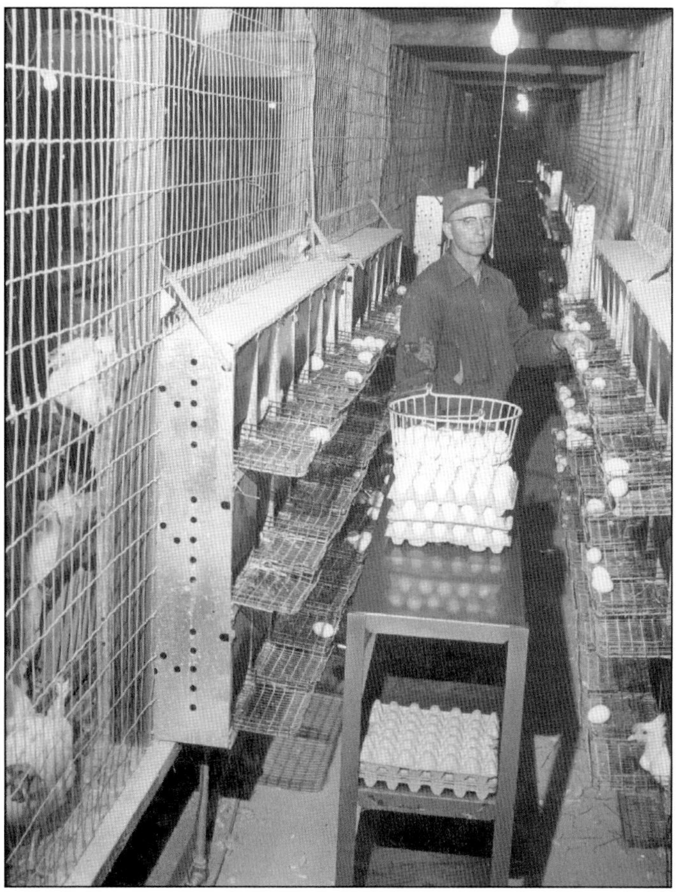

Both in town and on the farm, rural people raised chickens. For farm families, egg production provided additional household income. The c. 1925 photograph above shows Ruby Miller feeding chickens. The c. 1960 image at right shows Harold Miller gathering eggs from 3,000 caged hens that were fed and watered automatically. Despite efforts at automation, poultry farming swiftly declined in Andrew County in the 1960s. By then, most women purchased their eggs at the grocery store. The demise of the backyard henhouse was not mourned by many; in 2006, Dan Hegeman commented, "I remember grandmother Hegeman saying that she thought farmwives' greatest day was when they didn't have to keep a chicken coop anymore."

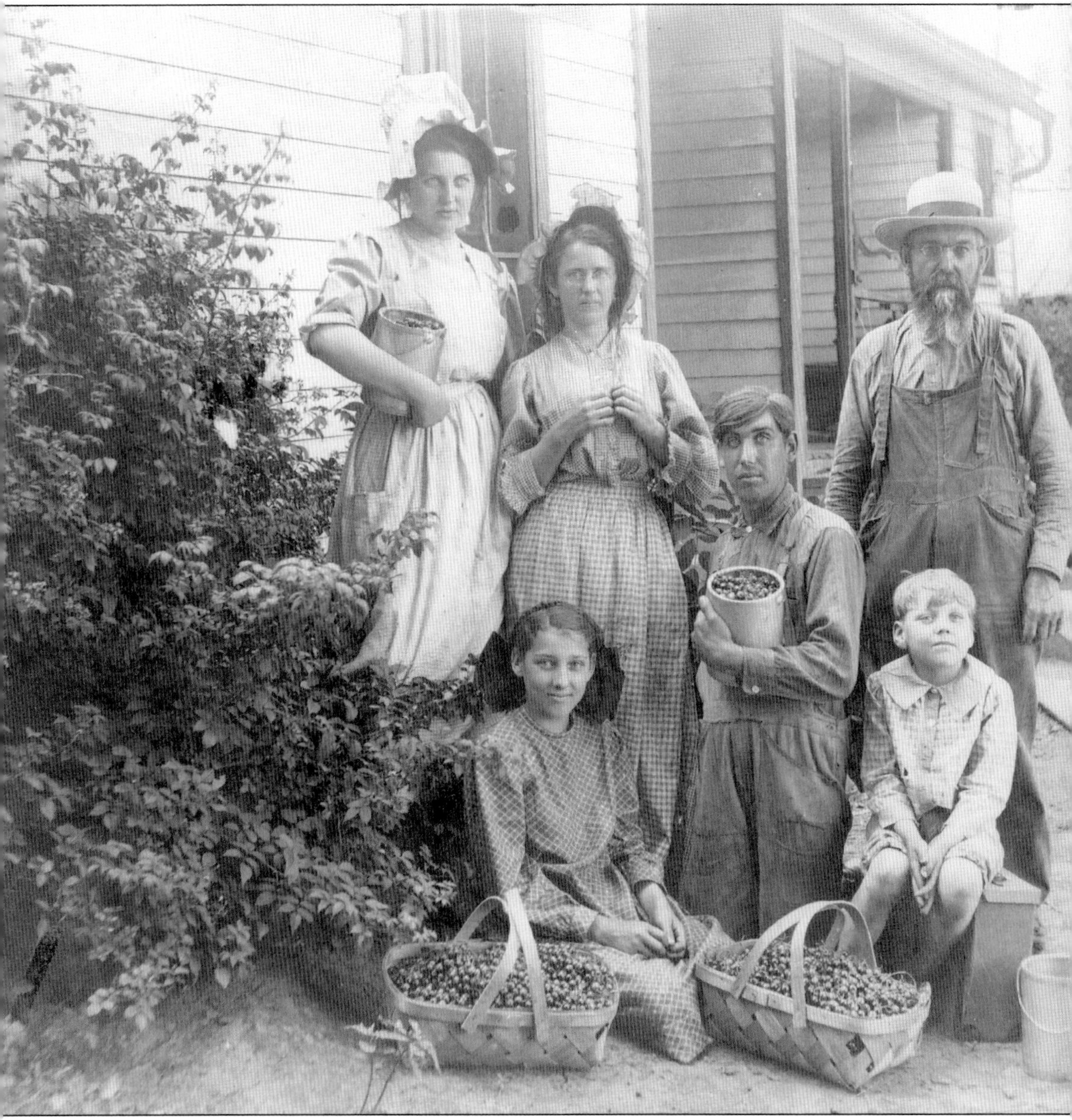

Apple orchards still dot the Andrew County landscape, but fruit production was once more diversified. In 1991, Crystal Schweizer Adkins observed, "The loess (fine-grained) soil in the western part of the county was particularly adapted to fruit trees and small fruit, making this area valuable to the fruit growers. Apples and peaches are still a very important cash crop in Lincoln Township." Lola Spohn Nielson confirmed the suitability of the area for fruit crops, recalling, "When the warm days came, all the fruit trees on our place burst into bloom—the pear, apple, peach, plum, and cherry trees." This c. 1905 photograph shows an unidentified local family with a bounty of harvested cherries.

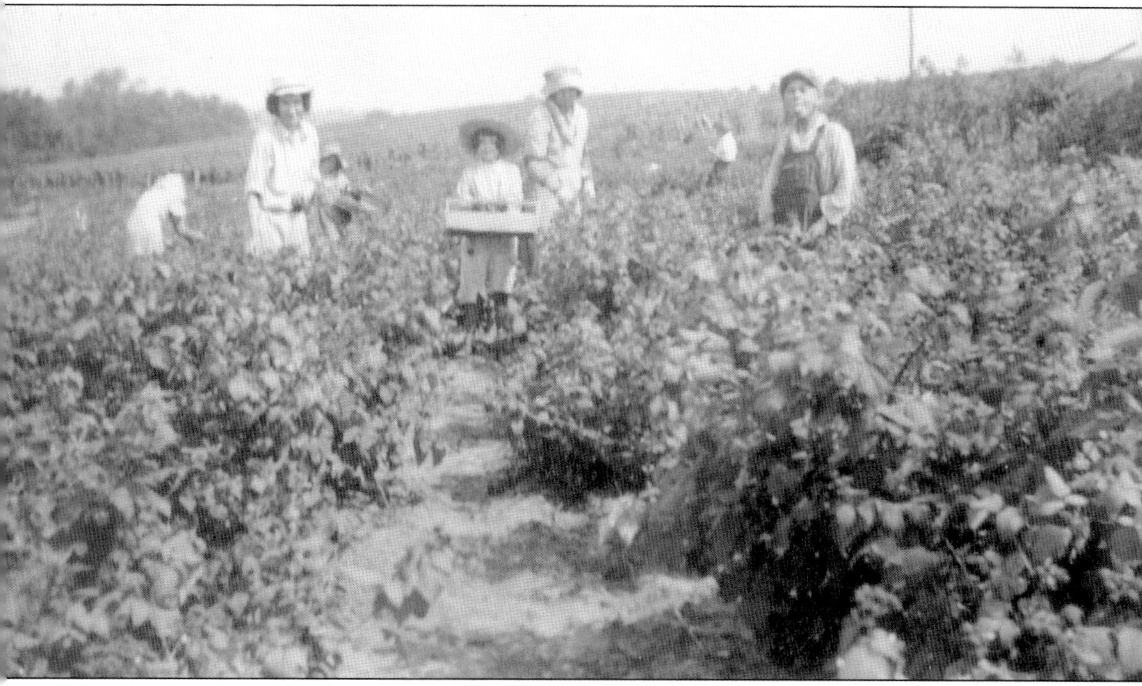

The Guy Sandusky family, pictured here in 1950, picked raspberries to earn Fourth of July firecracker money. In Andrew County, berries were not just picked for personal use. Farm families supplemented their income by selling extra fruit to local grocers. In 1994, Carl Rudolph remembered that his father had a big raspberry patch that produced more fruit than the family could use. He recalled that the patch yielded between 50 and 60 crates of berries. Rudolph noted, "We'd pick every other day, and I'm talking about 24-box crates!"

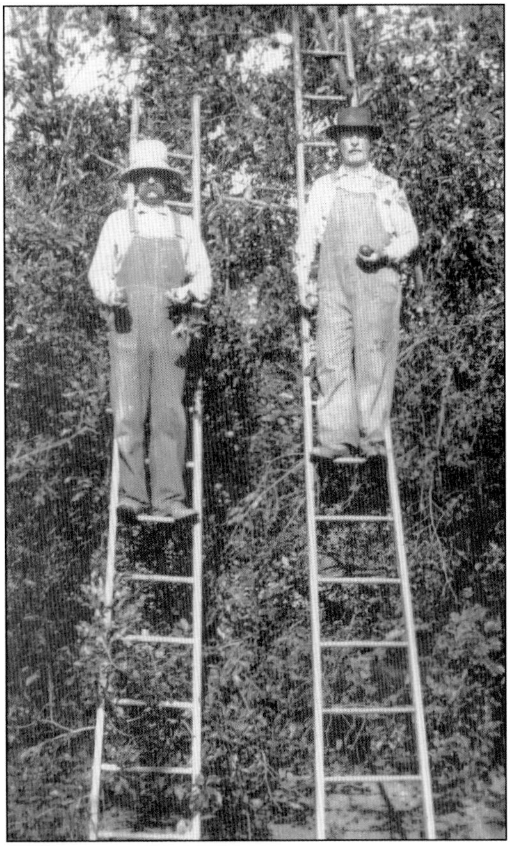

This c. 1920 image shows C.C. Davis and his hired hand as they pick apples on Davis's farm just outside of Fillmore. In Andrew County, apples became a preferred crop by the mid-19th century. In 1852, the *Savannah Reporter* informed readers that "cattle and hogs are fond of good apples as well as folks." Each autumn, many farm families turned some of their apples into cider.

In this 1986 photograph, a young woman picks apples at Schweizer Orchards near Amazonia. In 1976, the *Savannah Reporter* noted, "The apples are sold to local residents, Affiliated Foods, Gerber Baby Food Company, Stephenson's Apple Farm and many others. At one time or another, the Schweizers have shipped apples to every state in the continental United States."

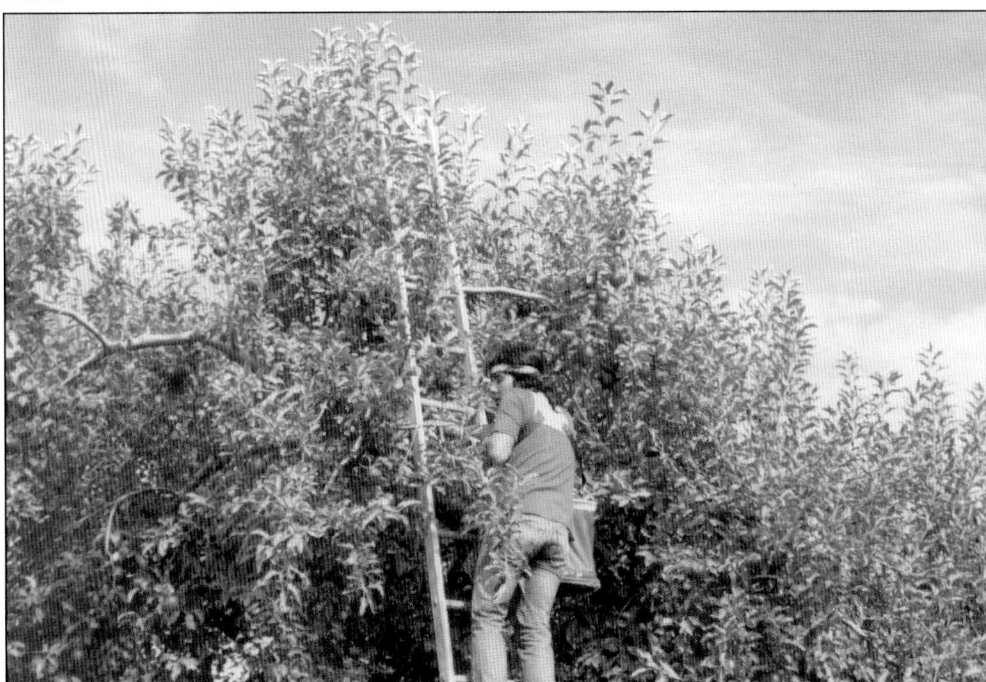

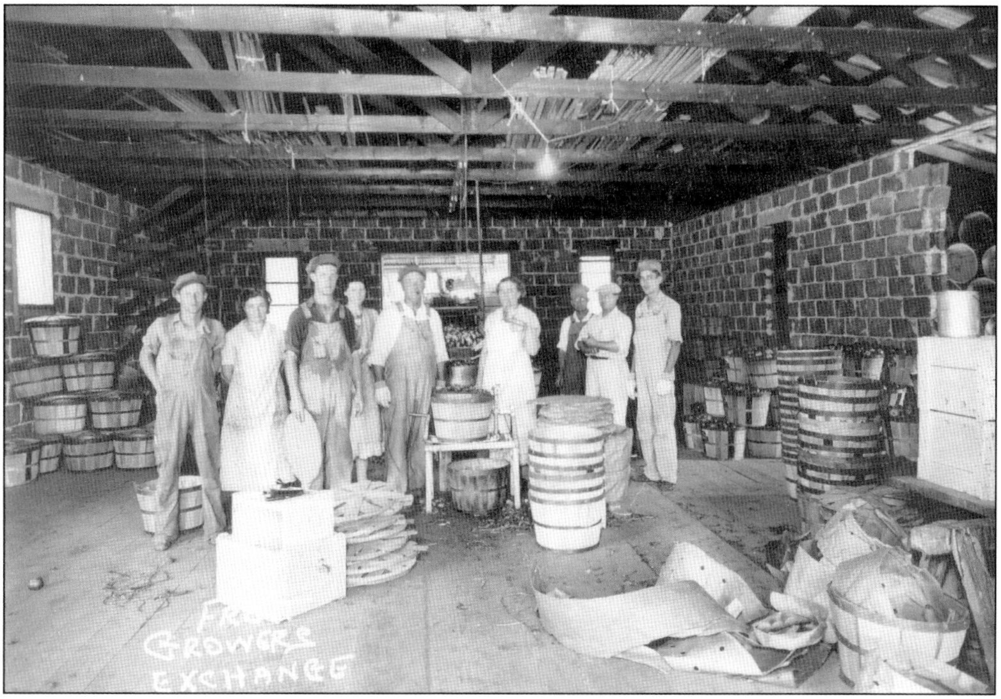

After apples are picked, they need to be sorted and packed for sale. The c. 1935 photograph above shows the local Fruit Growers Exchange in the packing shed at Schweizer Orchards in Amazonia. The 1980s image below shows two Schweizer employees sorting apples. In addition to wholesale sales, both Schweizer and Hunt orchards, near Amazonia, operate retail operations.

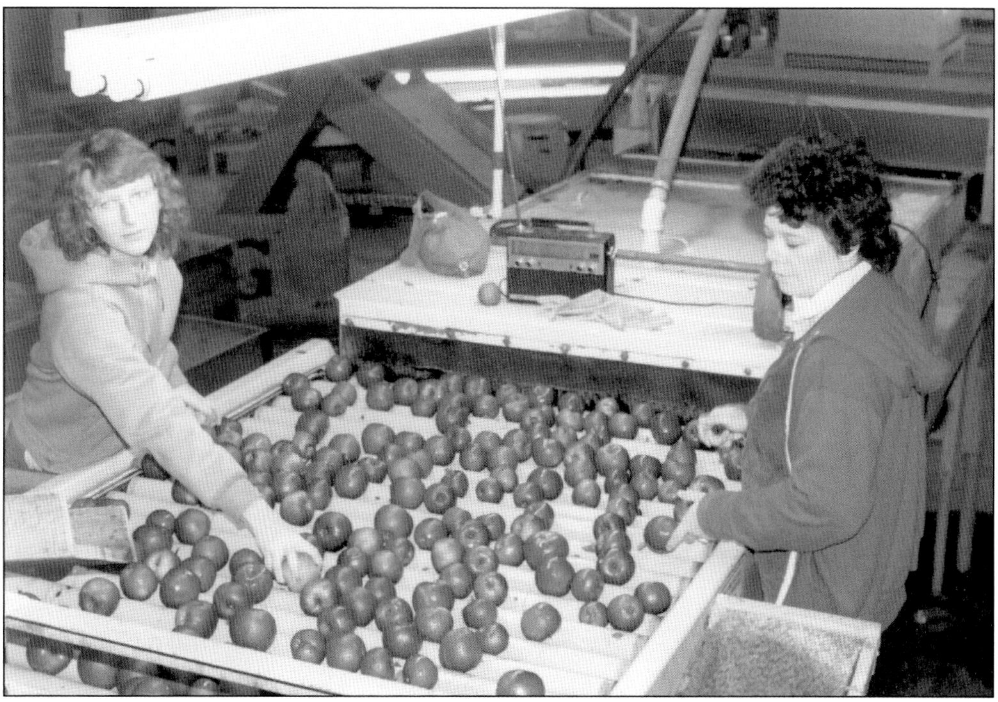

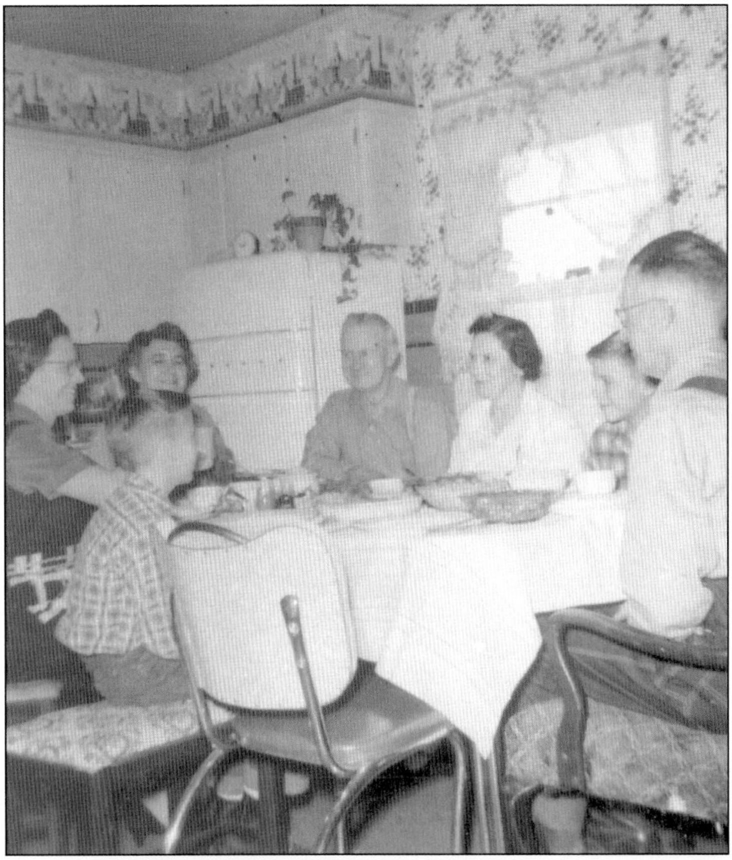

Farm families gather around the kitchen table to eat, read, discuss business, and chat with visitors. The c. 1950 family picture at left was taken at the Blakley farm. Other, unrelated guests were also invited in through the kitchen door. In the 1990s, Bill Herman recalled delivering heating oil to rural homes. He remembered, "I was welcome in all of their houses. Lots of times the lady would holler down and say, 'Come on up! We've got fried chicken!' " On the farm, family members produced the food. The c. 1946 image below shows Charles Miller (left) and his son Tom scalding a hog while butchering.

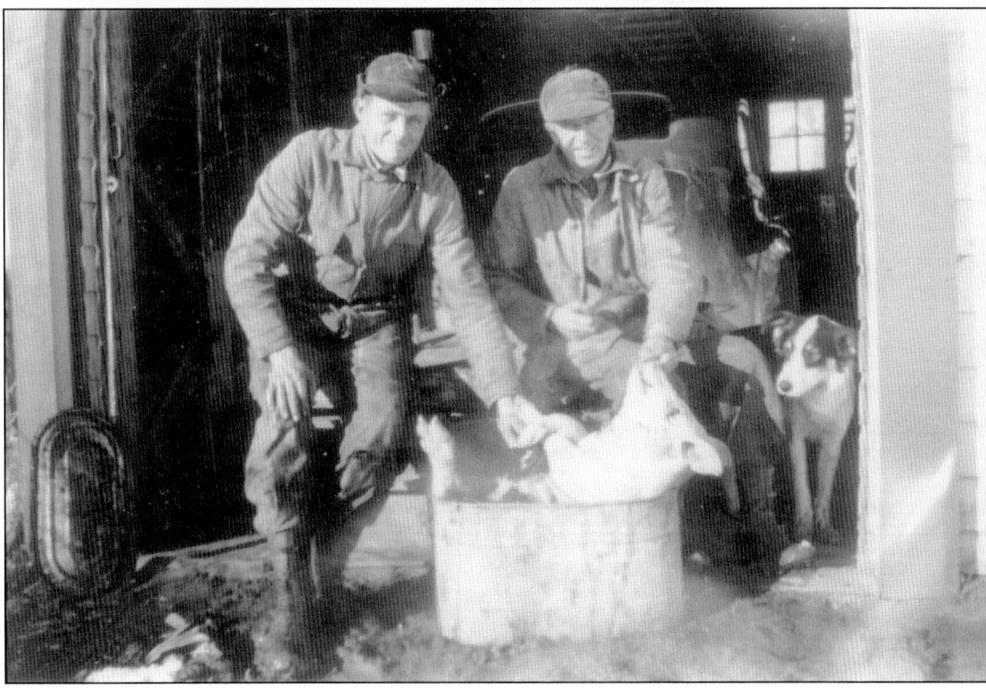

Two

Church, Courthouse, and School

In his novel *The Town* (1957), William Faulkner focused on the fictional county seat of Jefferson, Mississippi. He observed, "The courthouse was the nucleus of the town, the symbol of civilized society—church, courthouse, school, in that order, with the courthouse the 'catalyst,' without which there was no town."

Throughout 1898 and 1899, the citizens of Andrew County watched with anticipation as their new courthouse was constructed. Its Romanesque Revival style was popular for institutional architecture. Features of this style include semicircular arches on windows and entryways and "belt courses" of decorative stone.

As shown on the cover of this book, the county courthouse stood as the most elaborate landmark in any county seat. In Andrew County (and elsewhere), its importance was emphasized by its height. In most small towns, both downtown and residential streets were laid out on a flat grid. The courthouse was among the few structures that added a sense of verticality to the local landscape. Even today, the courthouse dome remains visible from many parts of town.

In the cover photograph, farm wagons appear in the foreground with carriages parked along another side of the square. In part, this is a striking image because the courthouse symbolized both town and country for Andrew County residents. The town benefitted economically from being the county seat. Court days brought business into town, and lawyers and title companies established downtown offices. County government, headquartered in the courthouse, provided basic services for those out in the country. It maintained country roads, over which farm wagons traveled, and offered police protection via the sheriff's office.

Church and school architecture symbolized a commitment to basic education and solid moral values. This was true in Savannah, but even more so in towns that were not county seats. Without a courthouse, a church or school might be the most architecturally distinctive building in town and a source of civic pride. Perhaps Faulkner should have imagined a setting beyond a county seat; since the courthouse symbolized both town and country, perhaps it was a catalyst without which there was no county.

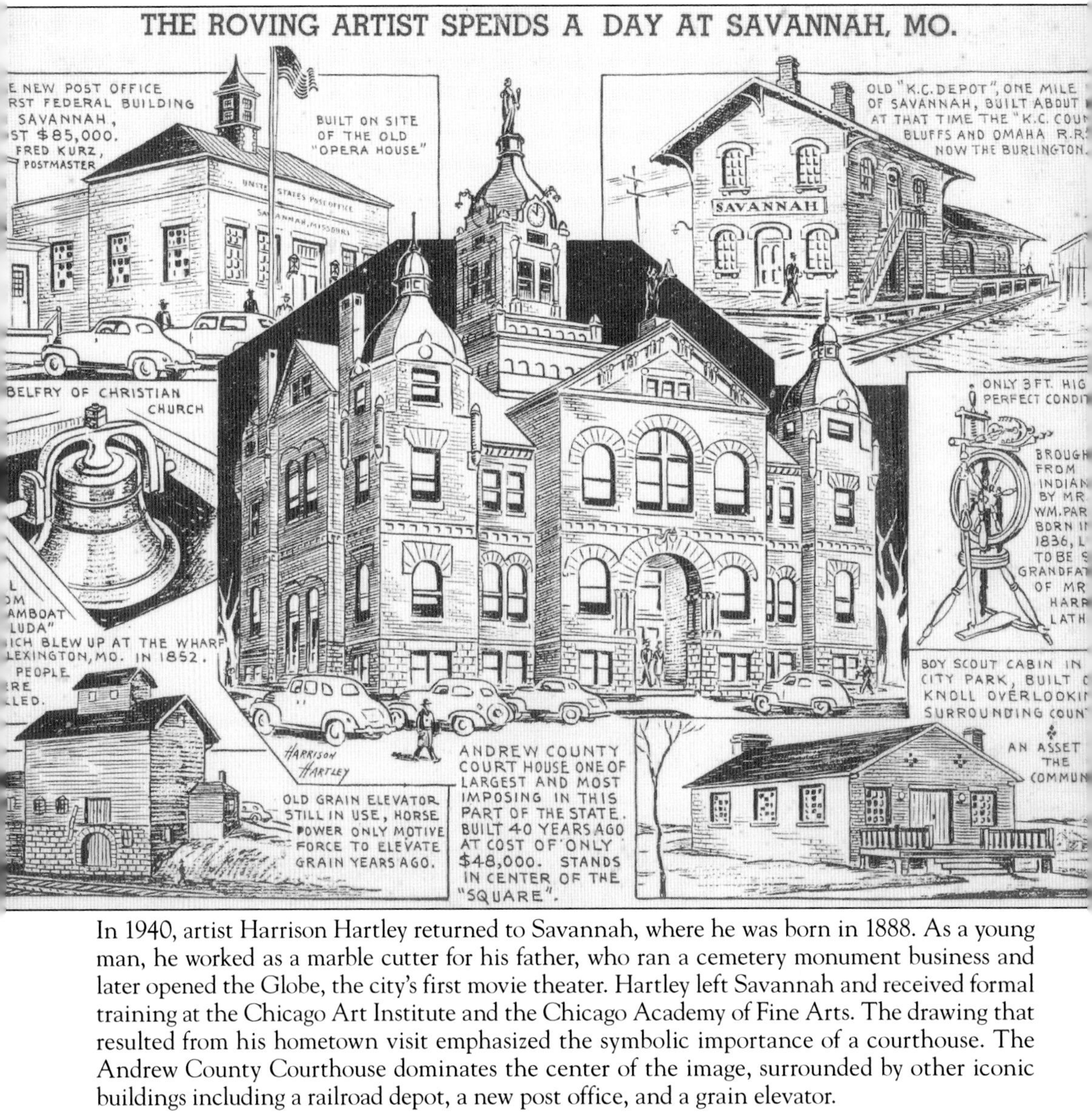

In 1940, artist Harrison Hartley returned to Savannah, where he was born in 1888. As a young man, he worked as a marble cutter for his father, who ran a cemetery monument business and later opened the Globe, the city's first movie theater. Hartley left Savannah and received formal training at the Chicago Art Institute and the Chicago Academy of Fine Arts. The drawing that resulted from his hometown visit emphasized the symbolic importance of a courthouse. The Andrew County Courthouse dominates the center of the image, surrounded by other iconic buildings including a railroad depot, a new post office, and a grain elevator.

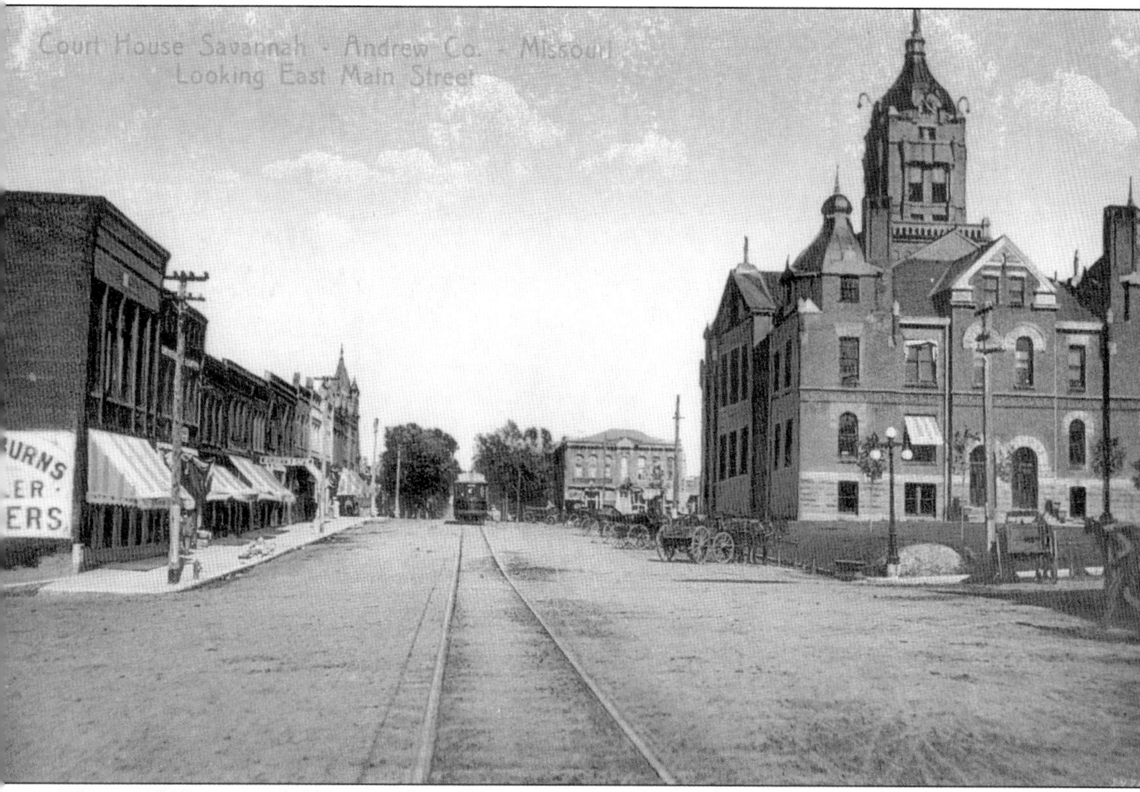

This c. 1915 postcard illustrates how the county courthouse lent a sense of verticality to the downtown street grid. In a description of the courthouse (then under construction) from 1899, the *Savannah Reporter* emphasized its 120-foot height to the top of the dome. The newspaper also highlighted the modern amenities inside the building, including steam heat, modern plumbing, and electric lights. In short, the people of Andrew County not only had a building to be proud of but one "worth every dollar to be paid for it." This image also includes farm wagons, illustrating the county seat's connection to the countryside. In addition, an interurban trolley rolled down Main Street, demonstrating that Andrew County maintained connections to larger cities and towns.

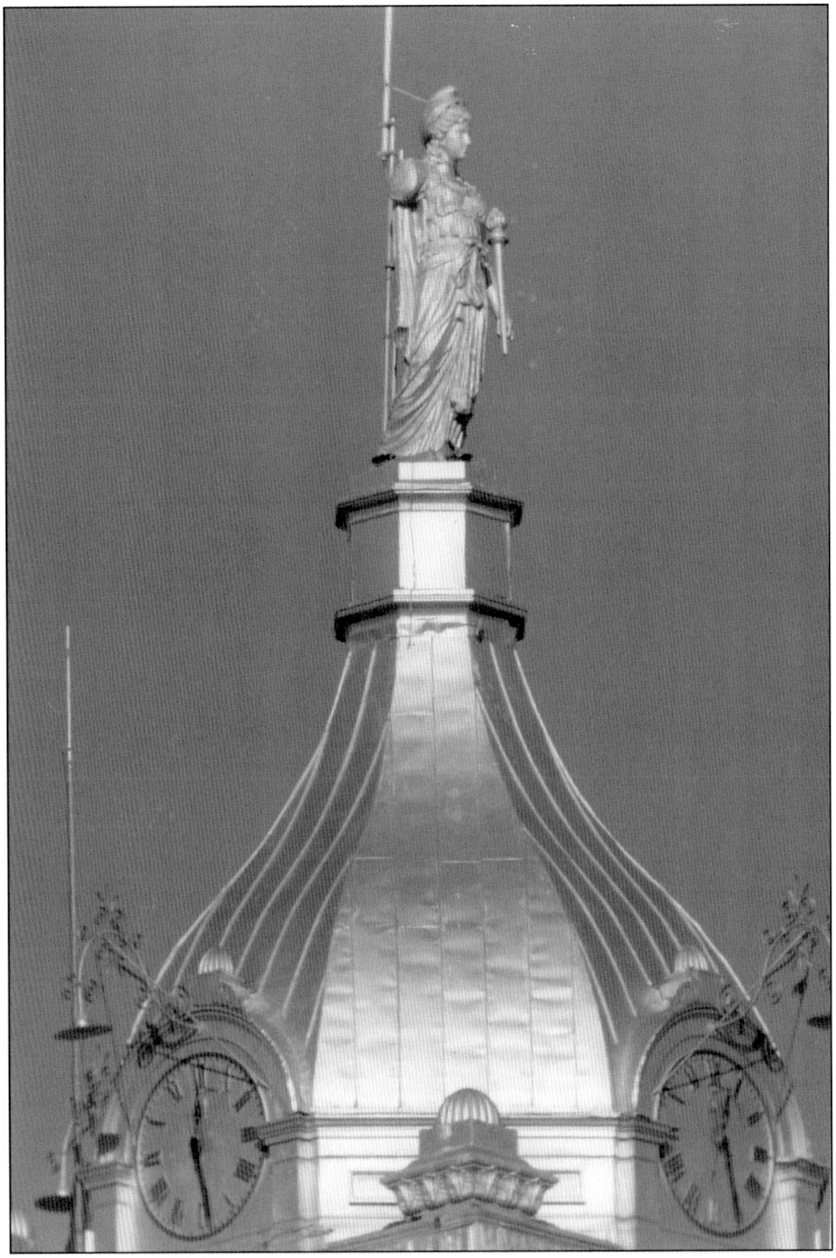

County courthouses demonstrated that rural citizens endorsed artistic expressions (beyond the merely useful and practical) on public buildings, churches, and schools. The Andrew County Courthouse befittingly featured statues of the blindfolded figure of Justice holding her scales above the Main Street and Court Street entrances to the building. The top of the tower sported a statue of Liberty. A local newspaper's letter writer, identifying himself as "Farmer Boy," took pride in the "magnificent structure" that had been erected in the county seat. He emphasized that on the courthouse pinnacle stood the "Goddess of Liberty whose sacred presence keeps peace hovering over the fair city." The only work left was to install a "fine large time-piece to put upon their structure." The four-faced clock on the courthouse tower continues to toll the hours in the present day.

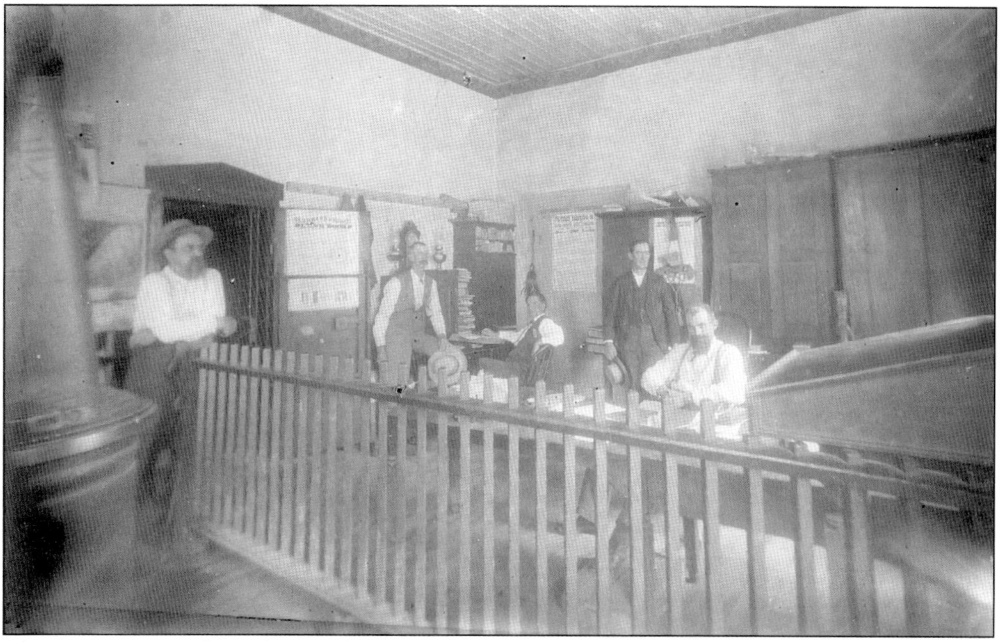

The c. 1910 image above depicts the circuit court clerk's office. The photograph below shows Jesse Roberts, Andrew County treasurer, standing at the counter in his office. As illustrated in the pictures, a county courthouse was predominantly a male-oriented space in the early 20th century. Women ventured into the building on legal business or to be involved in court proceedings. Early-19th-century courtrooms were often equipped with spittoons to collect tobacco juice. In 1900, according to the *Savannah Reporter*, the new and refined Andrew County Courthouse boasted furnishings of "white oak polished to what architects call an egg shell finish." Each county department was provided with an "airy and well lighted" office.

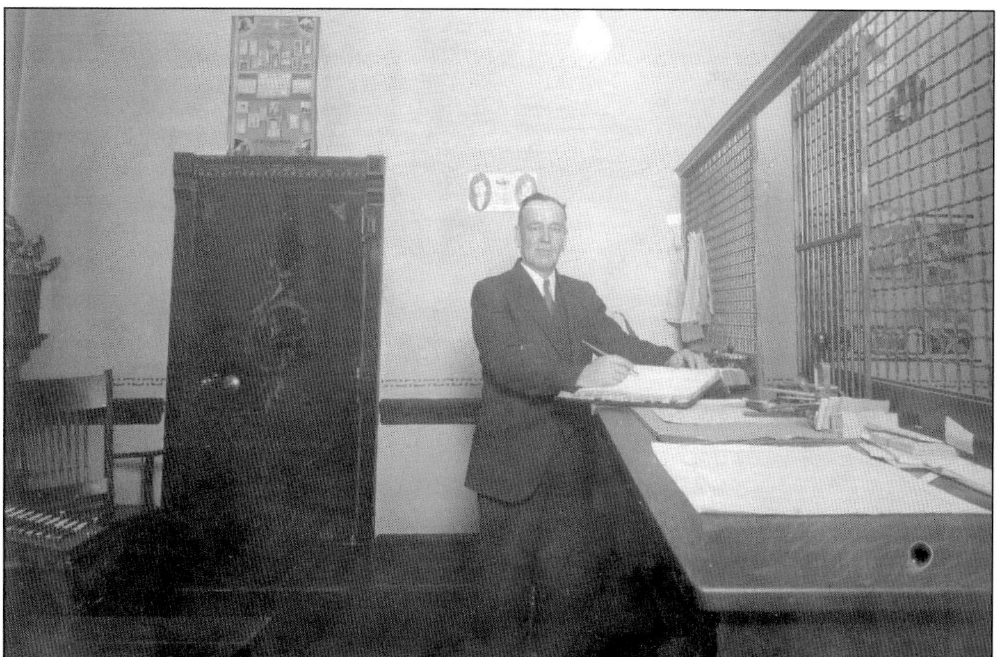

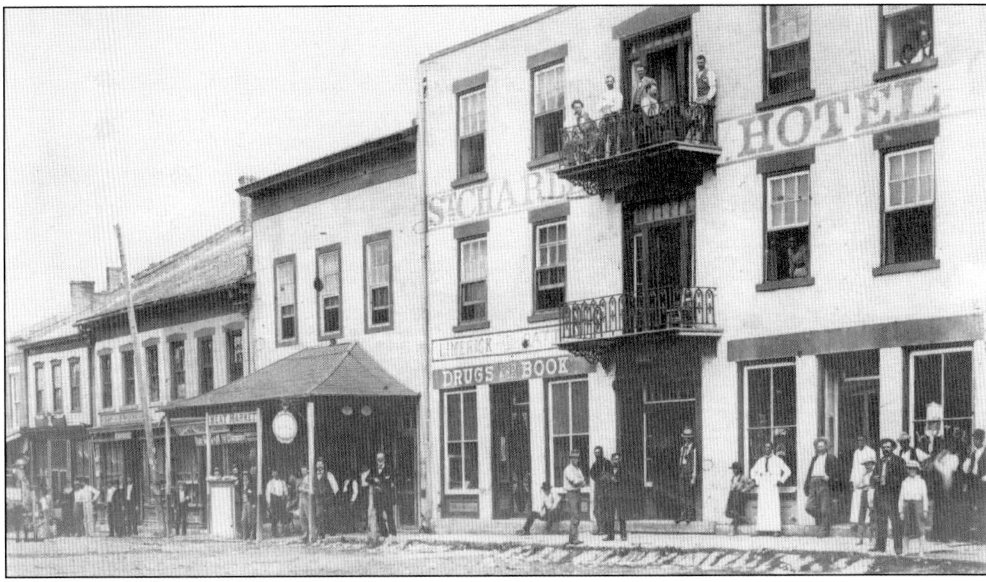

This post–Civil War image of the south side of the Andrew County Courthouse square features the St. Charles Hotel. Before the automobile age, rural people involved in court business often required overnight accommodations since travel to and from Savannah could not be accomplished in a single day. Hotels and boardinghouses met the needs of travelers and boosted the local economy.

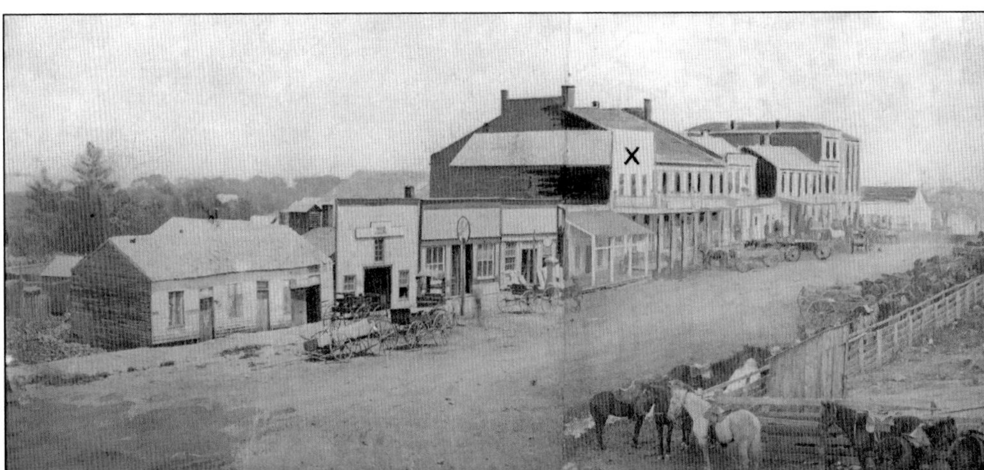

This 1868 photograph showing the north side of the courthouse square illustrates that Midwestern towns of the era were geared toward horse-drawn transportation. Dirt streets were wide enough to permit wagons with ample room to turn around. Hitching posts or fences provided opportunities to tie up a team of horses or a single steed.

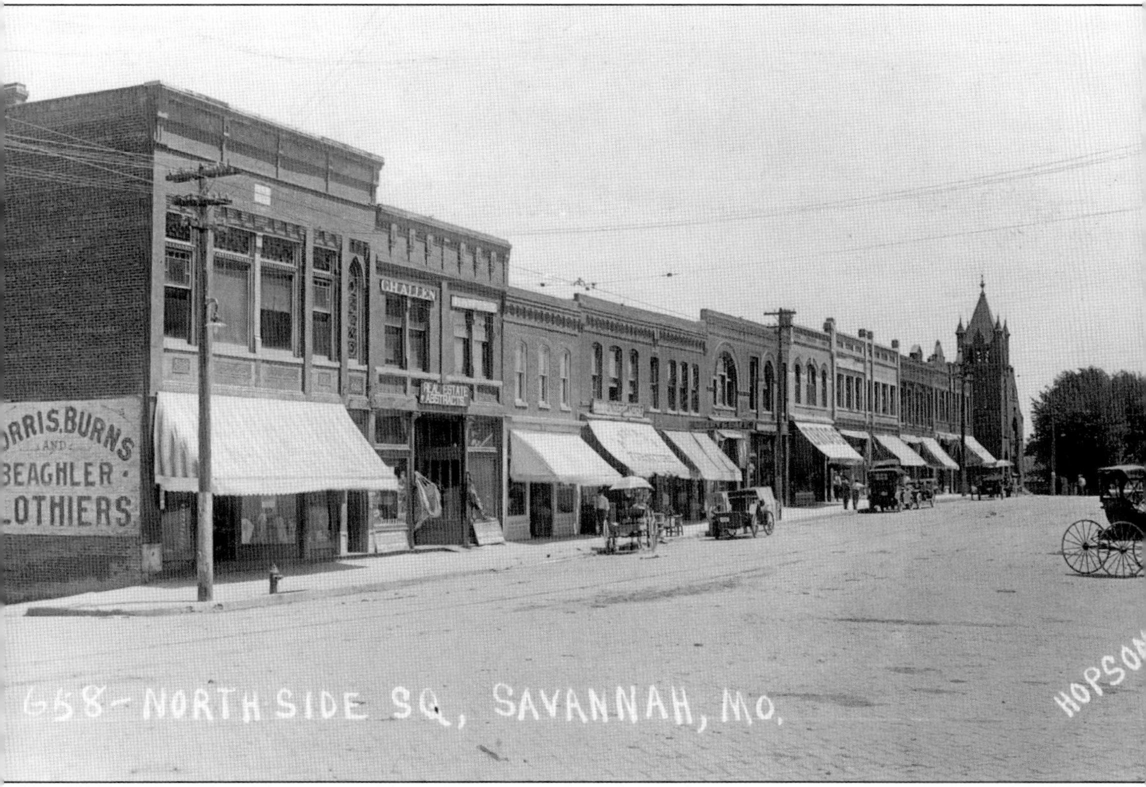

Early in the evening on Thursdays during football season, the present-day Savannah High School marching band practices on the county courthouse square. What the marching musicians and flag bearers may not know is that the storefronts and upper-story facades of the buildings on the square also once exhibited a unified "rhythm." This c. 1915 postcard image of the north side of the square illustrates that Midwestern downtowns were originally developed as appealing pedestrian spaces. Storefronts sported display windows flanking a center door entrance. Awnings shielded window shoppers from the sun or rain. The traditional storefronts and awning lines defined a street wall that created an attractive shopping environment. The resulting facade synchronicity was echoed by the alignment of second-story windows and cornice lines.

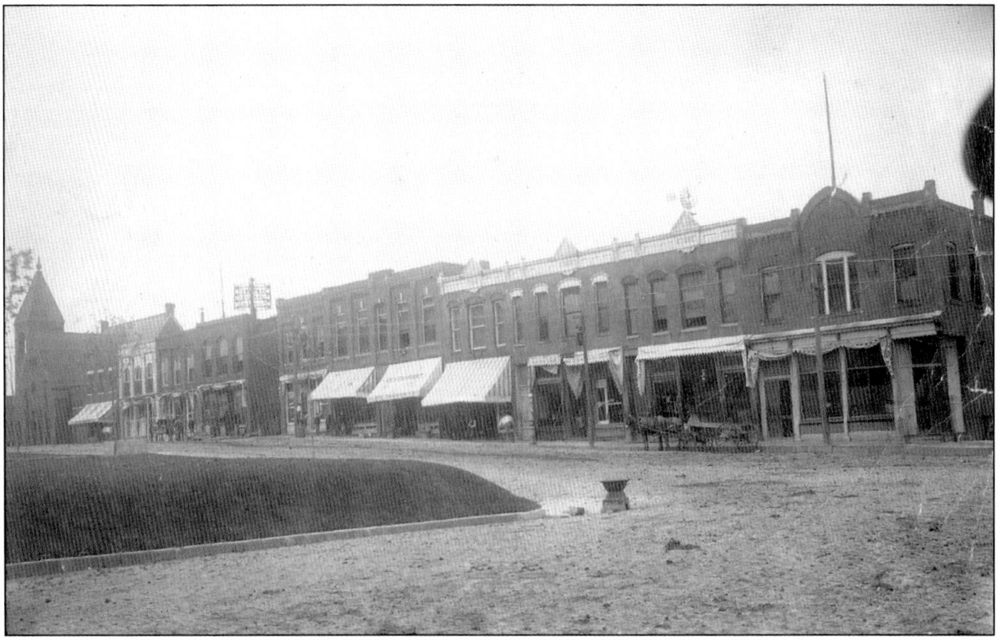

These postcard images of the west and north sides of the courthouse square date from about 1910 (above) and 1915 (below). They illustrate the unified street wall that defined a pedestrian-friendly downtown shopping space. Walt Disney recognized the nostalgic appeal of human-scaled downtown architecture when creating "Main Street, USA" at Disneyland, in California, and Disney World, in Florida. In the official 1983 guide to the Magic Kingdom, the author alerted visitors to not miss the "Walt Disney Story" housed in the yellow building on the town square. Here, visitors could view a "film that tells the story of the boy from Marceline, Missouri, who built a kingdom around a mouse." Unlike the Disney version of turn-of-the-century-small-town Main Streets, the street in Savannah does not lead to Cinderella's castle.

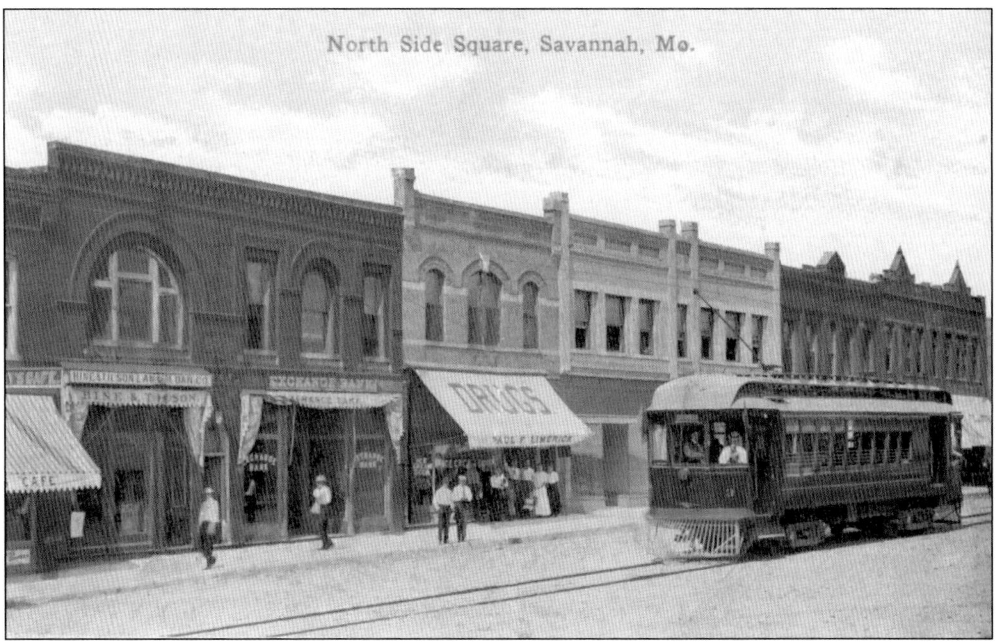

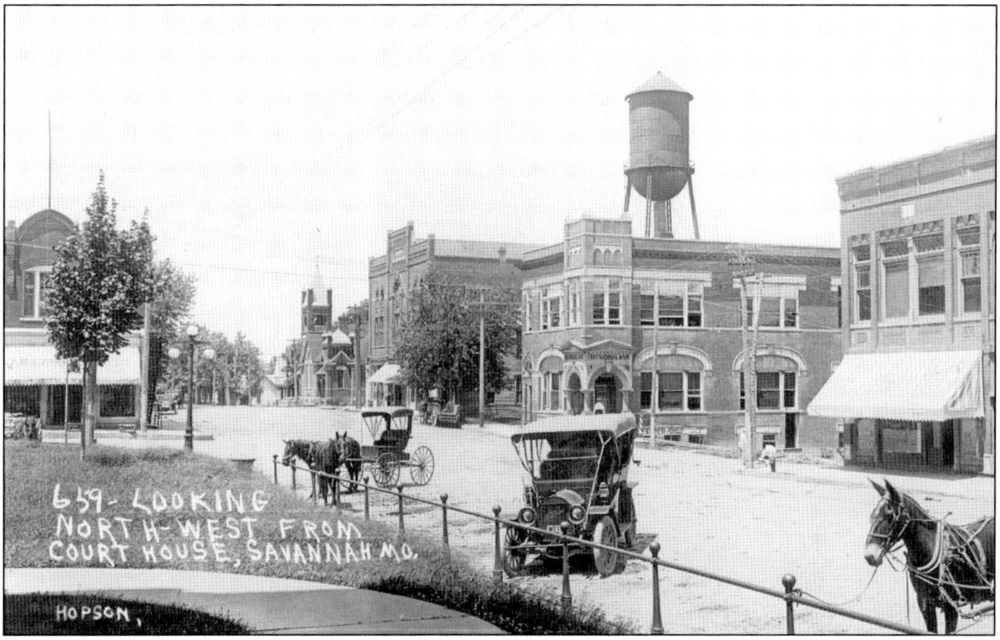

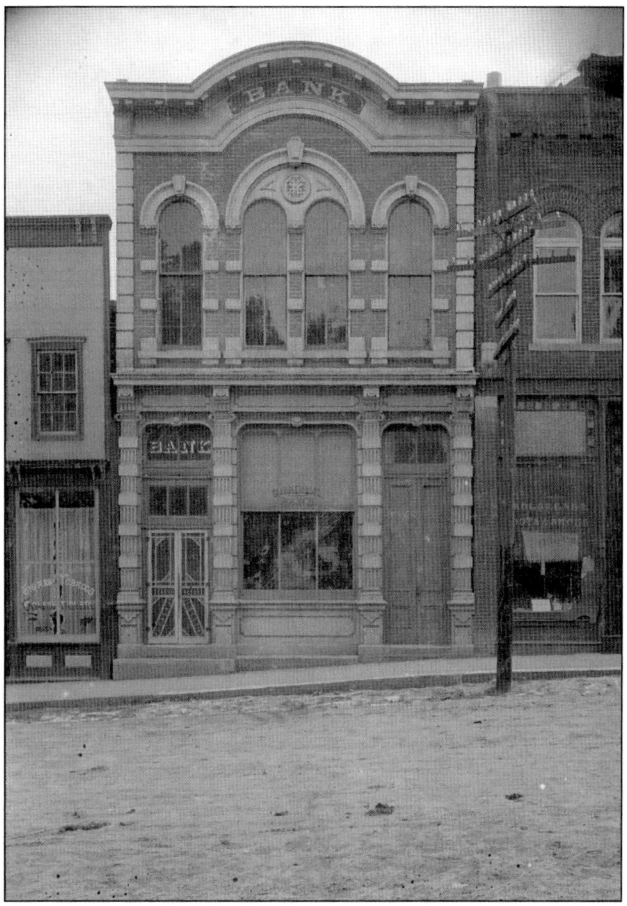

The c. 1925 postcard image above looks northwest from the courthouse and depicts structures that distinguished themselves from the standard downtown street wall. Beginning on the corner, the street included a bank building, an opera house, and a church. Rising above them all was the water tower. With one snap of the camera, the photographer captured structures representing religion, culture, finance, and public utilities. The c. 1890 photograph at right shows the Commercial Bank on the courthouse square. Bank buildings were among the most distinguished structures in many small towns; bankers recognized that their buildings needed to communicate a sense of strength and sophistication.

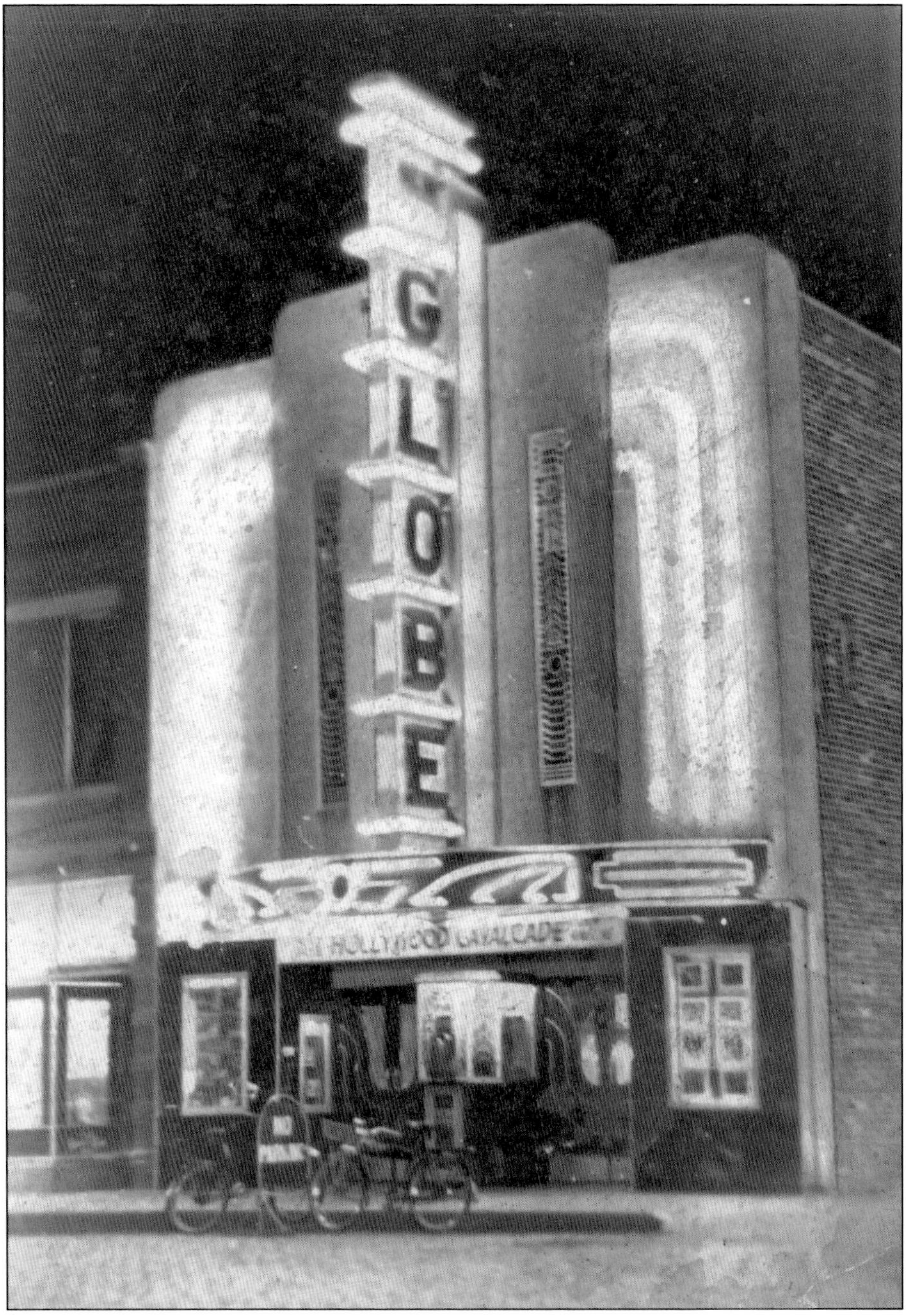

In the late 1930s, a new form of architecture arrived on the Savannah courthouse square. The movie theater pictured here originally opened as the Tivoli. M.B. Presley took over operations in 1938 and renamed it the New Globe Theater. Presley managed the Old Globe Theatre also located on the square and briefly kept both movie houses open. He inaugurated the opening of the New Globe by offering free movies at both venues. A crowd estimated at 2,000 showed up, more than could be accommodated at a single showing in both theaters combined. The neon-lit facade of the New Globe reflected off the stately Romanesque Revival county courthouse across the street. On the Savannah courthouse square, tradition and modernity existed in close proximity.

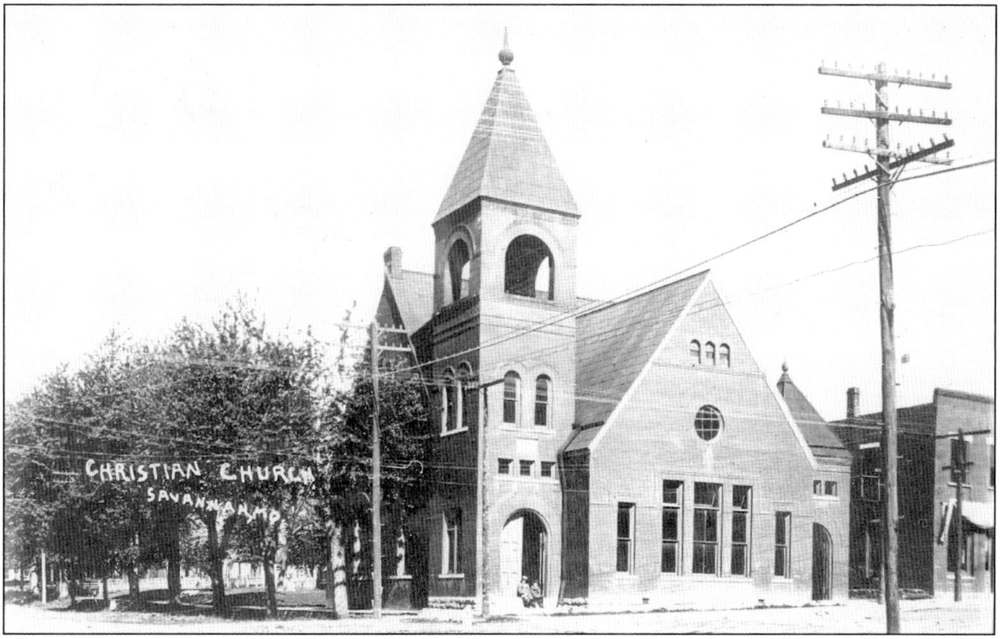

The 1911 image above shows the First Christian Church in Savannah. The photograph below, of the Methodist Episcopal Church South, dates from approximately the same period. Even now, drivers around the courthouse square can sense how churches served to indicate transitions between the downtown business district and residential neighborhoods. The current Methodist church, for example, is located on the edge of the square. Churches set a moral tone and provided opportunities for socializing. The local Methodist church, for example, offers an annual "salad lunch" open to everyone, where they can enjoy that historically significant Jell-O salad with tiny marshmallows in it.

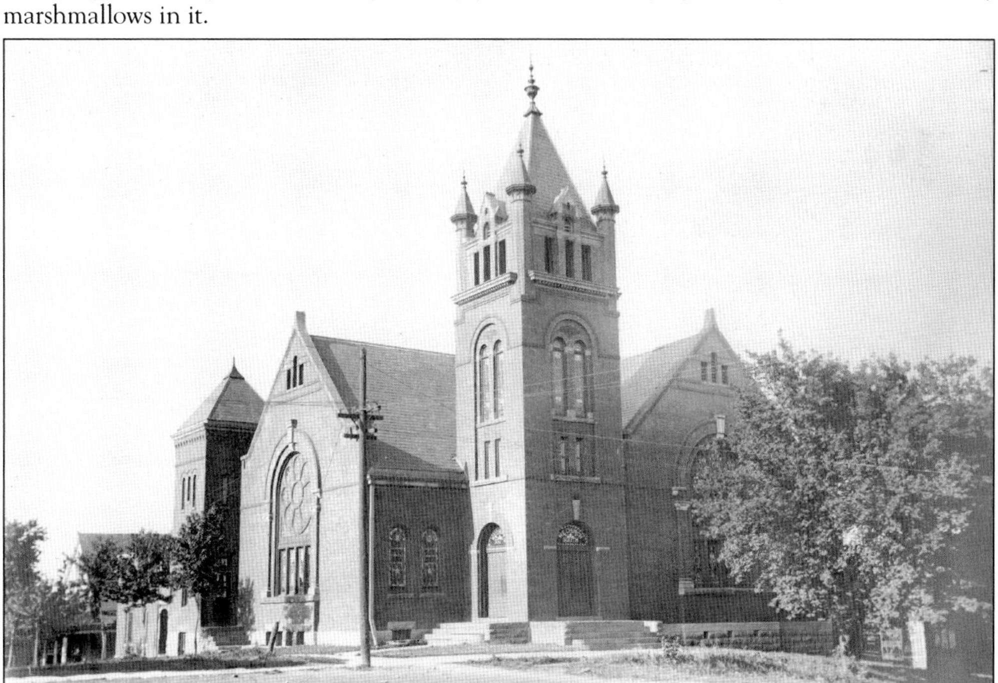

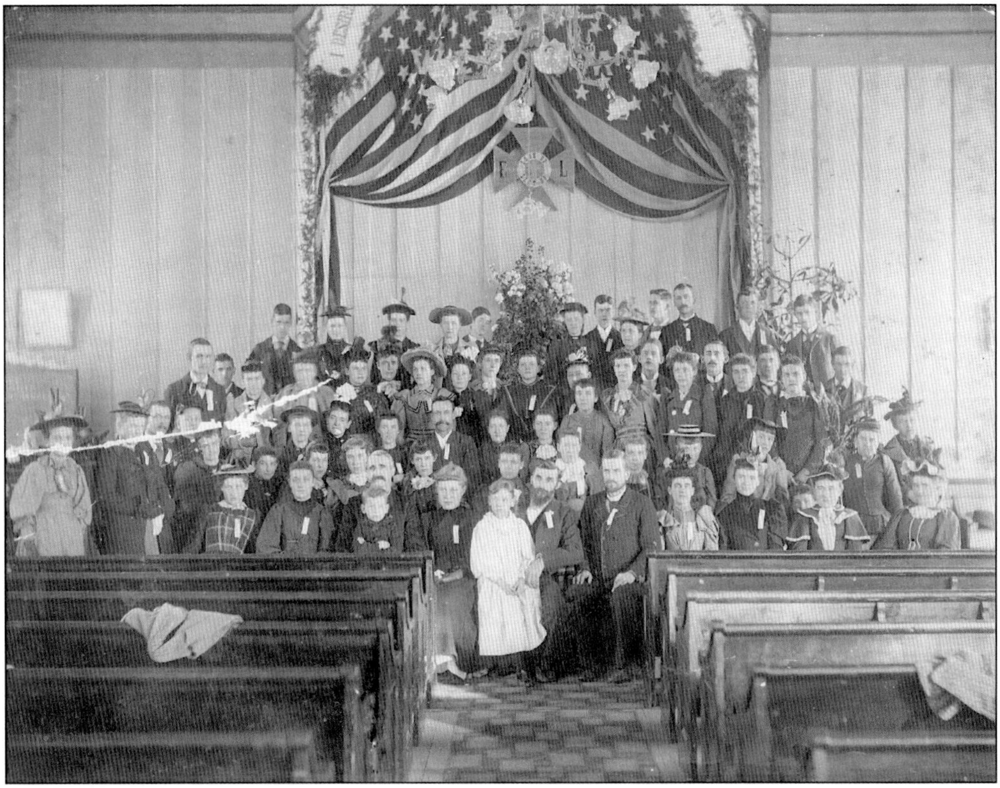

This c. 1909 photograph of the inside of the Savannah Methodist Episcopal Church depicts the leaders of the Epworth League, an organization intended to foster piety among young people. The flags draped behind the group were to illustrate that patriotism and religion were intertwined.

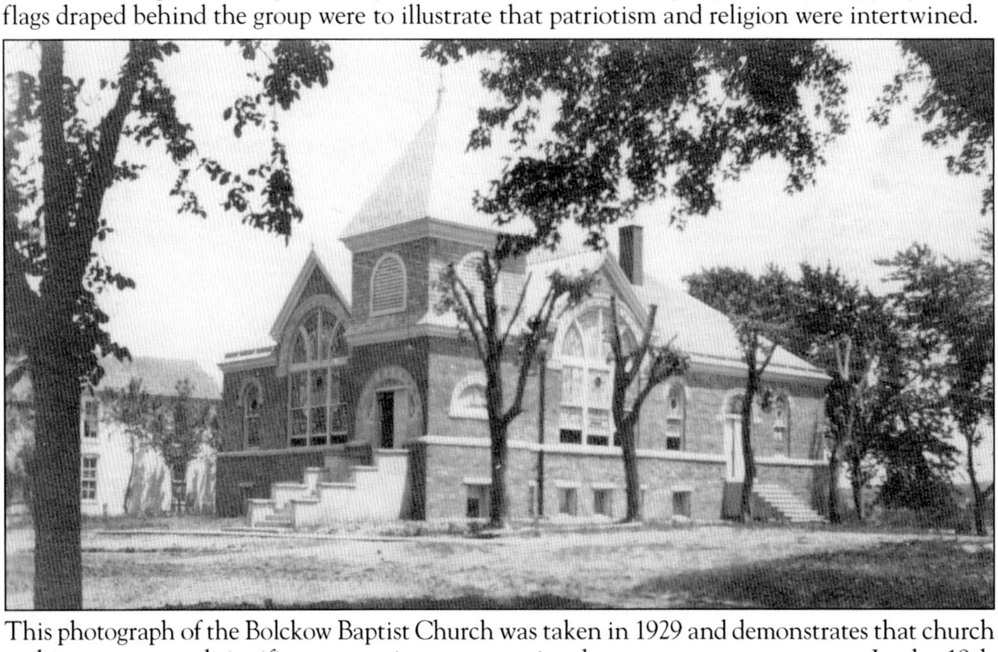

This photograph of the Bolckow Baptist Church was taken in 1929 and demonstrates that church architecture proved significant even in a community that was not a county seat. In the 19th century, the local church also often served as a school classroom.

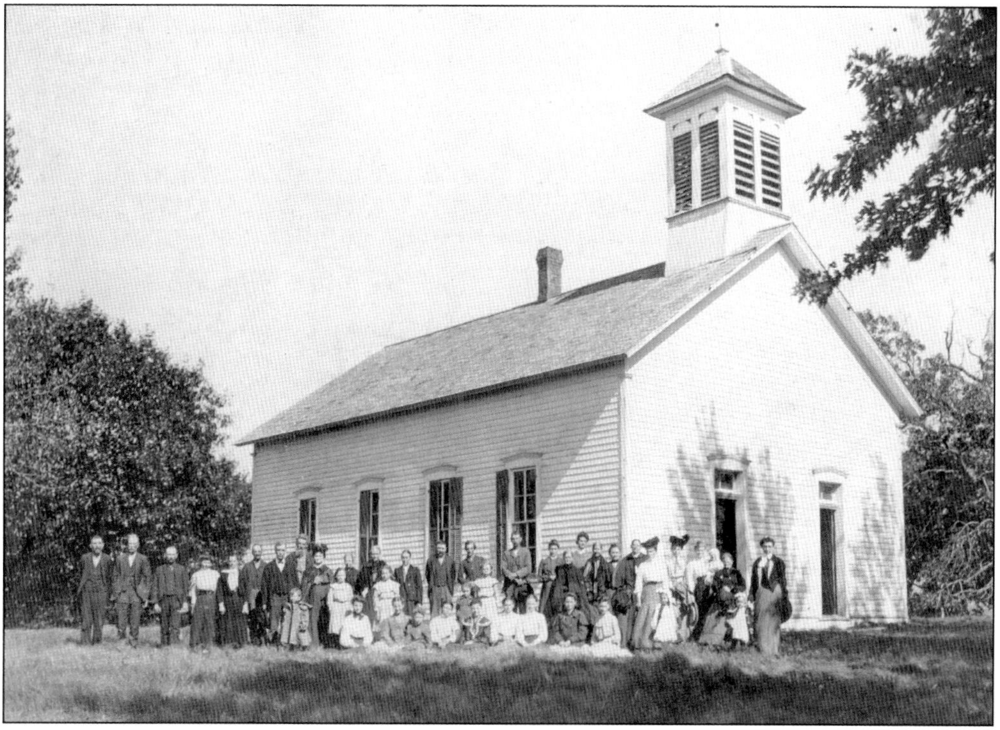

The c. 1900 photograph above shows the Bethel Church, located near Cosby. A similar image of the Rosendale Christian Church, seen below, dates from around 1945. Church affiliation both defined social status and offered socializing opportunities in small towns. As with youngsters in school pictures, photographs of church congregations might be the only images rural people ever had taken of themselves.

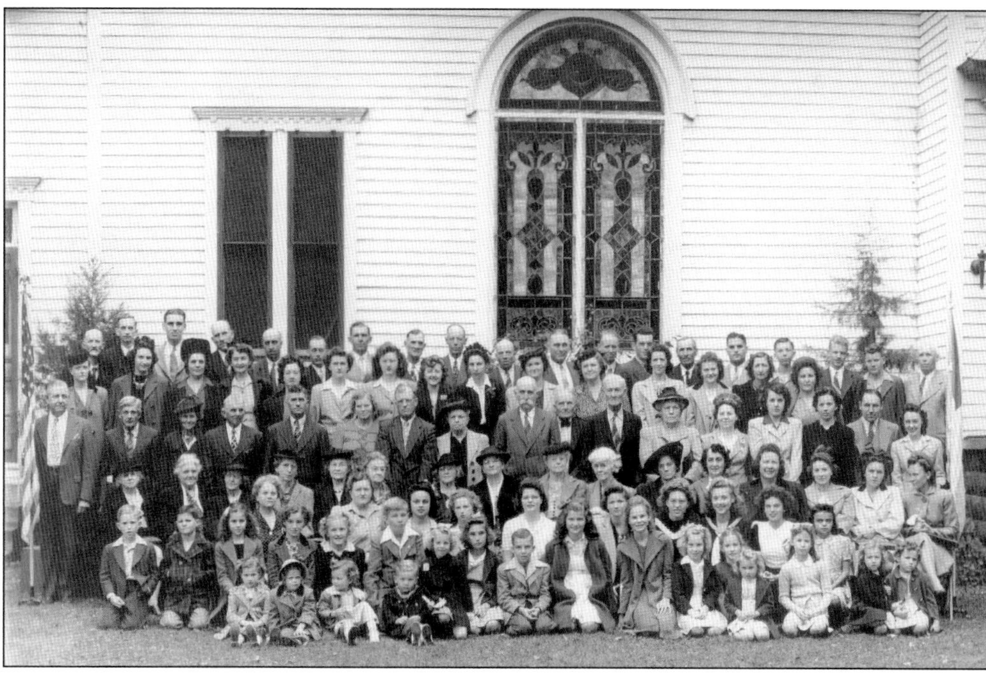

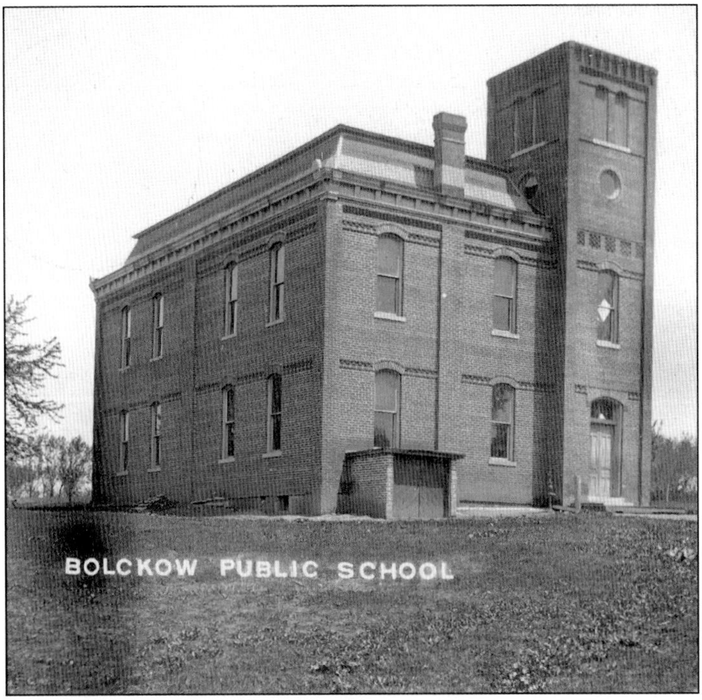

This postcard image of the Bolckow Public School illustrates the community's pride in a public school building. In 1912, a local resident mailed the card, produced by a local photographer, to Ona Davis in Clarksdale, Missouri. In the early 20th century, photographers produced small runs of localized postcards that permitted people to boast about their "progressive" communities.

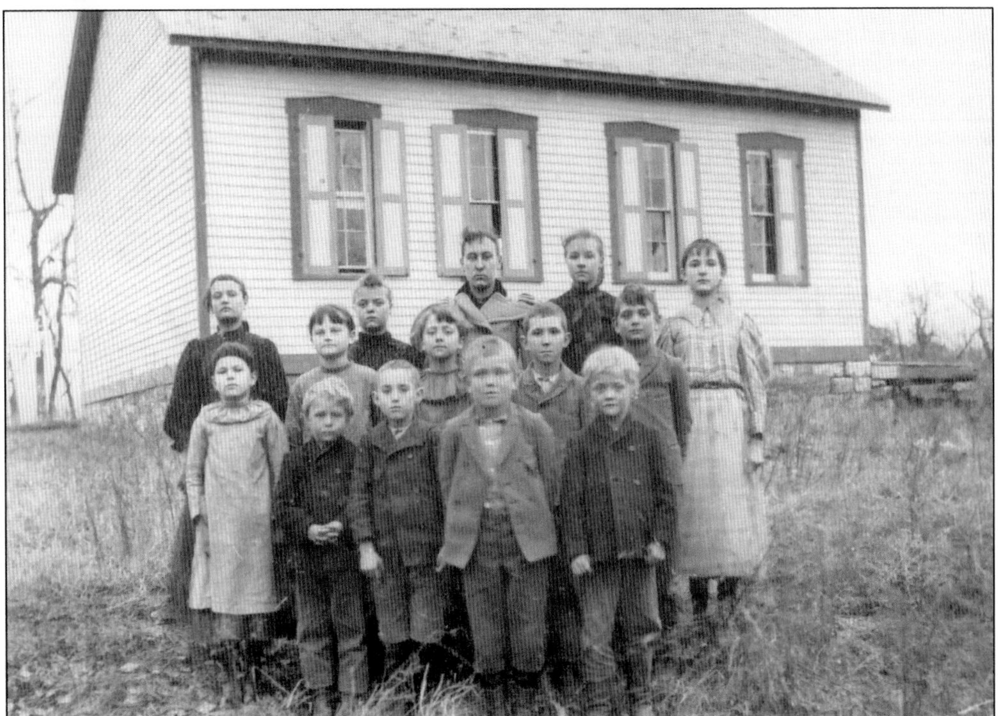

Americans embrace an idealized vision of a little red rural schoolhouse, but, as illustrated by this 1893 image of the Brand School, schoolhouses were often light colored or whitewashed. Rural school boards valued teaching the "three *R*s" but were notoriously parsimonious regarding spending on education; red paint simply cost too much.

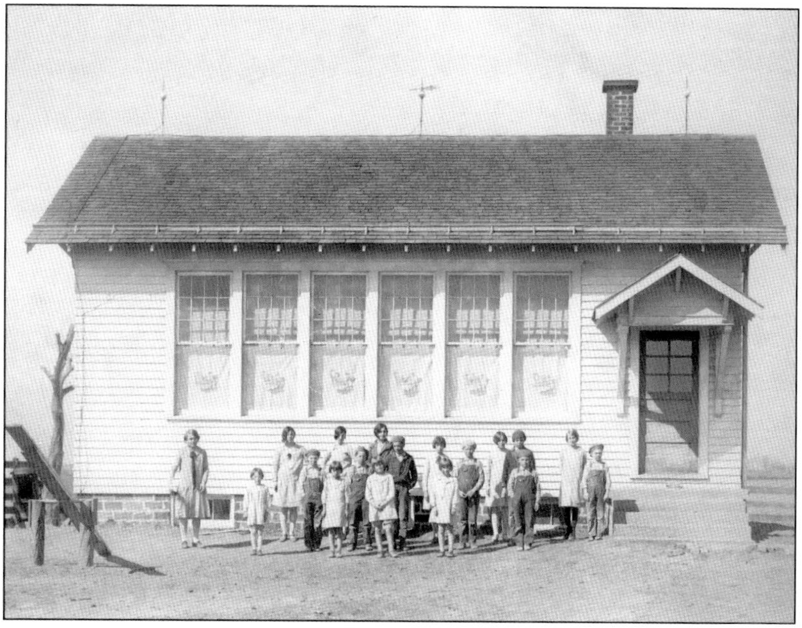

There are six windows and an entry door on the Housman School, pictured here in the late 1920s. Windows were sometimes grouped on the sunny side of a school to allow sunshine to illuminate the blackboards on the opposite interior wall. Teacher Katie Lett stands at far left.

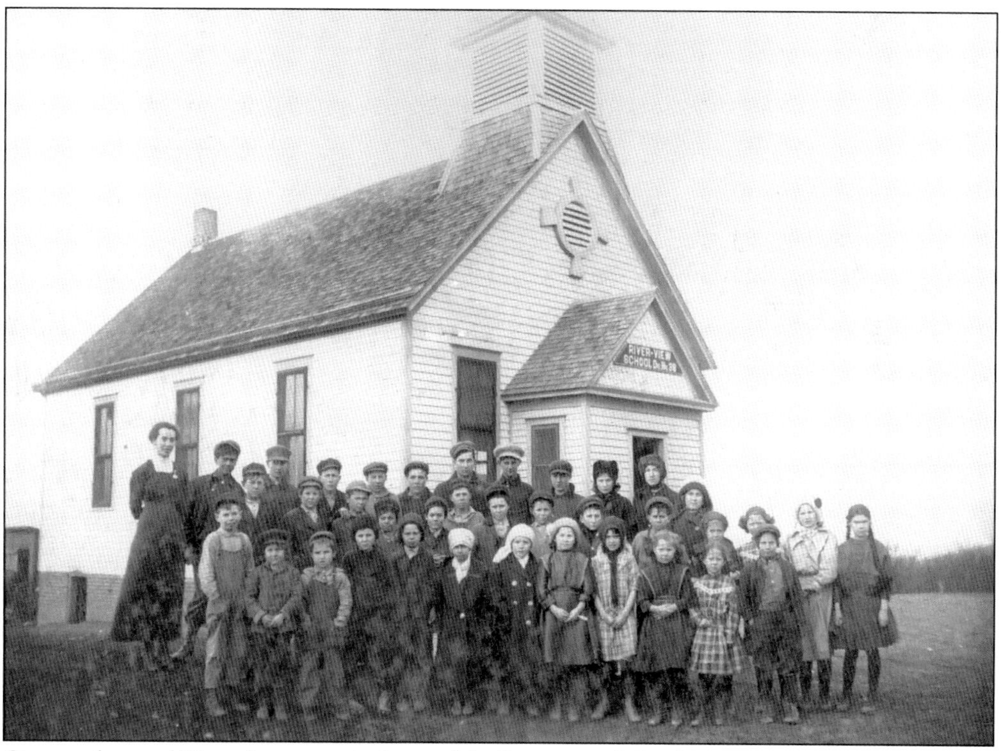

One teacher and 37 students pose in front of the Riverview School, near Amazonia, around 1915. Lewis Atherton, Missouri historian and author of *Main Street on the Middle Border*, noted that values defining country life were taught in rural schools like this, often through the well-known readers created by Rev. William Holmes McGuffey. Occasionally, the name of a locality in a rural county was taken from a school, which might be one of the few structures in an area.

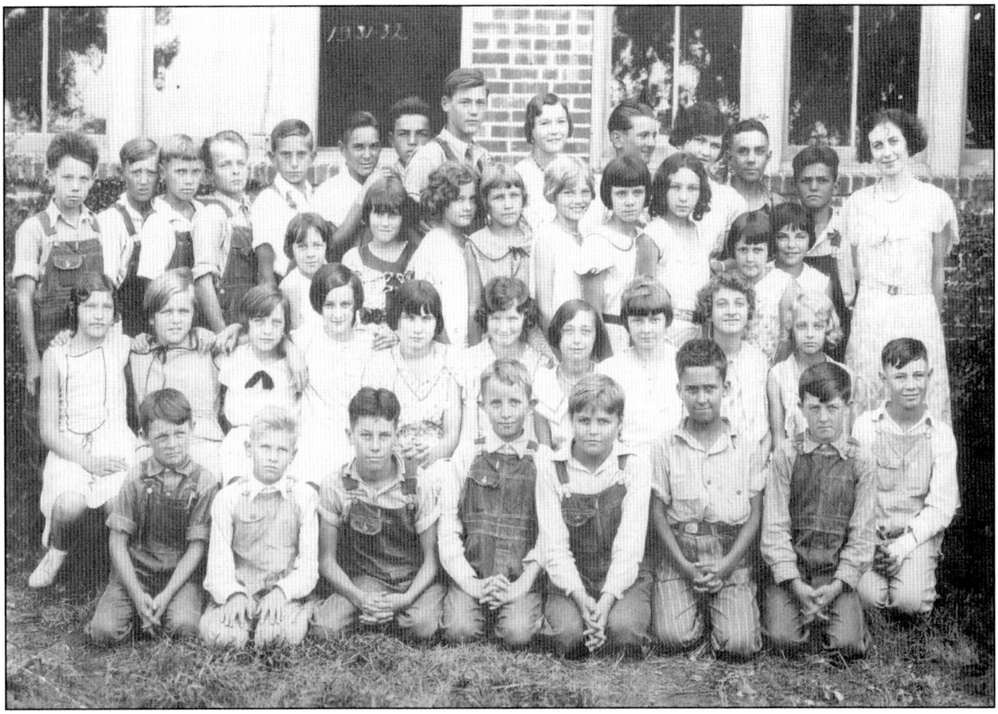

The 1931 photograph above was taken outside the Fillmore School. The 1938 photograph below shows teacher Wilma Robertson with her students at the Howard School. From the 19th century until today, professional school portraits remain an annual ritual. For some rural families, these pictures served as the only visual documentation of their children's school-age years. They were preserved in albums and shared with relatives.

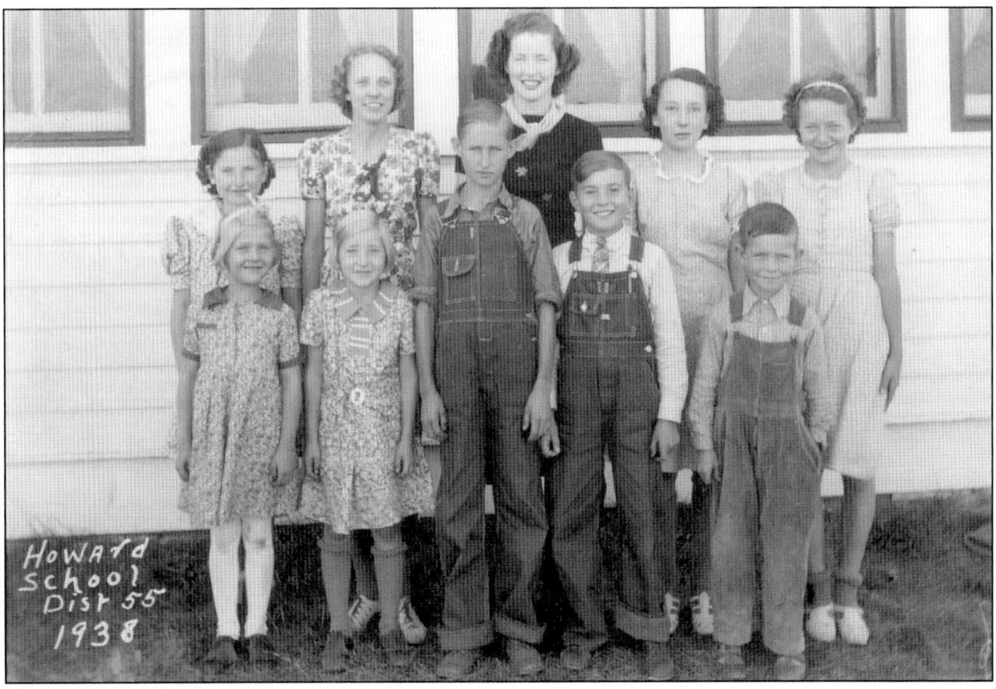

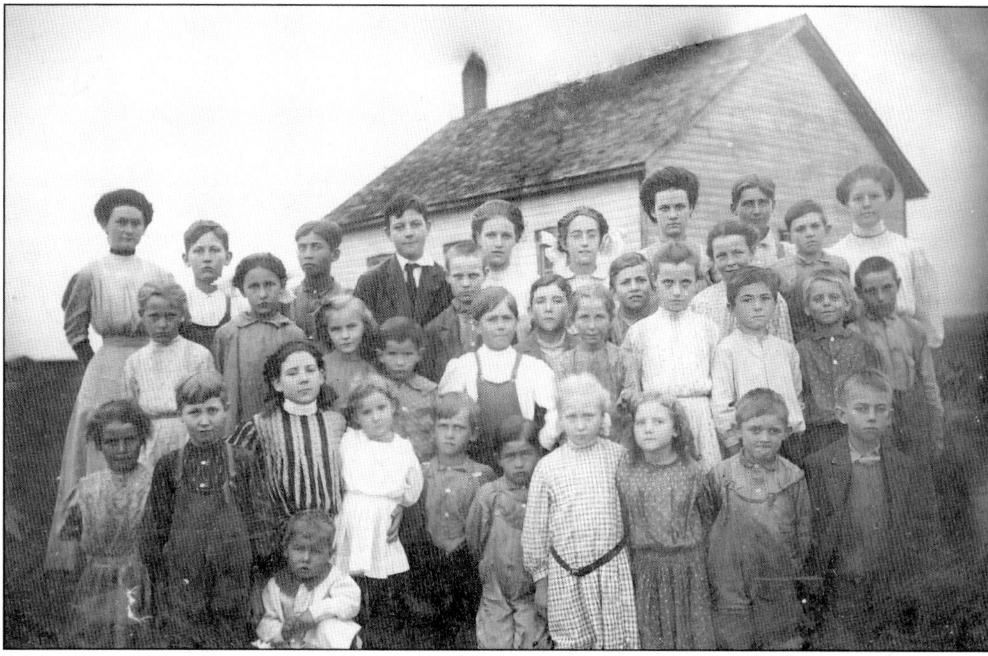

The above image shows students at the Murphy School in 1908. The photograph below was taken at the Deakin School around roughly the same time. Lewis Atherton traced learning to endorse the "cult of the useful and practical" to rural schools like these, referring to a story called "The Colonists" in Rev. William McGuffey's *Fourth Reader.* In the story, the founder of a new colony interviews potential colonists, quickly accepting farmers, millers, carpenters, blacksmiths, masons, brick-makers, and doctors. He adds a schoolteacher, since colonists must be educated. Lawyers, soldiers, and dancing masters, however, were excluded as social parasites. A "gentleman" was smugly dismissed with the statement that the honor of his company was not required. In classrooms like those in the Murphy and Deakin Schools, rural schoolchildren learned that it was better to make bricks than to dance.

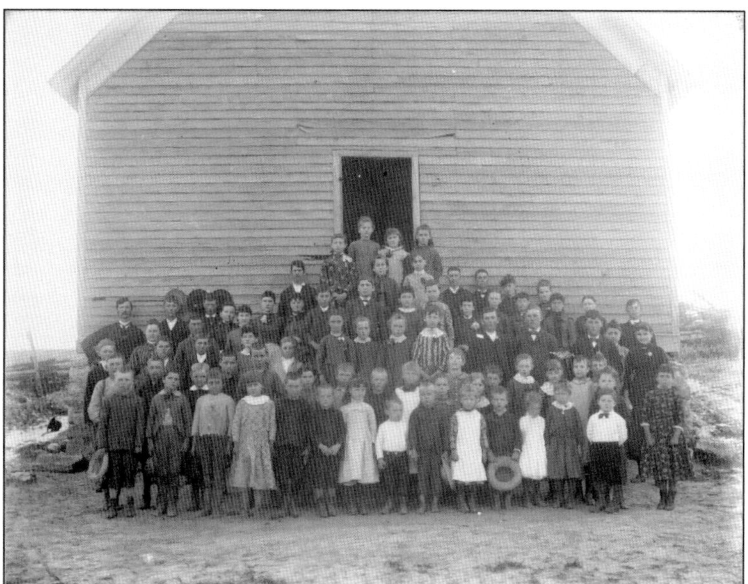

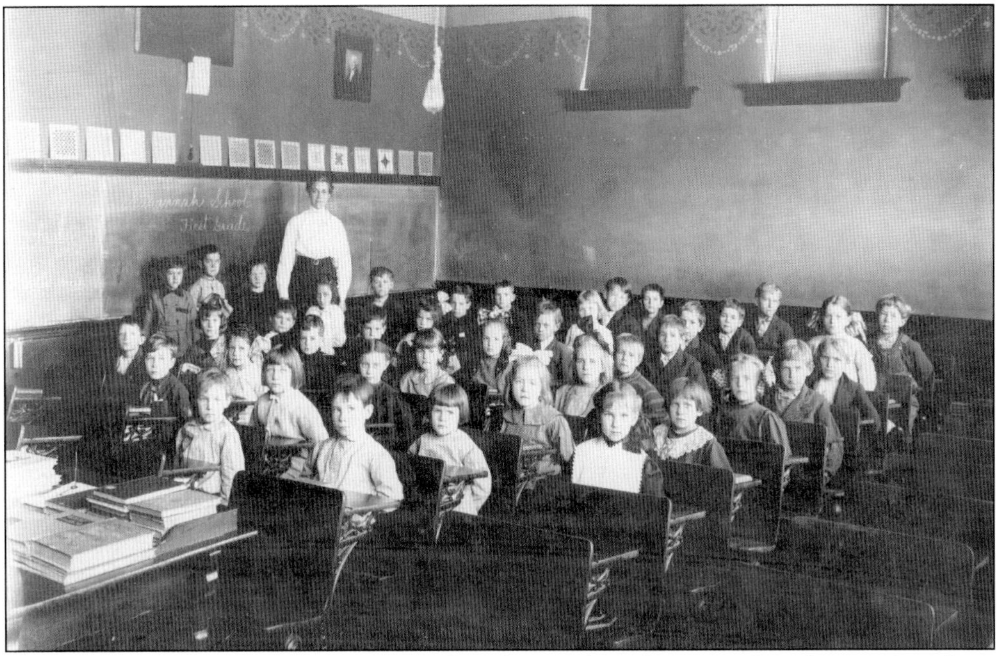

Classroom photographs are rare compared to the number of images of teachers and students standing outside schools. The c. 1914 image above shows teacher Minnie Cline in her first-grade classroom at Savannah Public School. The image below depicts a Washington School classroom in 1955. Note the number of boys in the image below; by the middle of the 20th century, schooling became a priority for both boys and girls in rural families, and boys were no longer pulled out of school for farmwork.

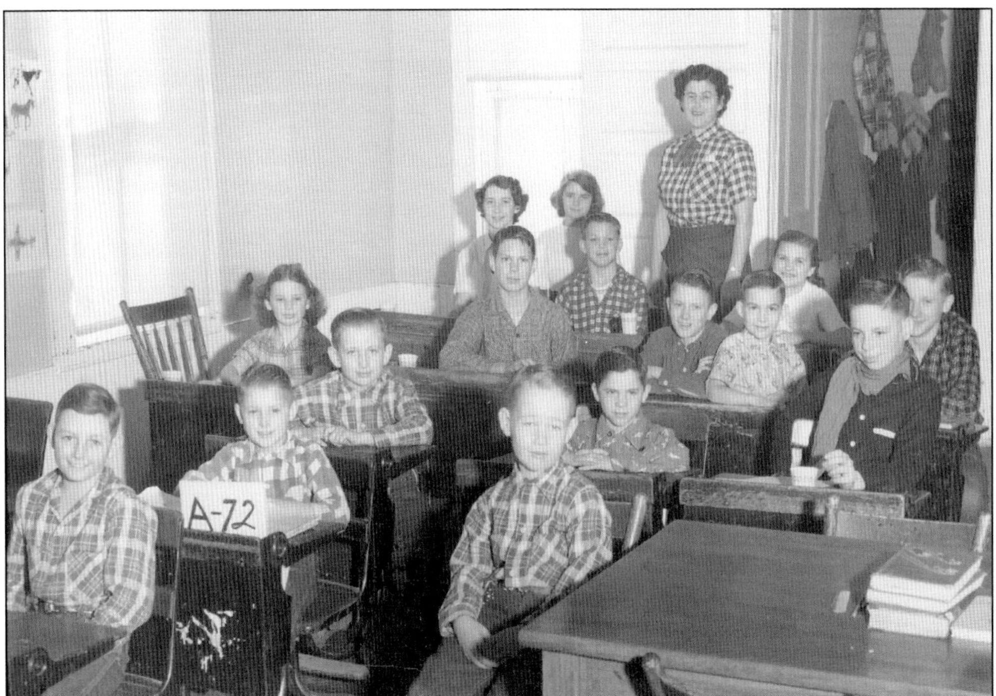

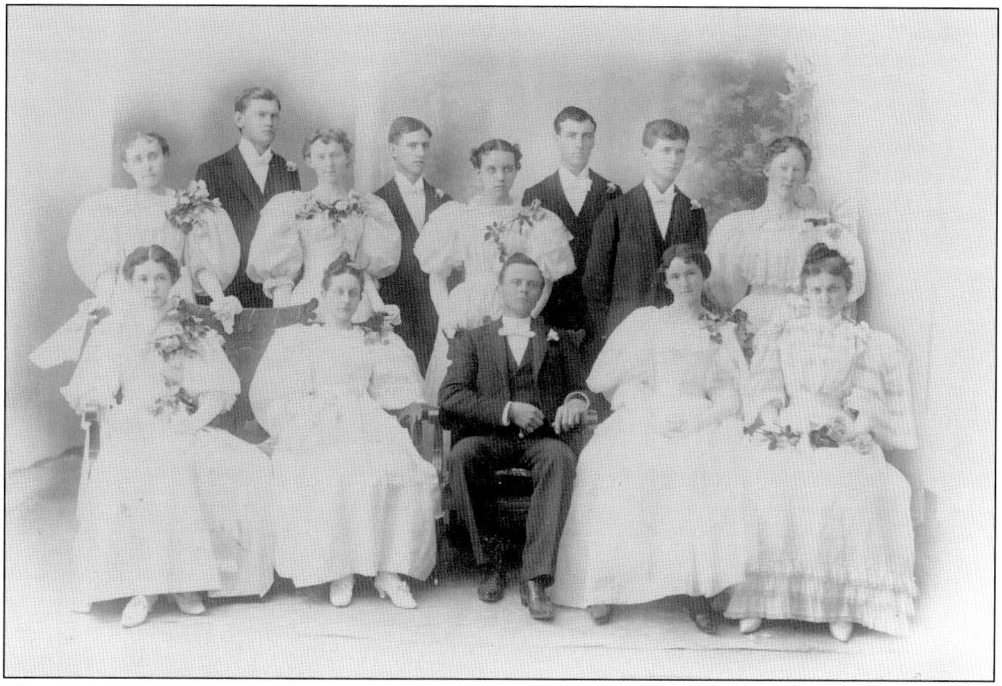

The image above shows the Savannah High School class of 1896. Pictured are, from left to right, (first row) Lula Dodge, Jessie Southerland, Supt. L.M. Garrett, Rose Schnetzius, and Nora Terhune; (second row) Edna Joy, Carl Christenson, Alma Hurst, Harry Beaghler, Gertie Clark, Will Kerr, Clyde Buis, and Helen Frodsham. The picture below shows Emma Vennekohl on the day of her high school graduation in 1943. In the 1896 photograph, the number of male students illustrates the increased emphasis on formal education for all youngsters. With the demands of modern farm management, young people now often graduate high school and study agricultural science in college.

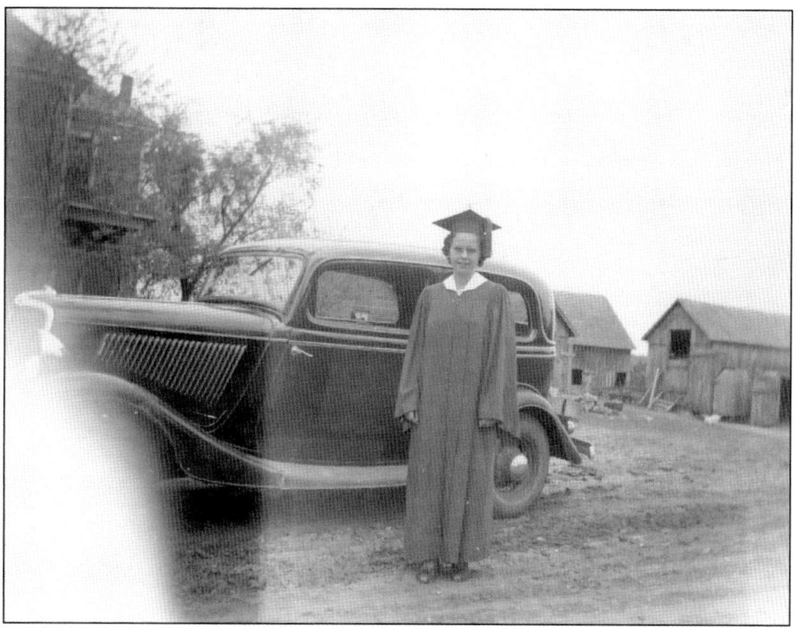

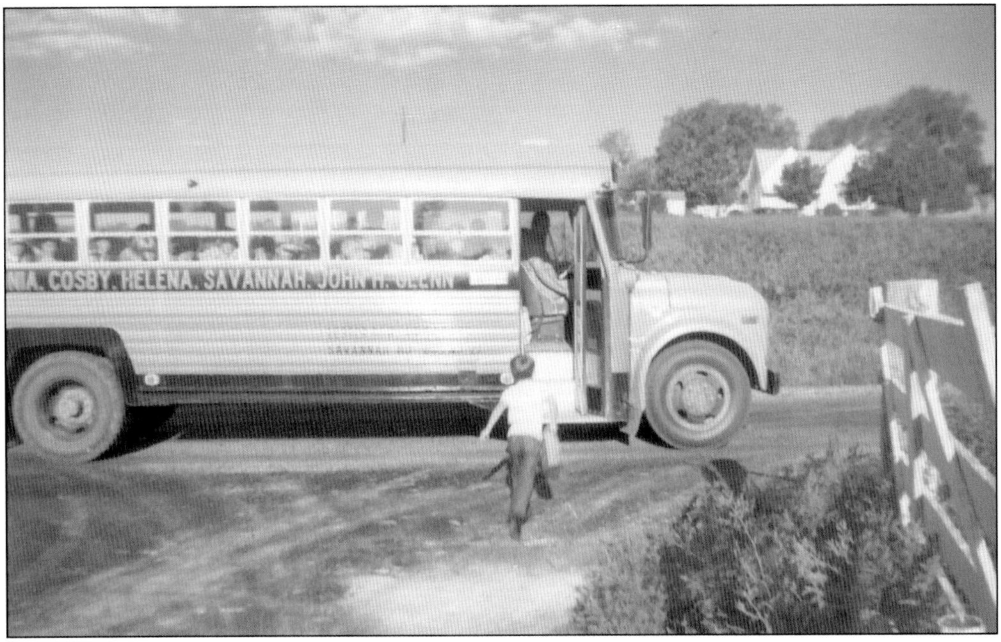

In the 1972 photograph above, Brent Kapp rushes toward a school bus. The photograph below captures a computer classroom taught by Renee Gorman at Savannah Middle School in the 1990s. In the late 20th century, consolidated school districts replaced the one-room schools that once dotted the rural landscape; consolidation was made possible by those yellow school buses. At school, students were introduced to the same computer technology as their big-city cousins. Lewis Atherton noted that in the mid-20th century, scientific thinking displaced the moral certitudes from the McGuffey readers—a trend that continued into the computer age. In 2004, Herb Clizer remembered, "We kept our farm account records in a shoebox. Sometimes we, and others, kept them in cigar boxes." Given the investment in ever-larger farms and sophisticated agricultural technology, even rural students need to master the latest computer skills.

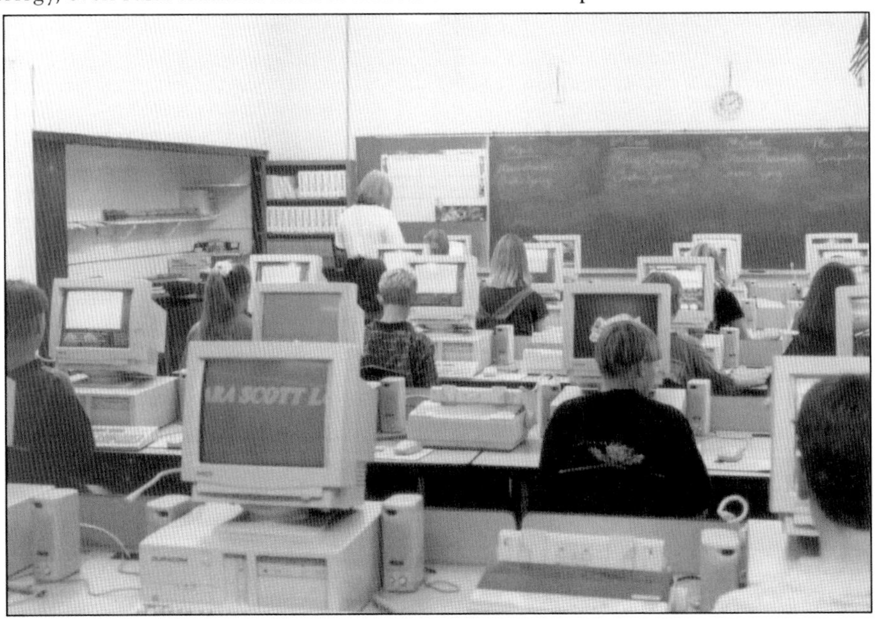

Three

Down Main Street

The first image in author and photographer Sam Breck's book about Midwestern towns, *It's A Small Town If . . .* , is of a main Street. The perception he offers is that one knows one is entering a small town "if from where it begins, you can see where it ends."

In larger towns like Savannah, landmark buildings—a courthouse, a bank, an impressive church edifice, or an opera house—served as visual magnets drawing people downtown. Often, these structures were clustered around a major intersection. In smaller places, like Whitesville, principal streets were not marked by landmark structures; they simply continued out into the countryside.

In the horse-drawn and early-automobile eras, most small towns served as market centers for nearby farm families who traveled from the countryside down roads that connected to Main Street. They shopped at the general store, which often also served as the local post office. Town centers also provided farmers with needed services. For example, in tiny Rea, which currently has a population of fewer than 100, the grain elevator is still in operation.

While small-town business owners helped families to meet practical needs, the places of business served a social function as well. In 1980, Cleo Simmons remembered a store in Rea that was operated by Mr. and Mrs. Homer Russell (or some member of the Russell family) from 1937 to 1958. Simmons recalled, "The store did a good business selling the things the people of the community needed, and buying their produce. It was a favorite meeting place for people on Saturday evenings." The stereotypical image of the country store—where locals gather around a stove to exchange gossip or play checkers—has a ring of truth to it.

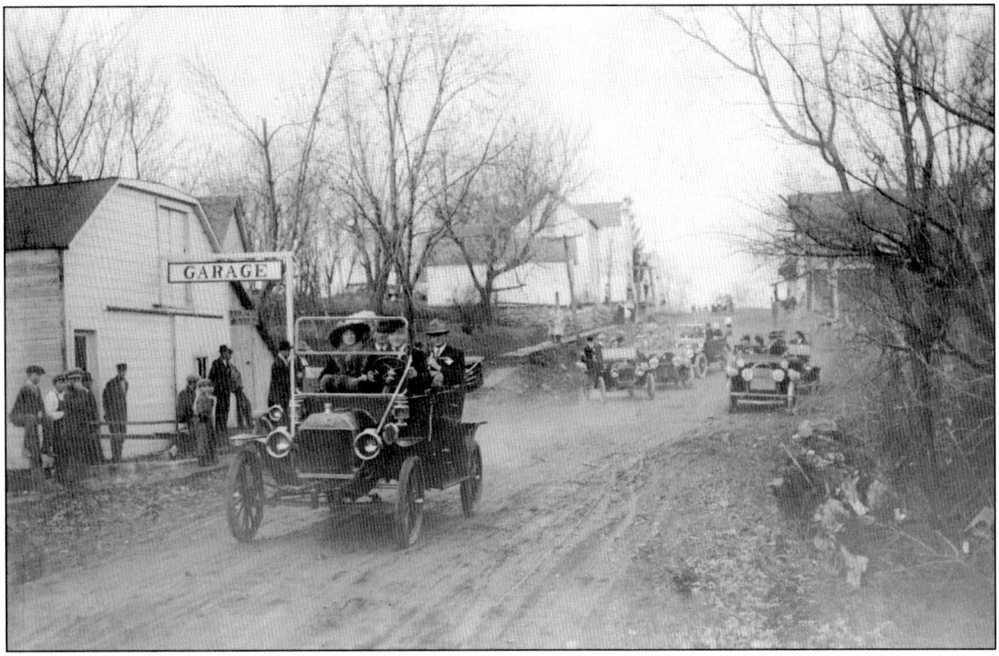

These photographs of Main Street in Whitesville date from about 1913. In many cases, a viewer could look down a small-town main street and see where the town ended and the countryside began, which illustrated the connection between a town and the farm families living within a 5- to 10-mile radius. Families came to town to shop at a general store, which was among the first places to offer access to communication technology. In 1993, Lyman Bill pointedly remembered that the Wyeth general store had a telephone.

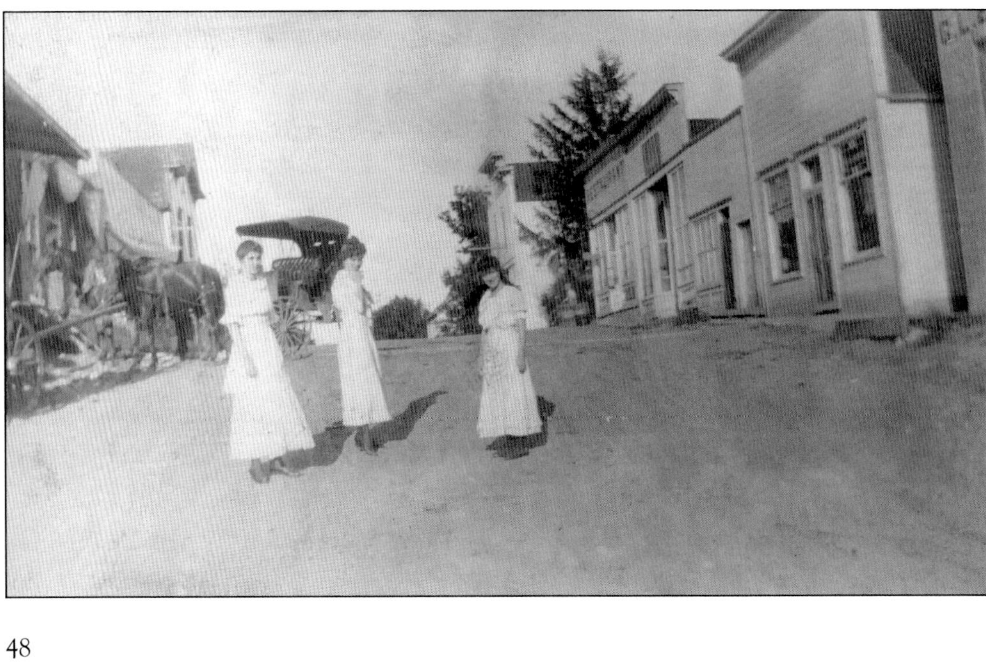

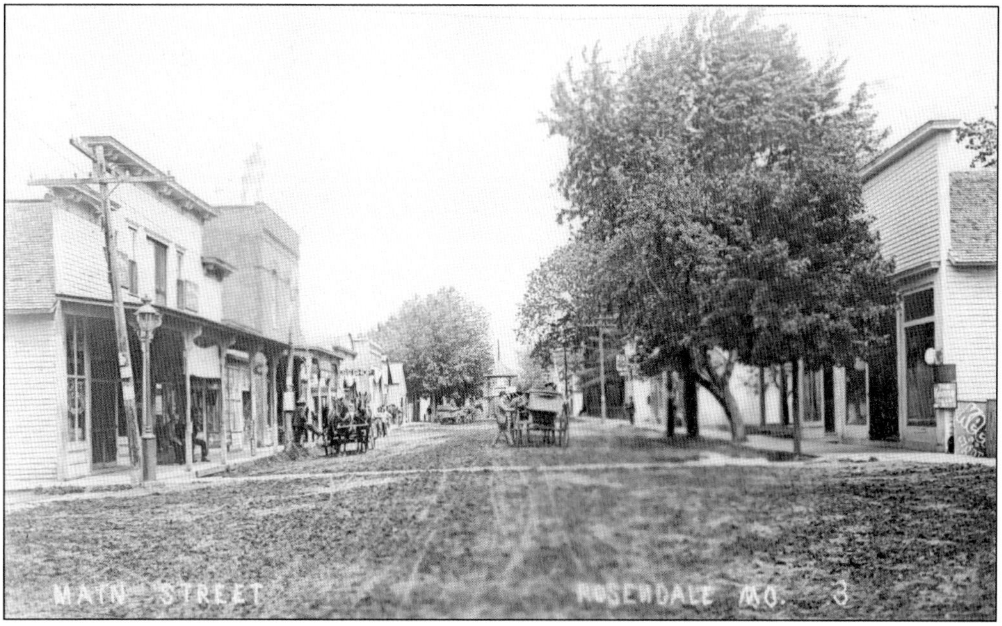

The 1916 photograph above shows Main Street in Rosendale. The image below, of Main Street in Fillmore, is from about the same time. In the below photograph, the second building displays the letters "IOOF" above the second-story windows, which stand for the Independent Order of Odd Fellows, a fraternal organization committed to charitable acts and civic betterment. In small towns throughout Andrew County, people who shared interests formed social clubs to promote camaraderie and civic involvement. The resulting familial atmosphere created strong, hard-to-break bonds among people.

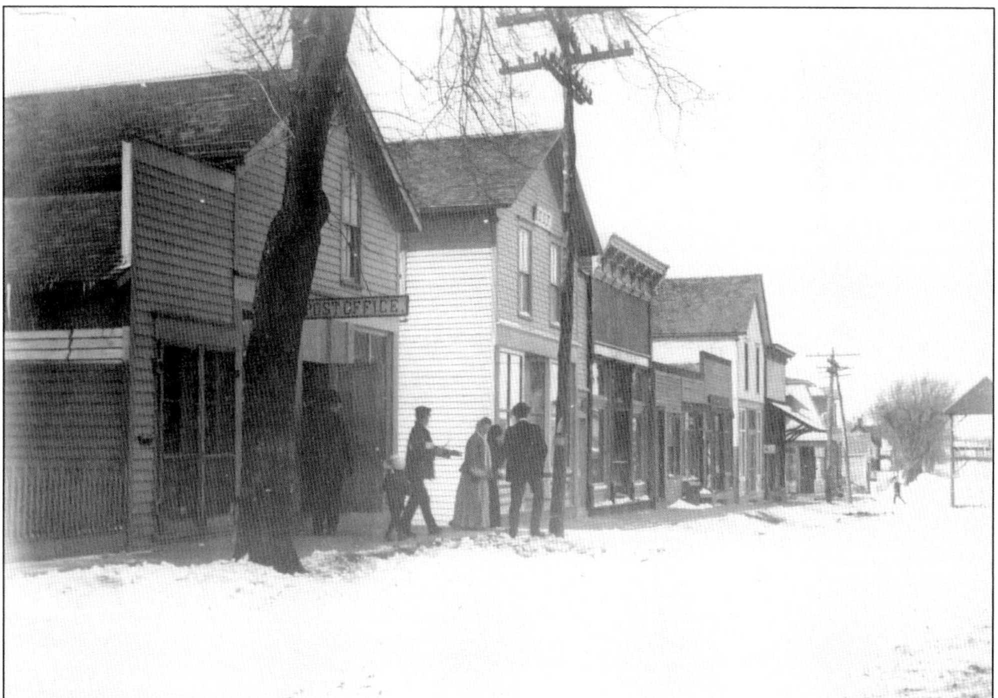

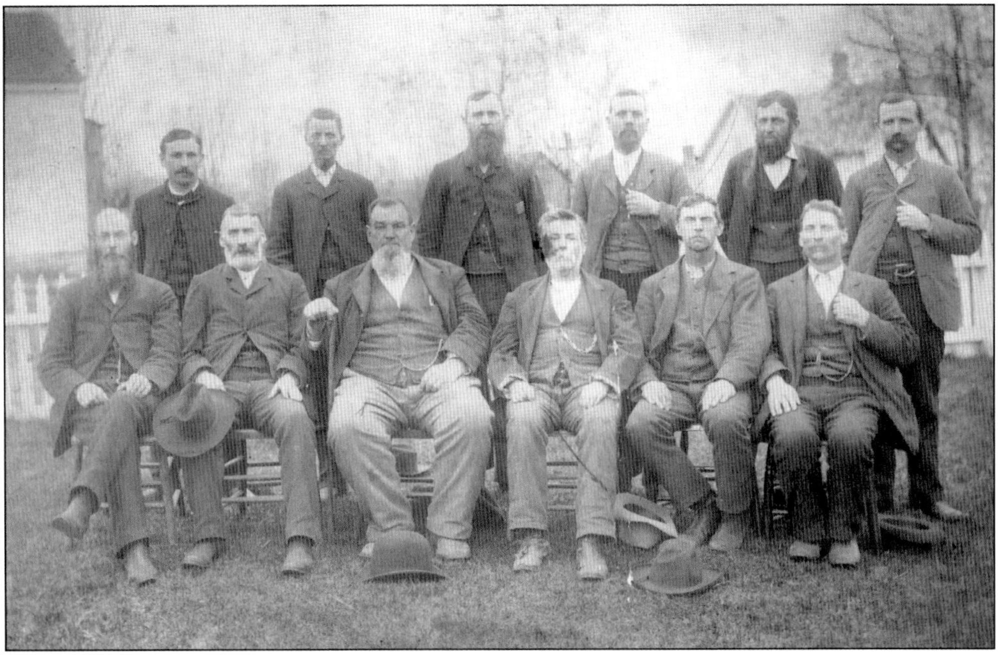

Local merchants assumed a leadership role in boosting the fortunes of a town in the late 19th and early 20th centuries. They formed boards of trade that eventually transformed into chambers of commerce. This is a group of Fillmore merchants around 1885.

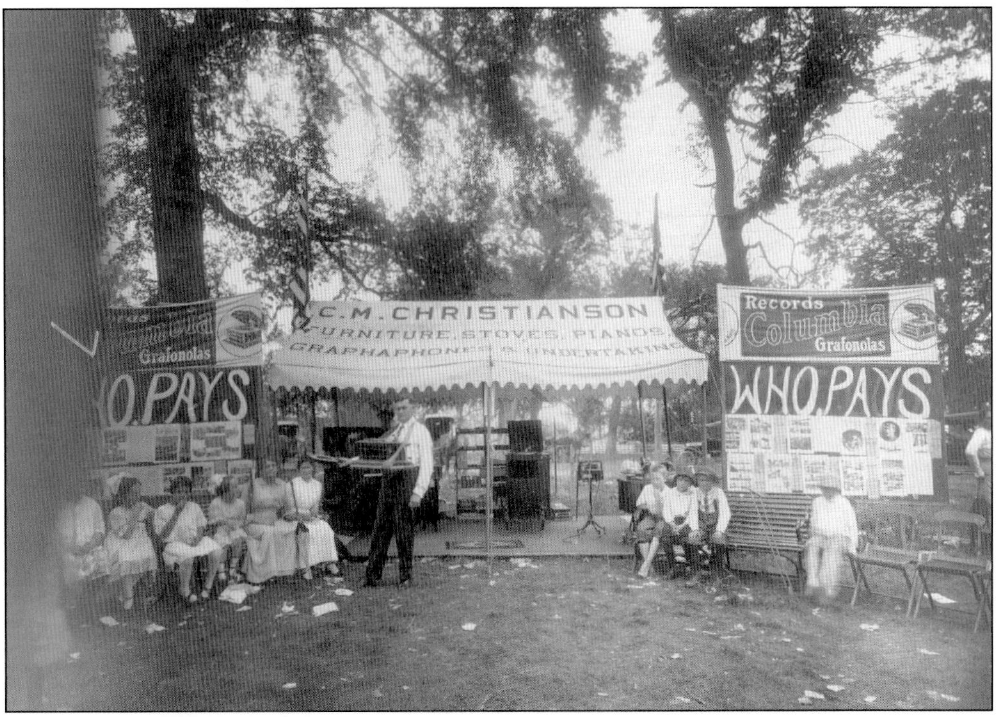

Very often, a small-town merchant needed to engage in several different lines of business in order to make a living. In this c. 1920 image, C.M. Christianson promotes his business in a Savannah public park. He sold furniture, stoves, pianos, and "graphaphones"; he was also an undertaker.

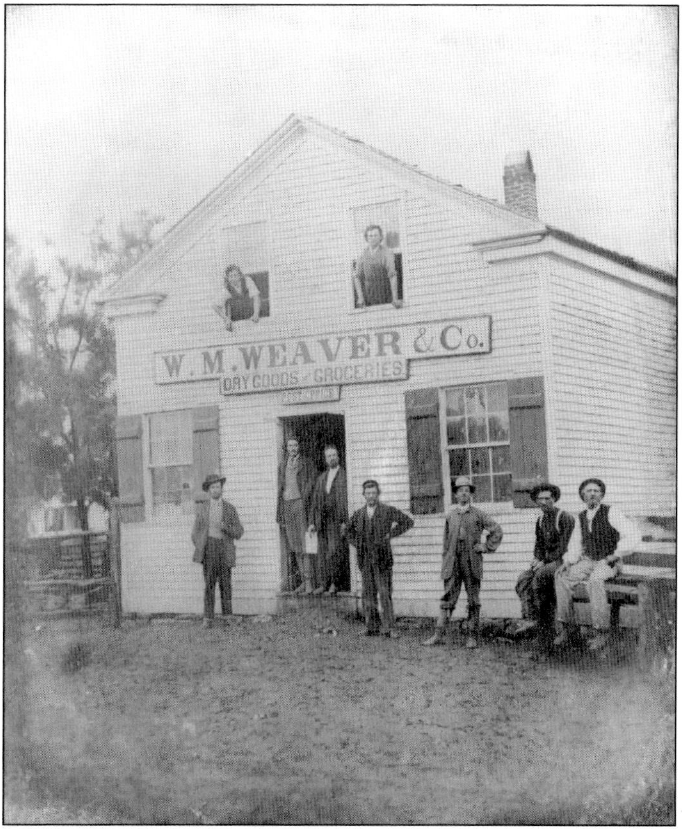

This c. 1910 image shows the W.M. Weaver & Co. general store in Whitesville. Although stores like this were small and product selection was limited, the service was personal and the atmosphere social.

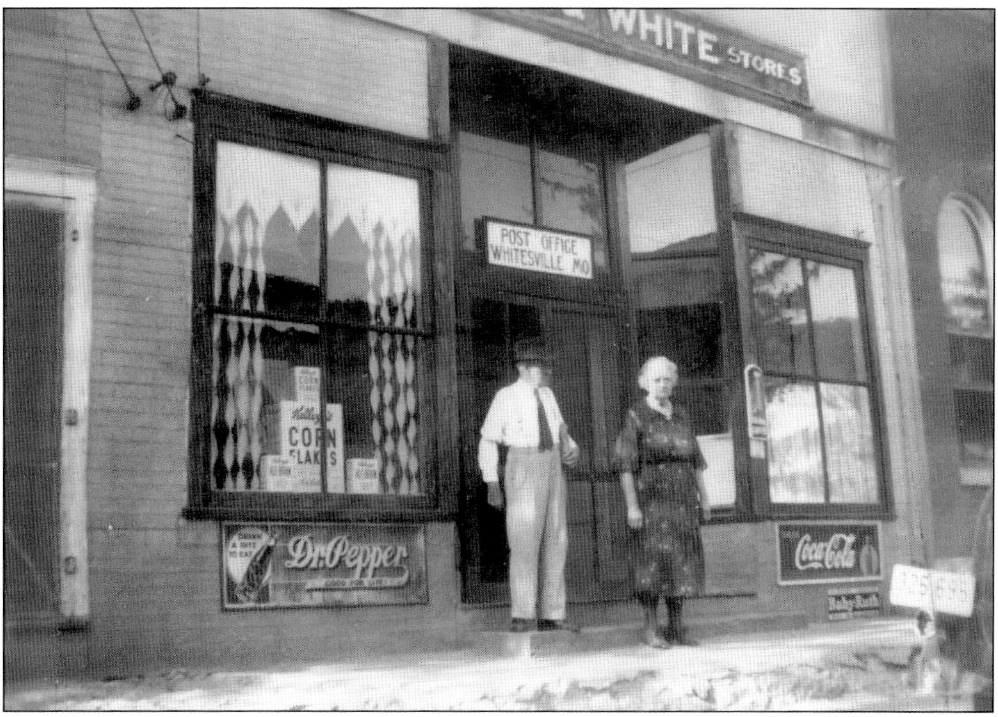

By the 1930s, the Whitesville general store sported a traditional storefront, with two large display windows flanking a central entry door. The windows included advertisements for Corn Flakes, Dr. Pepper, and Coca-Cola, illustrating the shift from selling goods in bulk to offering prepackaged brand-name products.

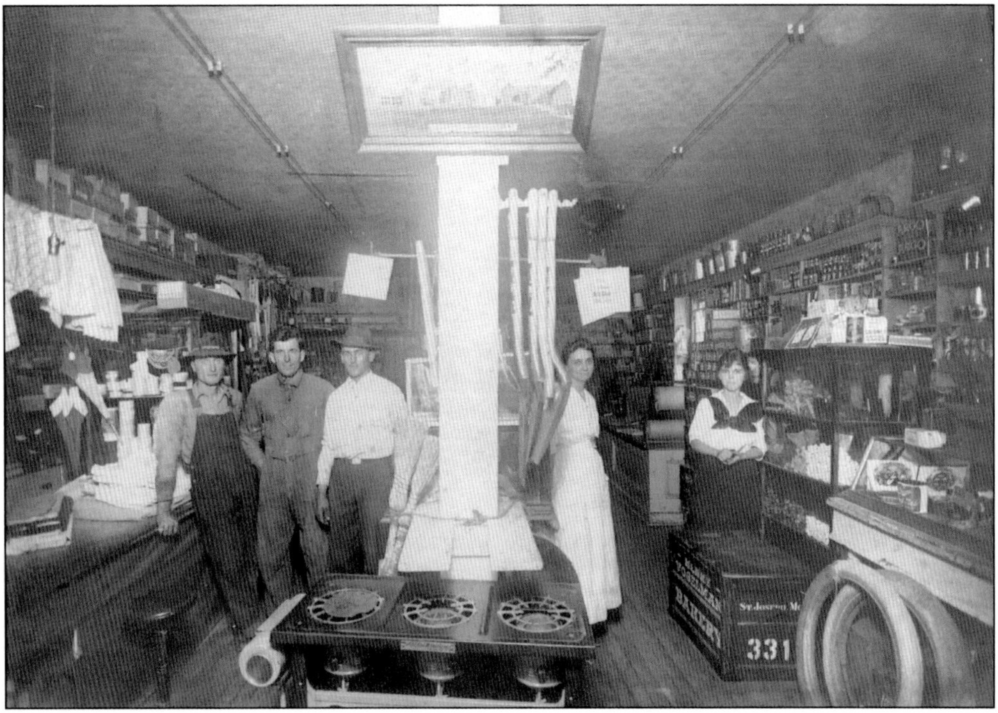

The c. 1916 photograph above shows the interior of the Amazonia general store. Pictured within are, from left to right, Adolph Egger, Albert Yenni, Clarence Schenks, postmistress Minnie Yenni, and Ida Kurz. The photograph below depicts the interior of the Cosby general store around the same time. In the 1980s, Henry Bunsen remembered the range of merchandise carried in a local store. He recalled, "Imagine going into Mr. Kline's general store. Under the grocery counter was a set of bins for sugar, beans, perhaps flour and other articles. There were very few canned goods. There were no fresh fruits or vegetables; on another counter were some dry goods as bolts of gingham, calico, overalls and shirts and other things. The other side of the store was for hardware."

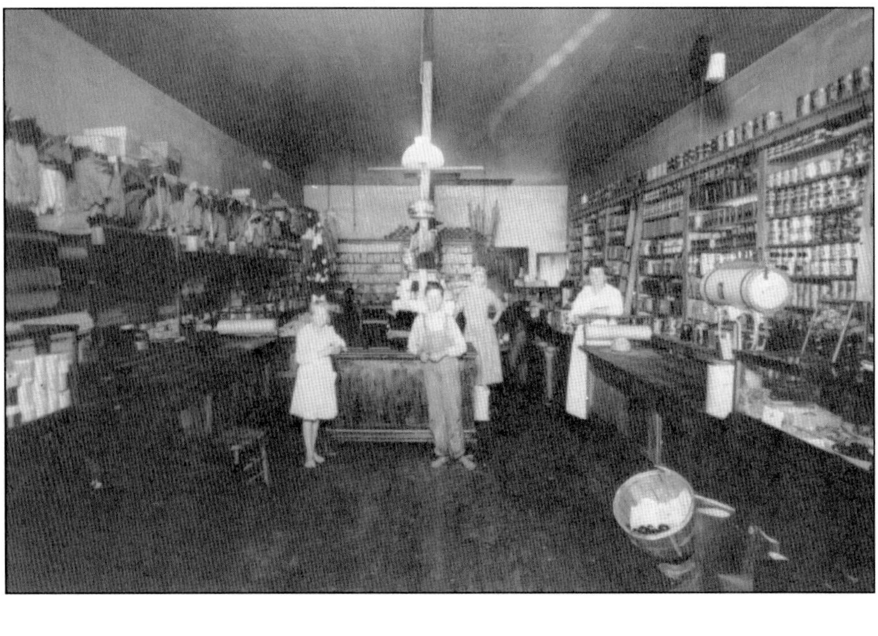

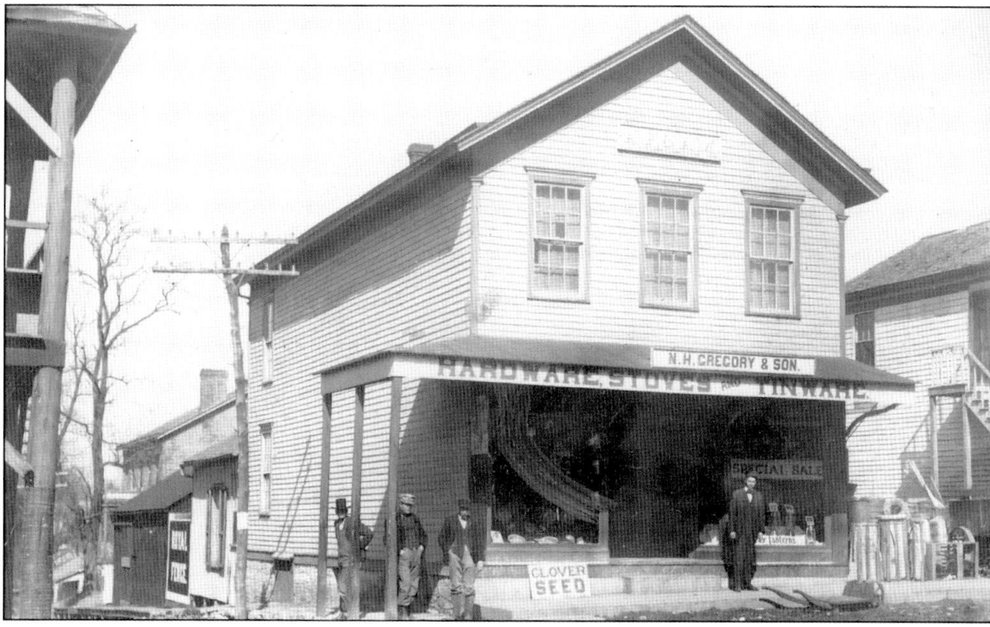

The image above of the exterior of the Gregory Hardware Store in Fillmore dates from about 1925. The photograph below was taken inside Gregory Hardware in 1955. In small-town Andrew County, many businesses were operated by the same family for several generations. In the below photograph, Horace Gregory, wearing his bow tie, stands on the far left. In the center, a customer waits for service from a longtime employee. The photograph illustrates the wide range of merchandise available in a hardware store in any quantity the customer wanted. If he needed one nut and bolt, he could purchase one, not six in a blister pack.

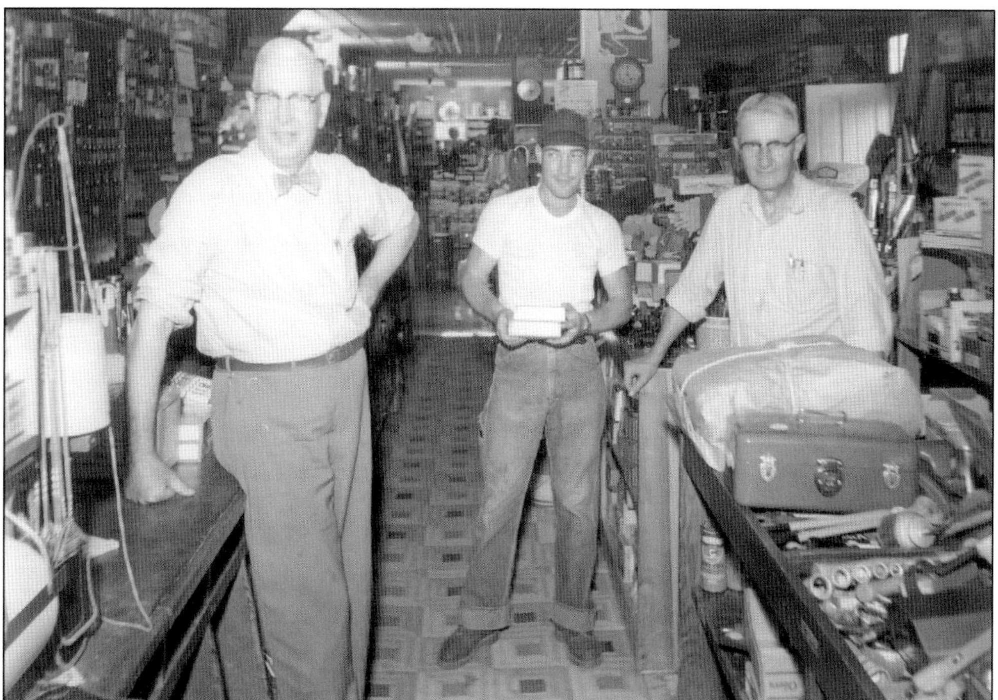

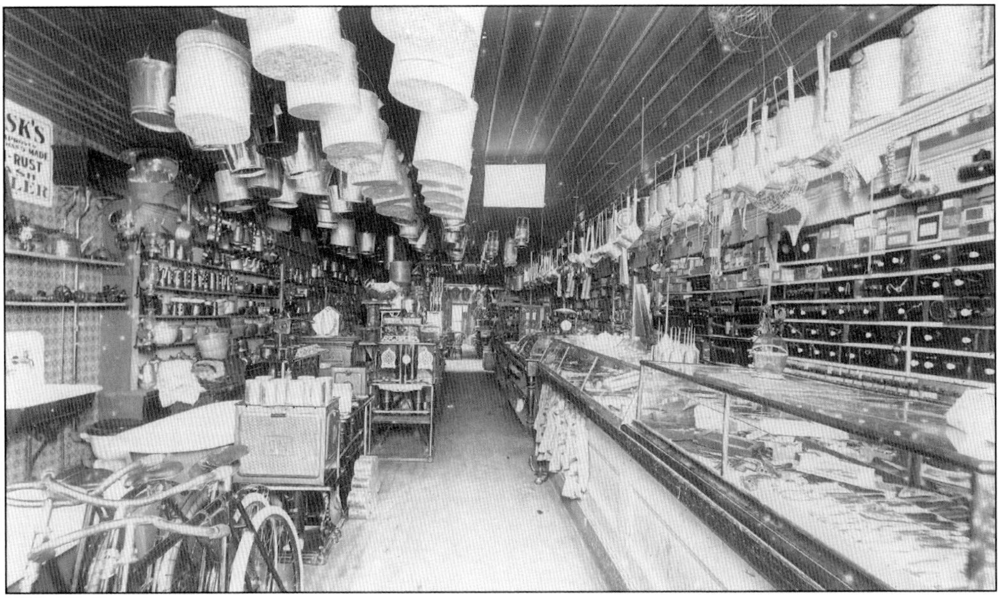

The photograph above shows Clasbey's Hardware Store in Savannah in the early 1900s, illustrating the range of merchandise offered at these types of stores. That range expanded over time: for example, bicycles appear in the foreground of the above photograph. Many people purchased bicycles as a form of basic transportation. In the 1930s, when radios became widely available, rural people might have purchased their first radio set at the local hardware store. The c. 1920 image below depicts the interior of Frank Gilmour's bakery in Rosendale. C.F. "Frank" Gilmour stands behind the counter on the left. These photographs illustrate traditional store design. Behind the display windows that faced the street, store interiors were basically long rectangular boxes with merchandise stacked along both walls.

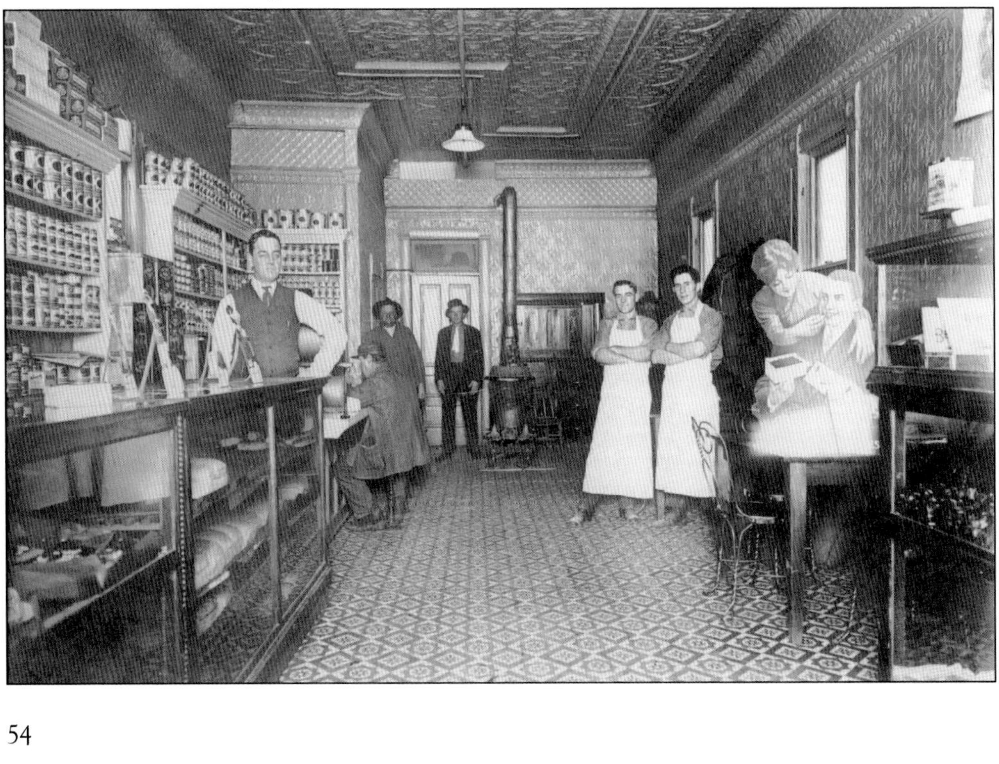

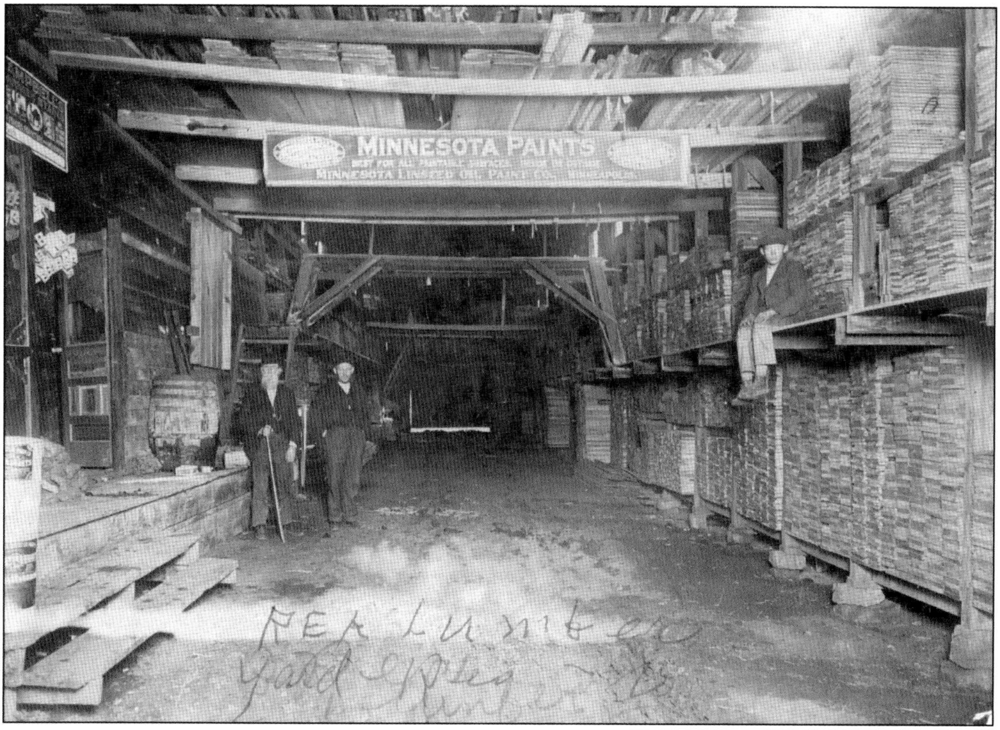

The image above shows the interior storage area of Rea Lumber in the early 1900s. The photograph below, from 2001, is of the grain elevator in Rea. A town could develop around businesses that met basic needs for rural people. A modest downtown district provided country people with a general store, a bank, a small church, and perhaps a rural school. In the 1980s, Lyman Bill remembered the people who populated such a town. He recalled, "The people of the Wyeth community were warm, wonderful, colorful. [They] were somewhat typical Missourians who were inclined to say what they thought, mincing no words."

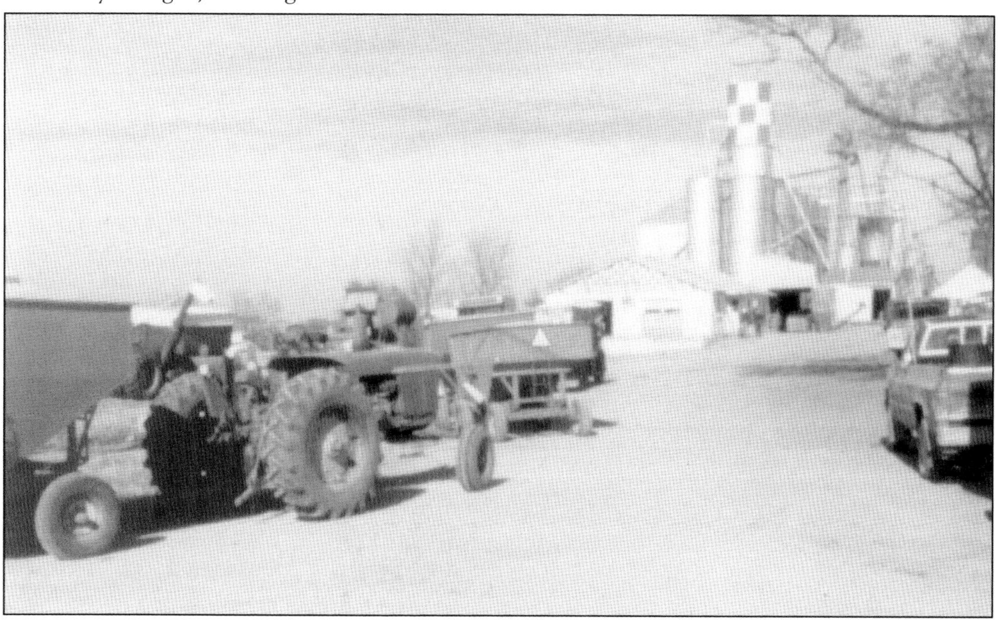

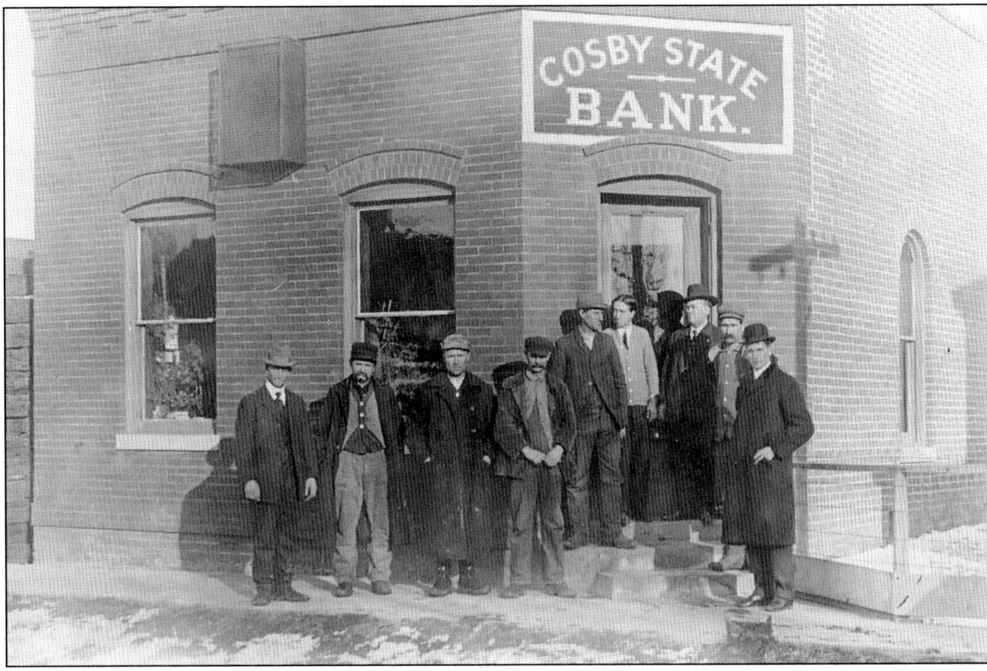

Given farmers' seasonal need for credit, local financial institutions operated in even the smallest Andrew County towns. The c. 1912 image above shows the exterior of the Cosby State Bank. While they were usually not as elaborate as bank buildings in larger places, small-town banks made some effort at architectural distinction. In Cosby, for example, the state bank boasted a decorative course of brick along the cornice line and rounded window openings. The 1915 photograph below offers a peek at the teller's cage in the bank interior. Along with the oversized alarm box on the outside of the building, the teller's cage communicated a sense of security to bank customers.

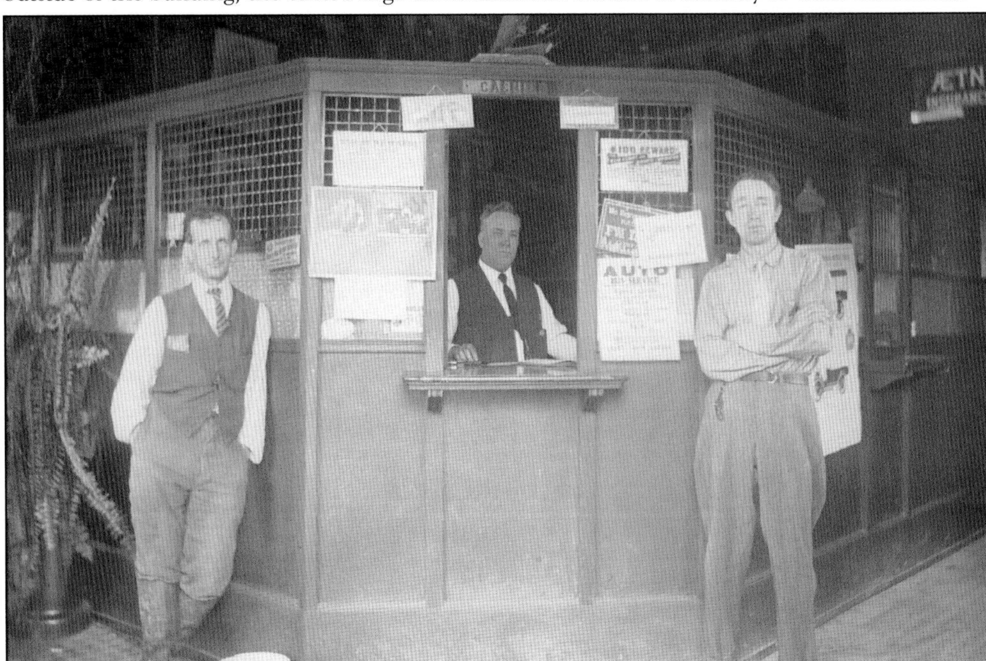

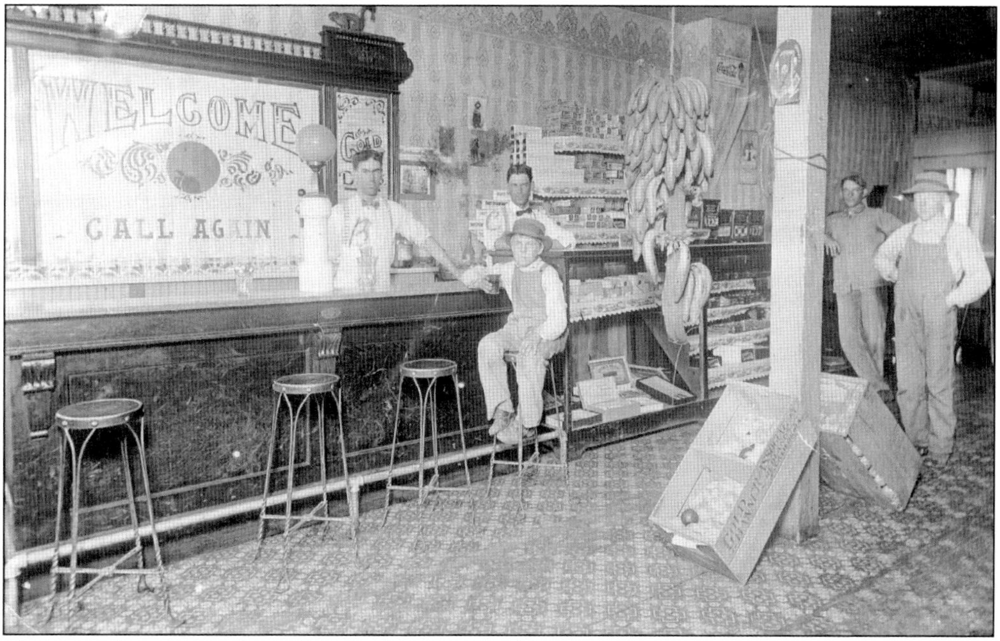

The 1913 photograph above depicts the interior of the Beattie and Castle Restaurant in Cawood. The picture below, taken two years later, is of Clyde Ferguson's Restaurant in Rosendale; Ferguson stands behind the counter on the far right. In the Beattie and Castle photograph, restaurant employees are wearing long-sleeved white shirts, aprons, and bow ties. The unidentified boy and two men wear work clothes. For rural people, dining at a local eatery was an extra perk during town visits; eating at a place like the Beattie and Castle was the equivalent of the cherry on top of the banana split that was a trip into town.

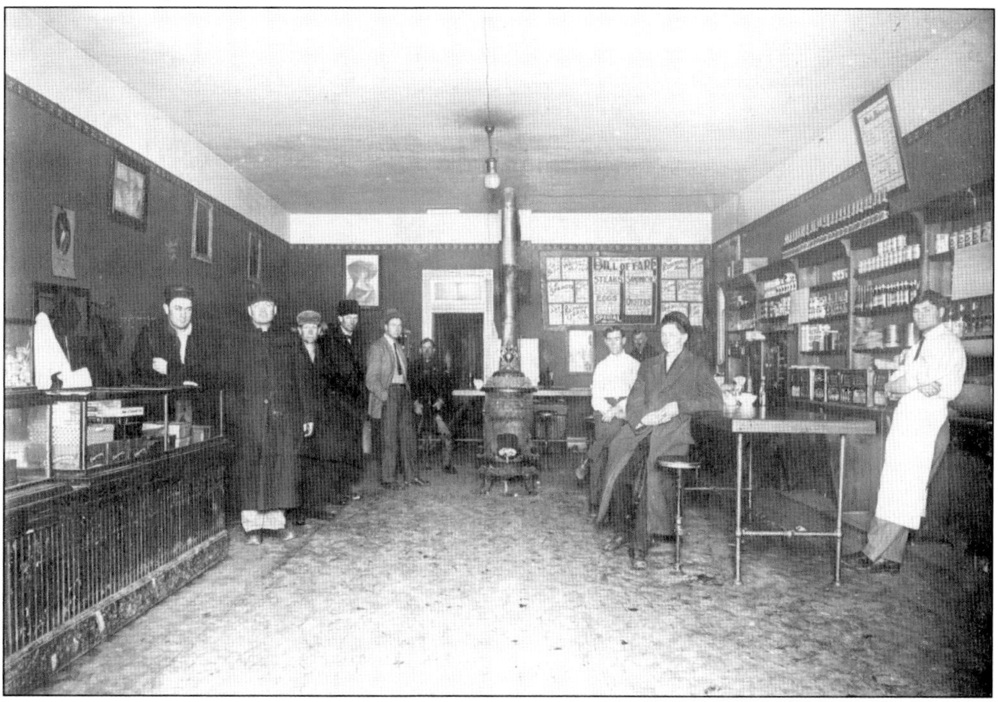

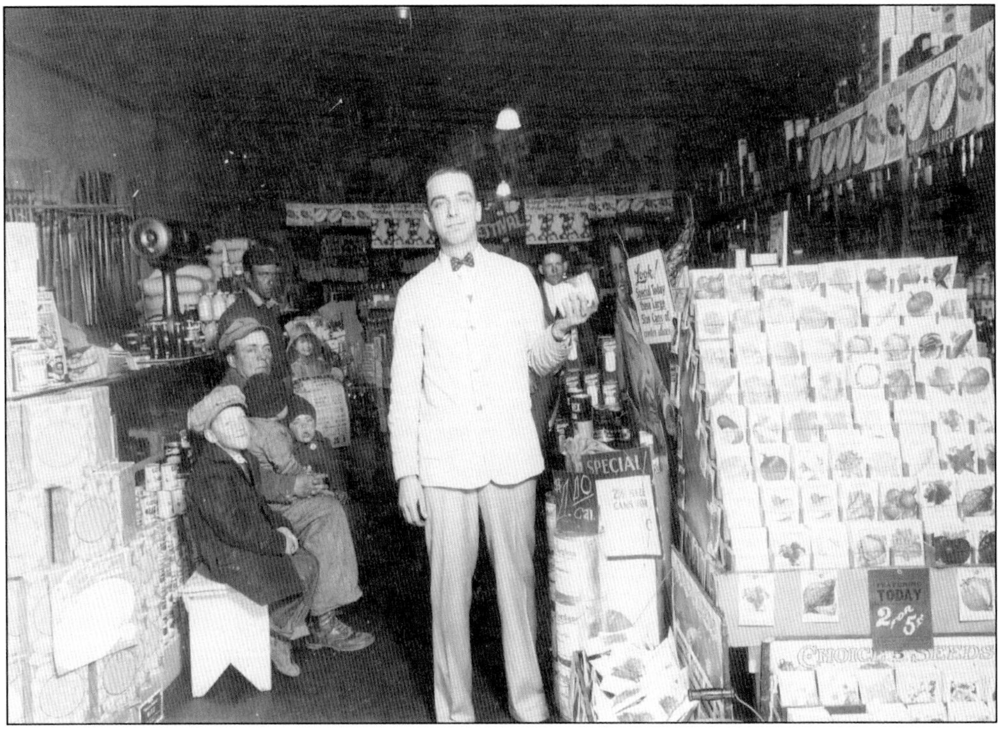

In the 1930 photograph above, grocer O.R. Roberts holds some canned goods sold in his store. Eight years later, in the image below, Ray Ramsey (left) stands beside owner Kenny Lentz in the Red & White Store in Fillmore. Red & White was a chain of independently owned and operated food stores. Lentz holds a loaf of Wonder Bread, much like how Roberts grasped canned goods. Both images illustrate the shift that small-town grocers made from selling bulk goods once stocked in general stores to selling pre-packaged, pre-priced foodstuffs. A clerk no longer filled a customer's order from a shopping list. By the 1930s, shoppers themselves filled their baskets with pre-packaged, name-brand items.

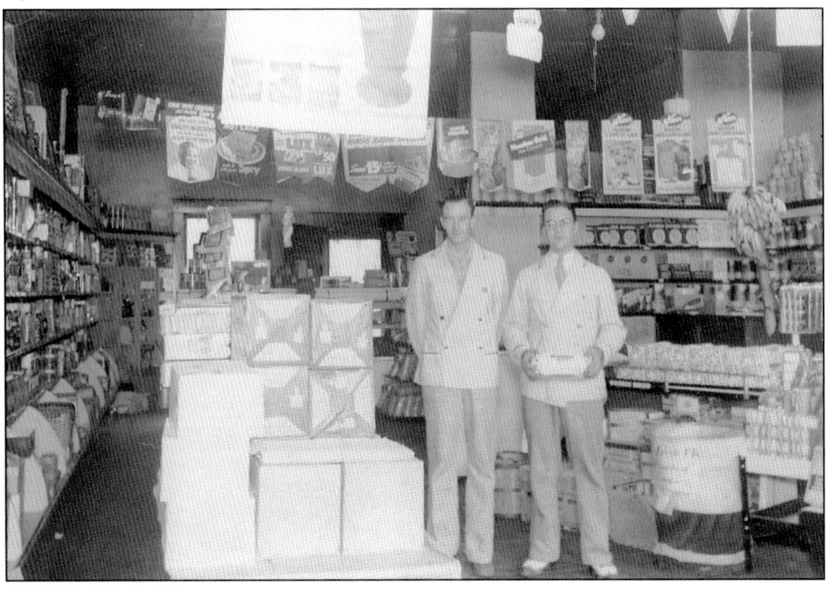

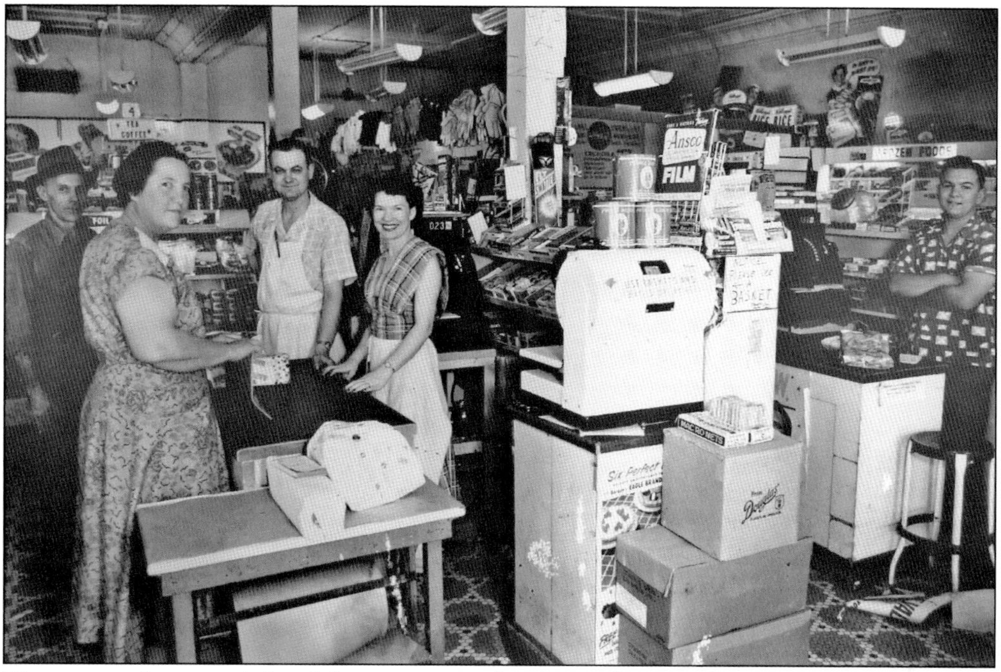

The man and woman behind the counter in the above photograph are W. Jean Stanton and his wife, Helen. The c. 1950 image was taken in the Stanton A.G. Market in Savannah. The photograph below shows Swanson's Grocery Store just before its grand opening in 1953. Swanson's moved from downtown Savannah to Highway 71, on the edge of town. The new supermarket was a bright, enlarged shopping space with an expanded product selection. Its location also illustrated a shift in preference for business owners from a pedestrian-oriented downtown shopping space to a location convenient for consumers in automobiles.

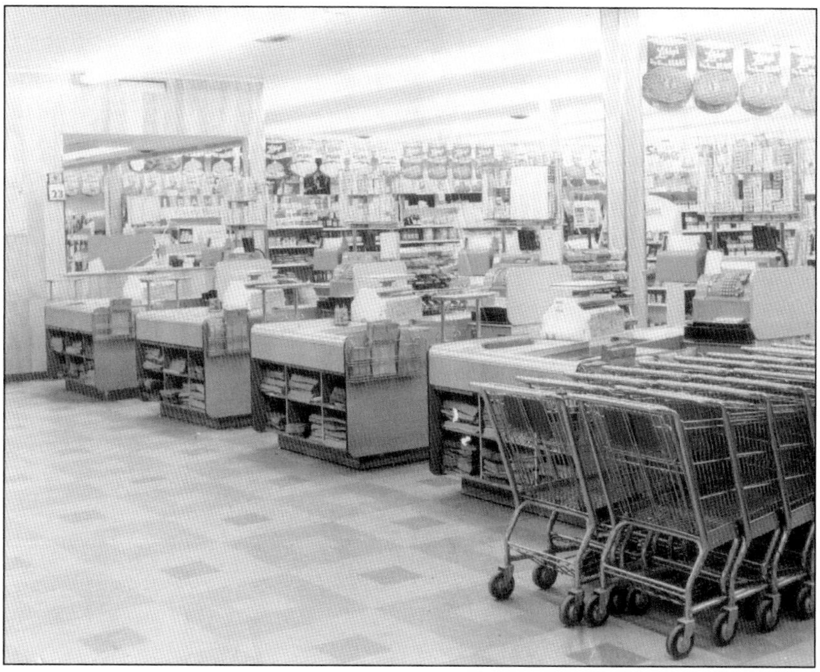

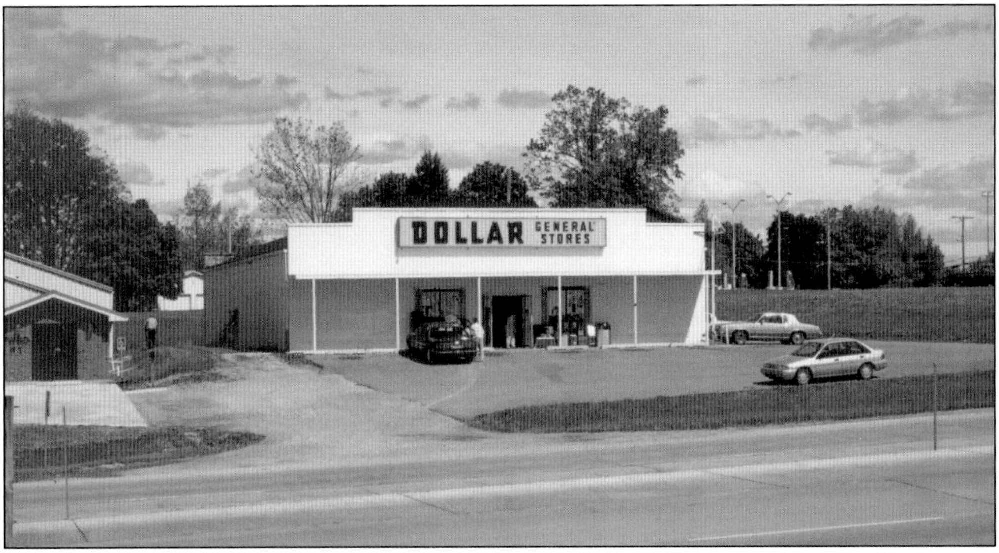

While locally owned businesses like Swanson's Grocery Store were located on Highway 71, national retail chains also appeared along the route, providing price competition for local independent retailers. The c. 2000 photograph above shows the Dollar General store on Highway 71. The image below documents the opening of a Hardee's Restaurant in the 1980s. Consumers could shop locally on the highway and also use the road to reach shopping destinations in nearby cities and towns. In 1957, the Home Bank attempted to boost local commerce by encouraging people to patronize businesses in their own communities. An advertisement in the *Savannah Reporter* emphasized that dollars spent in Savannah worked to the benefit of everyone, supporting "better stores, better schools, better churches, better streets, and better recreational facilities."

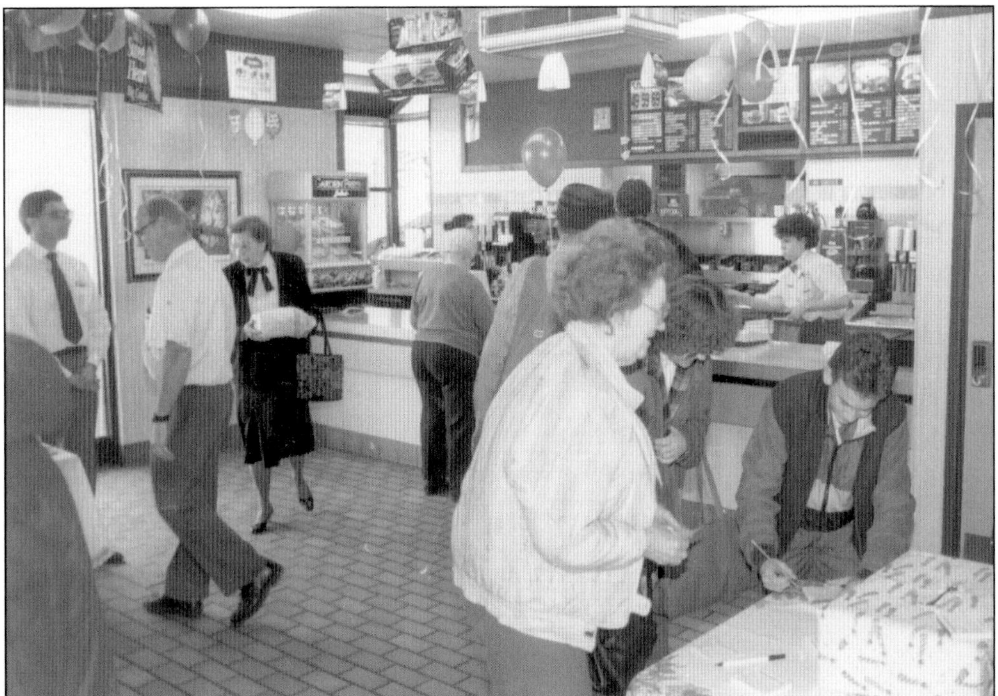

Four

NEIGHBORHOODS AND "NEIGHBORING"

Rural people joined formal organizations to pursue specific goals and enhance a sense of community, including fraternal groups, boards of trade, the Grand Army of the Republic, and the Women's Christian Temperance Union, to name a few. Children enjoyed activities sponsored by the Girl or Boy Scouts or Future Farmers of America.

Informal networks among rural people were equally important. Scholars refer to them engaging in "neighboring": an exchange of information facilitated by frequent interaction among people over time. Outside of academia, this activity is referred to as "gossiping." Gossip both provided a stream of information and served as a form of entertainment. There were specific locations in which to gossip: women exchanged information at afternoon tea or in the beauty parlor, while men did so at the barbershop or the pool hall.

In *A Northern Countryside* (1916), Rosalind Richards offered a poetic description of how information found its way into a small-town neighboring network: "The wall that guards one's citadel of inner privacy needs, in a small town, to be made of strong stuff; it is subjected to hard wear. Indeed, we share some of the privations of royalty, in that we lead our whole lives in the public eye. We see each other walk past every day, greet each other in shops and at street corners, and meet each other's good frocks and company manners at every church supper and afternoon tea."

Richards admitted that she enjoyed visiting the city. Her greatest pleasure, however, was not associated with the bright lights of theaters or palatial department stores. Richards most enjoyed the anonymity of the crowd, a chance to breathe a little. While savoring such a respite from small-town scrutiny, she insisted that the closeness of rural people offered "unspeakably precious" advantages. She noted, "Our neighbors' joys and troubles are of instant importance to us, each and all." This chapter explores when and where people learned about such joys and troubles.

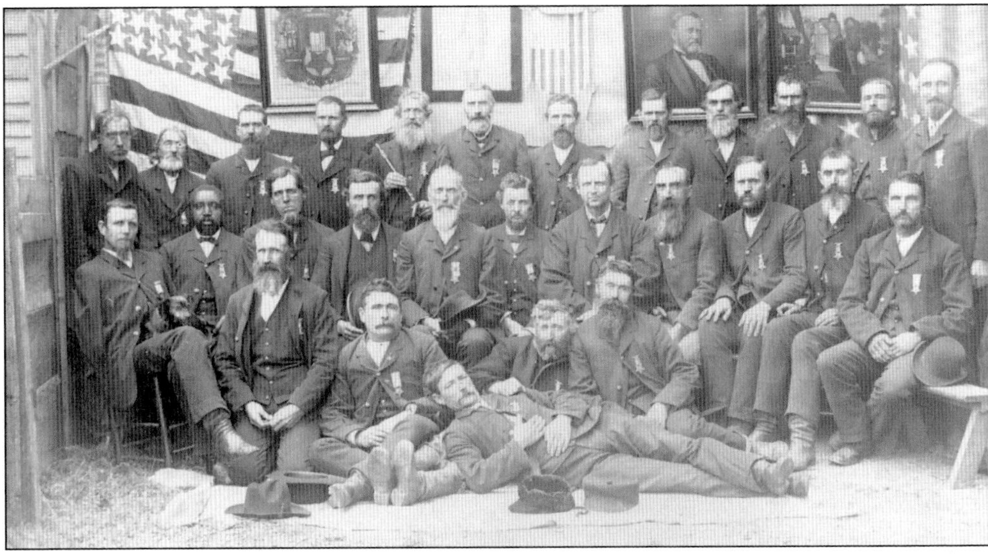

In the years after the Civil War, veterans frequently staged reunions. The c. 1890 image above shows members of the Grand Army of the Republic in Fillmore. The GAR, an important formal organization in rural areas, was among the nation's first lobbying organizations that advocated in favor of issues such as veterans' pensions. Union veterans joined the GAR, and African Americans were welcomed as members. For example, Sam Carriger, seated second from the left in the second row, was an ex-slave and a Union veteran. The photograph below is from a 1900 reunion of Andrew County Civil War veterans.

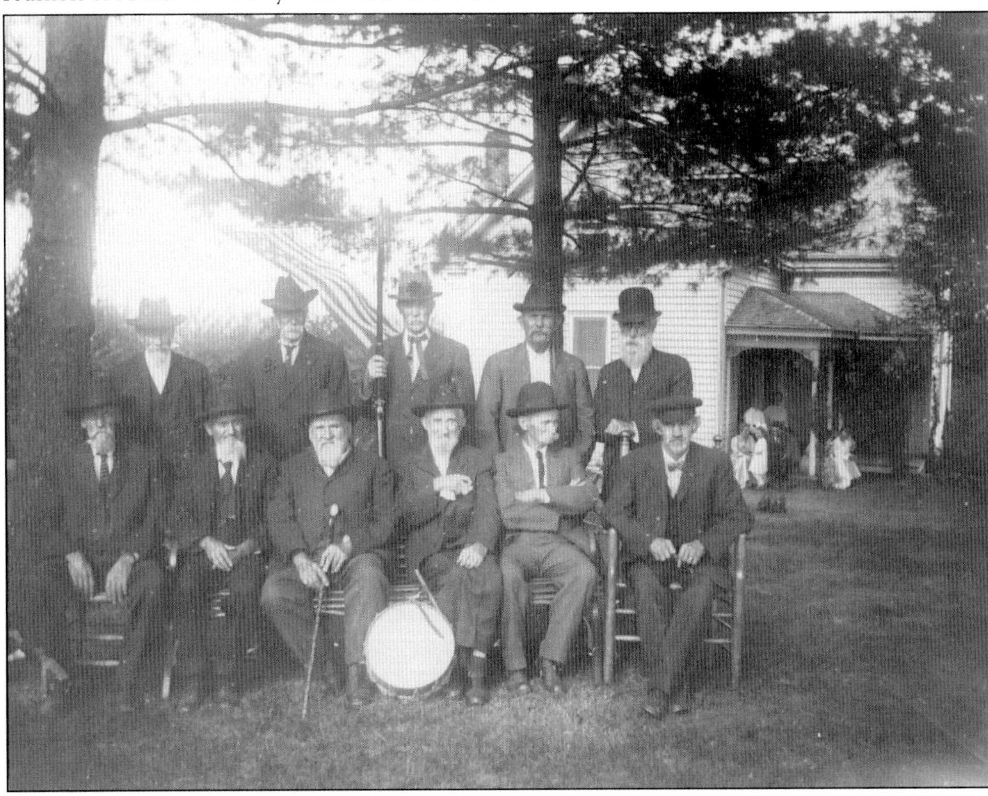

After the Civil War, the prominence of the GAR signaled the ultimate triumph of Union forces in the minds of some county residents. Before the conflict, Missouri was a slave and border state that eventually stayed in the Union. Loyalties, however, remained divided. In a *History of Andrew and DeKalb Counties* (1888), the author recounted an 1861 confrontation involving the raising of Old Glory on the courthouse square that was countered by Confederate sympathizers hoisting a rebel flag. A "well-known Southern man" made "many sneering remarks about the Yankee flag." The bombardment of Fort Sumter "fired the patriotic heart" in Union men, who organized military companies; rebel sympathizers did likewise. The photographs, from the early 1860s, show Capt. Frederick Becker (right), in his Union uniform and Thomas Clasbey (below) in his Confederate gear.

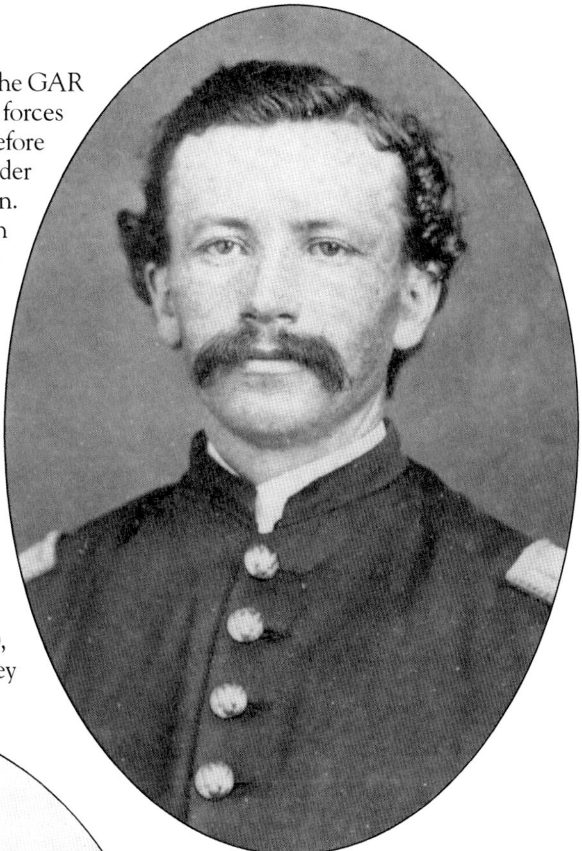

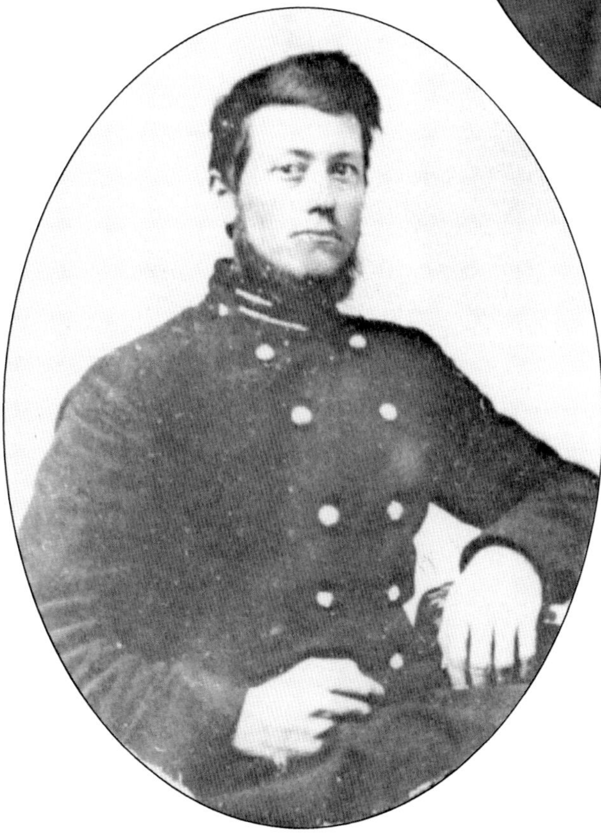

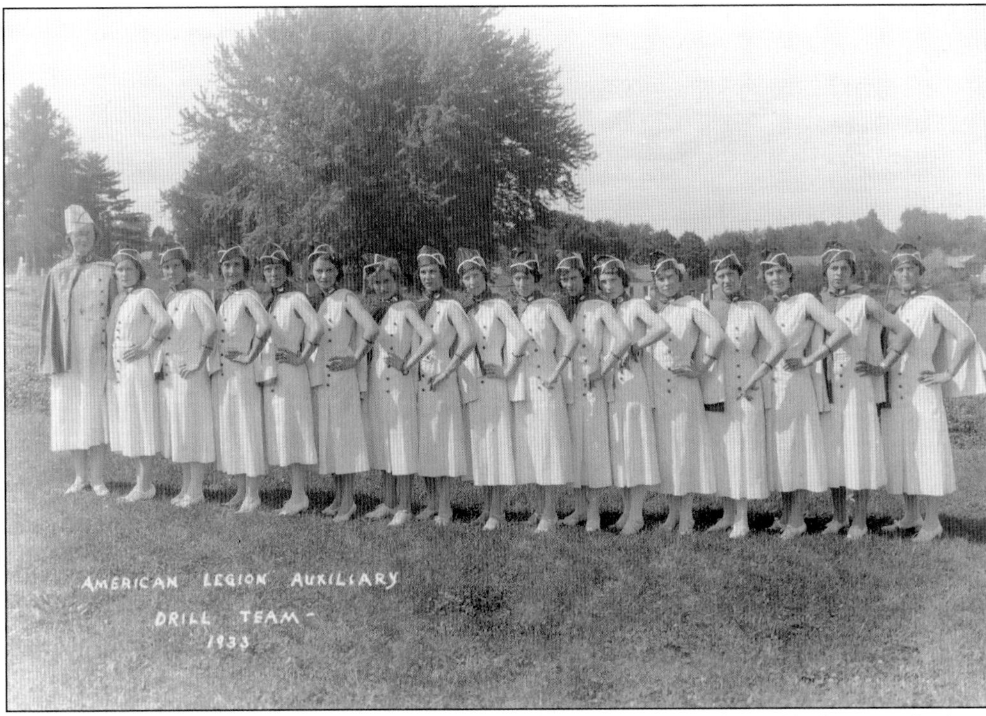

In Andrew County, young people also joined formal organizations. The 1933 photograph above shows the American Legion Auxiliary Drill Team. Returning World War I veterans established the American Legion in 1919. Its auxiliary now engages in a wide range of civic projects. The photograph below shows the Rosendale Boy Scout troop that was first organized in the 1920s.

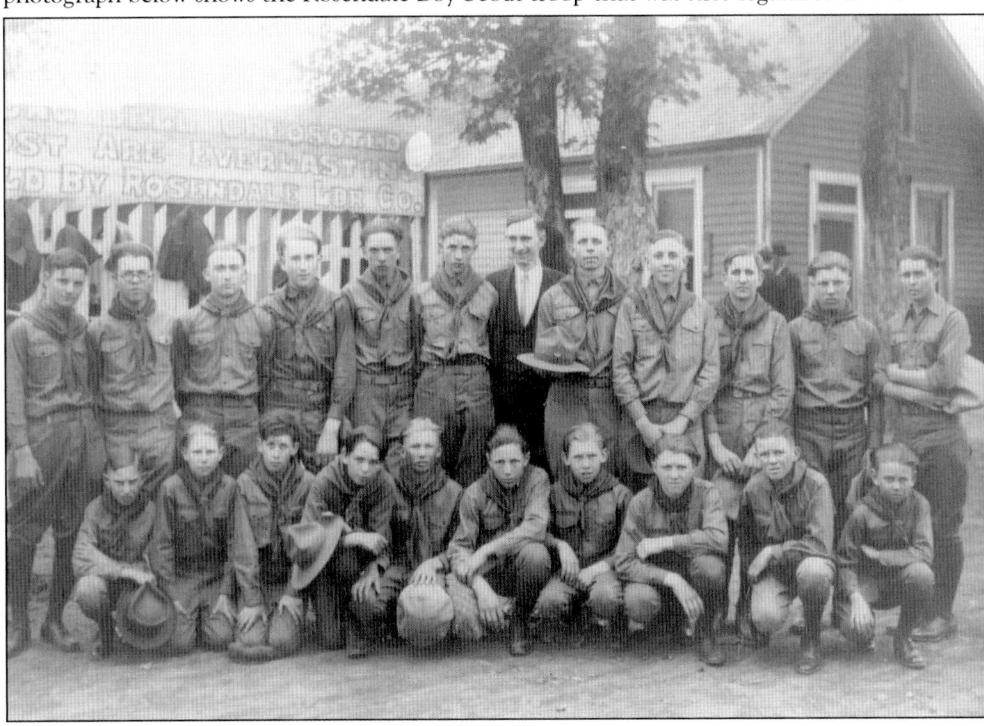

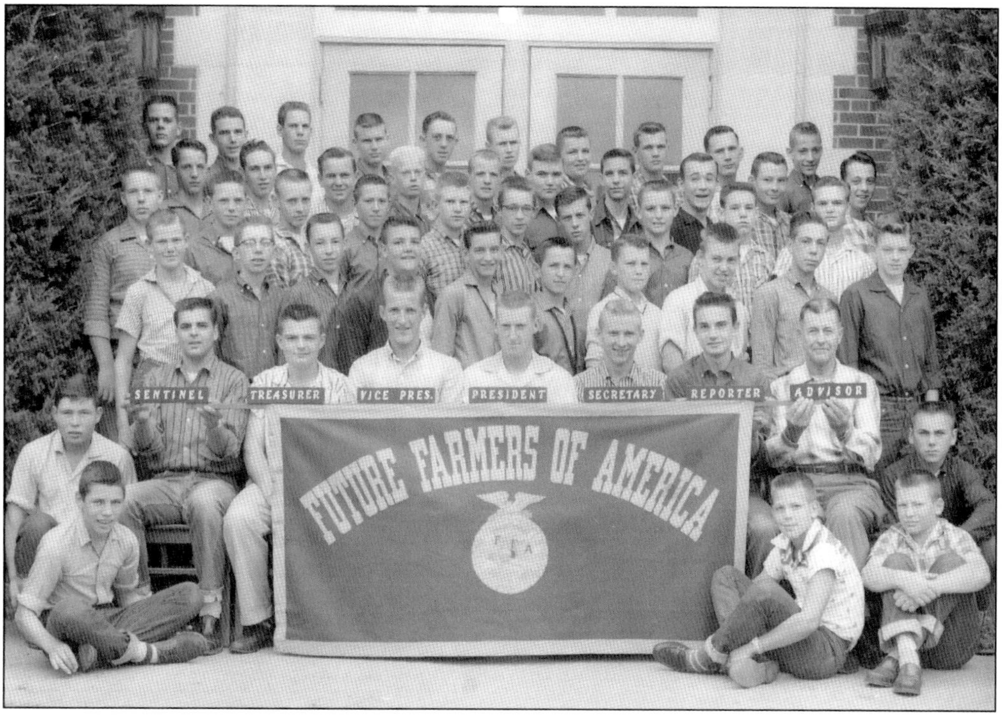

In rural areas, organized activities for youngsters often focus on farming. The 1950s photograph above shows a Savannah Future Farmers of America (FFA) group in front of a school. The FFA was founded in 1928 in Kansas City with the aim of promoting "vocational agriculture" and preparing students to manage the ever-changing needs of farming operations. The image below depicts the Beef Calf Club Show at the Andrew County Fair in 1924. Such competitive displays encouraged participants to develop skills in animal husbandry and farming in general.

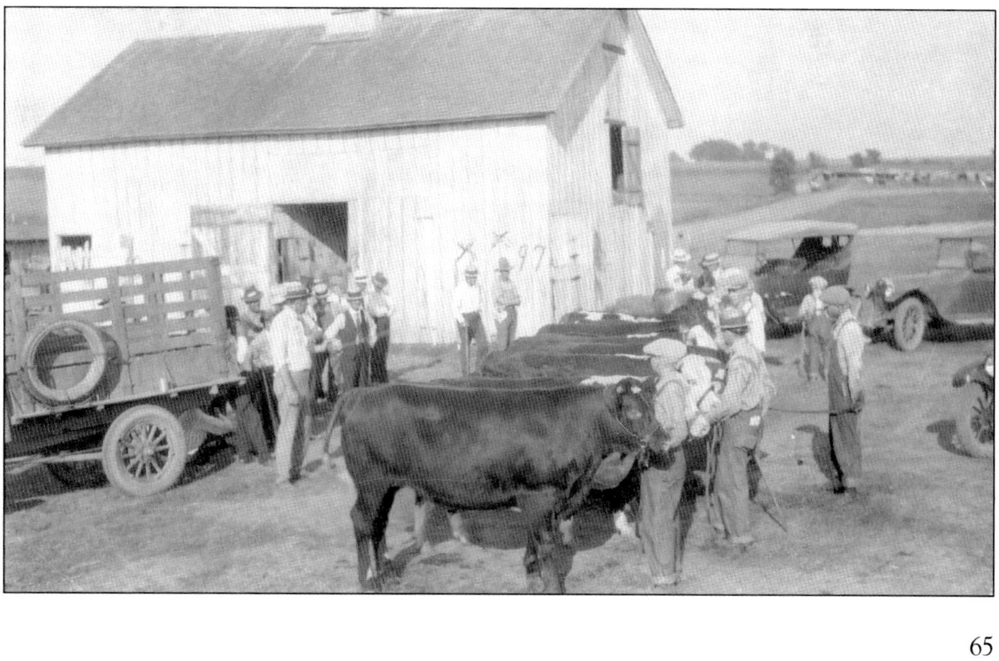

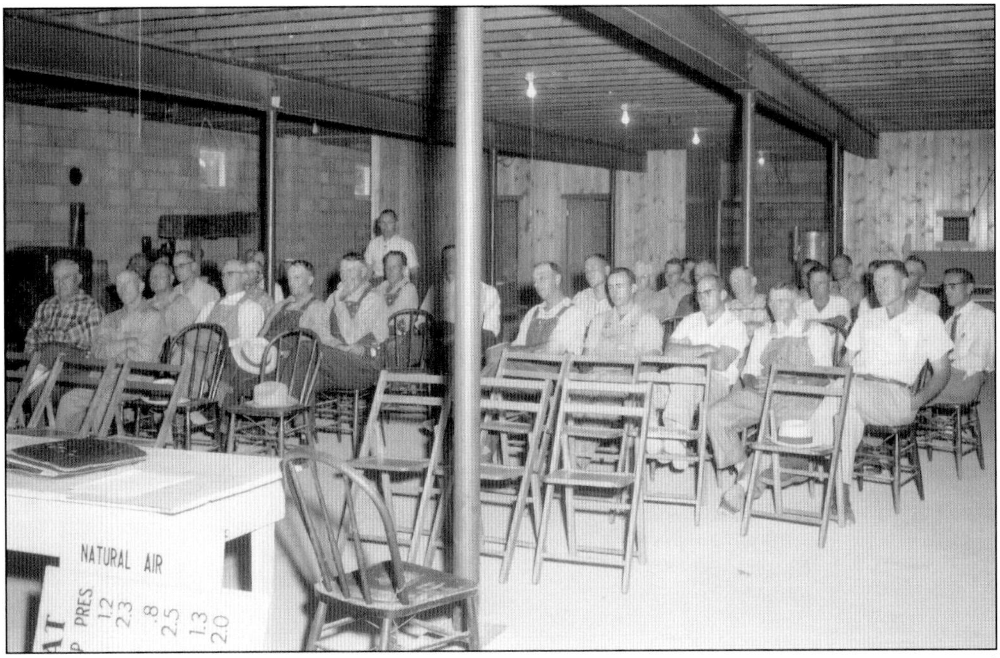

Learning about the latest developments in farming did not end with lessons in vocational agriculture. The 1950 photograph shows a group of Andrew County farmers attending an "ag lecture" organized by the University of Missouri Extension Service. In the photograph below, extension agent Ruby Larson (standing) leads a "home meeting" for local women in 1948. The women at the table are, from left to right, Nan Walker, Helen Fothergill, Goldie Fothergill, Agnes Weaver, and Maris Pittman. As the two images illustrate, questions can be asked about whether state agricultural agencies fell victim to gender stereotyping in the 1940s and 1950s. Men attended ag lectures while women engaged in home meetings appropriate for their roles as homemakers.

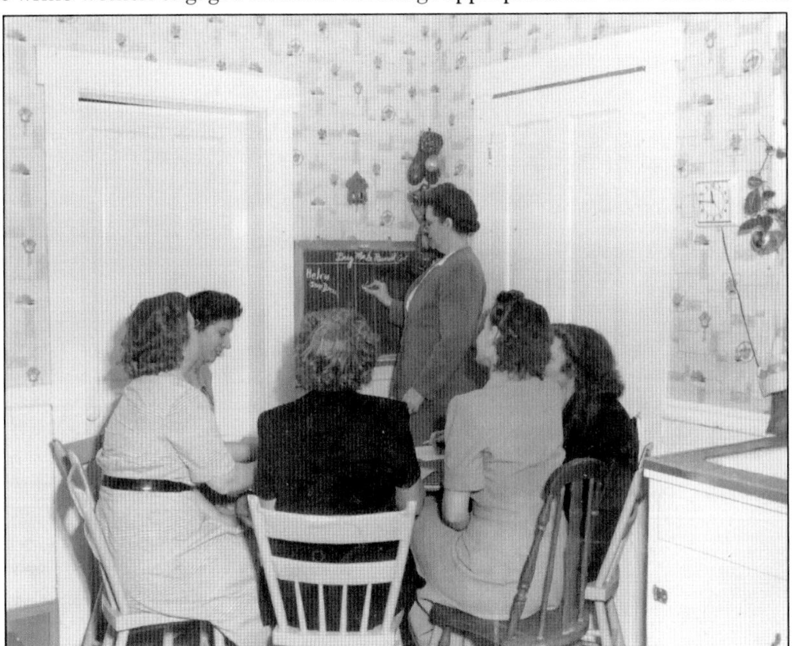

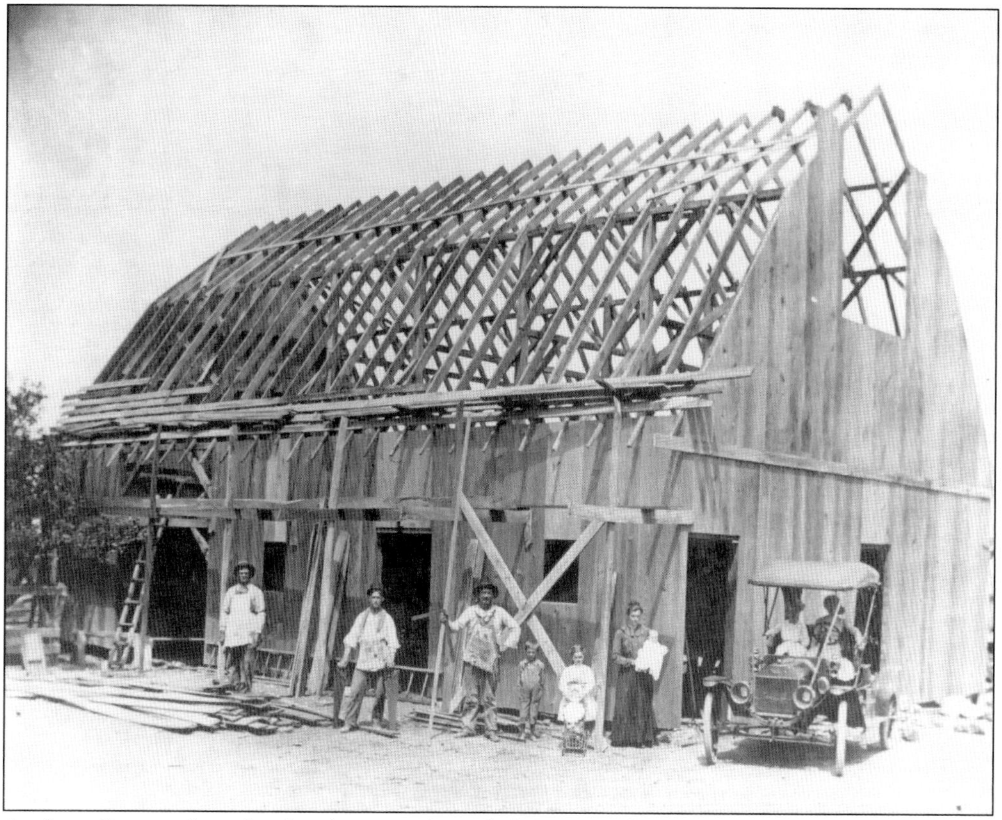

Andrew County farm families knew and needed their neighbors. Well into the 20th century, neighbors united to help build barns, butcher livestock, thresh wheat, make soap, saw wood, and can corn. In the image above, William Bunse (far left), his helpers, and family members pose for a photographer during a barn raising in 1910. In the 1923 photograph below, Ruby Roderick (left) and her neighbor Hallie Swartz (second to left) pose with Audry ?, Myrtle Swartz, and Evea Adkins after a canning session; Edward Norman Swartz and his dog Grip are underneath the table.

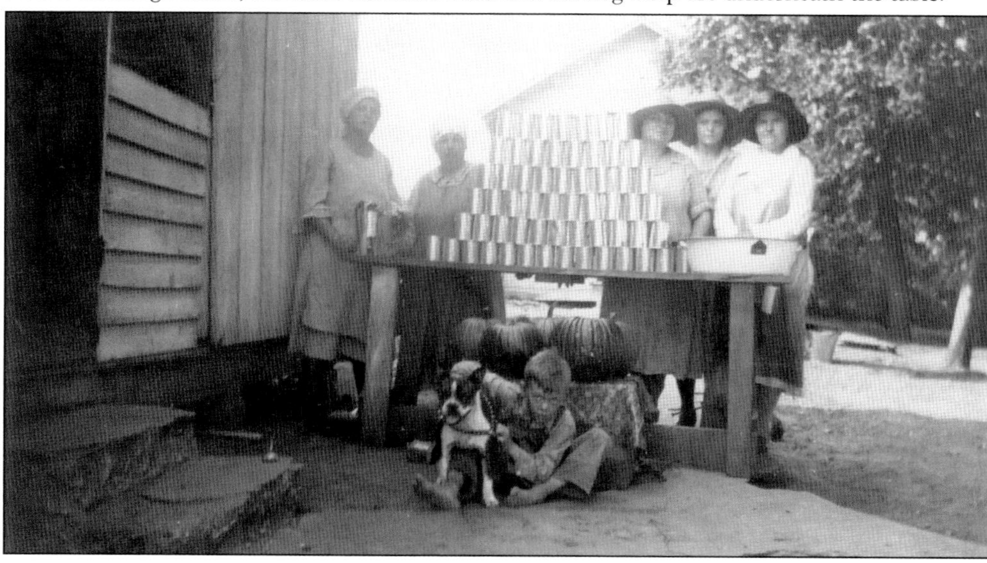

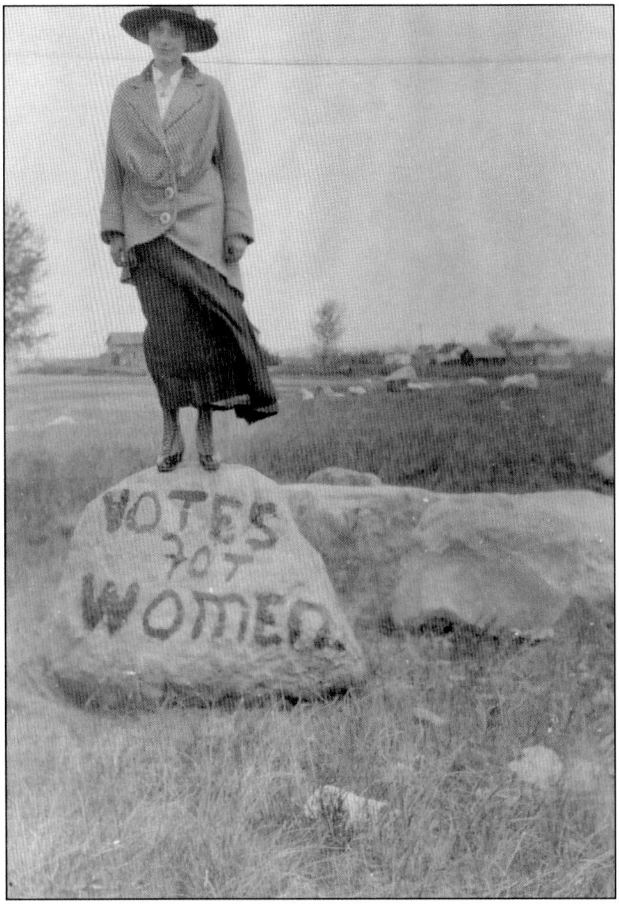

The c. 1918 photograph at left shows a suffragist standing on a rock; in many rural areas, support for women's suffrage was linked to the Prohibition campaign. In Andrew County, the Women's Christian Temperance Union was active for decades. In 1887, a local option campaign included speakers who described the "terrible curse of the rum traffic." Voters, however, endorsed the continued sale of intoxicants; many of those votes were generated in the blacksmith shops and livery stables that served as loafing places for men. The Moran and Son Blacksmith Shop is pictured below in 1901. As for livery stables, historian Lewis Atherton observed that they were universally condemned by pious mothers, who rated them only slightly above the town saloon. The card playing, bawdy humor, and occasional betting on horses enjoyed by a stable's denizens shocked "those refined people who spoke of bulls as gentlemen cows."

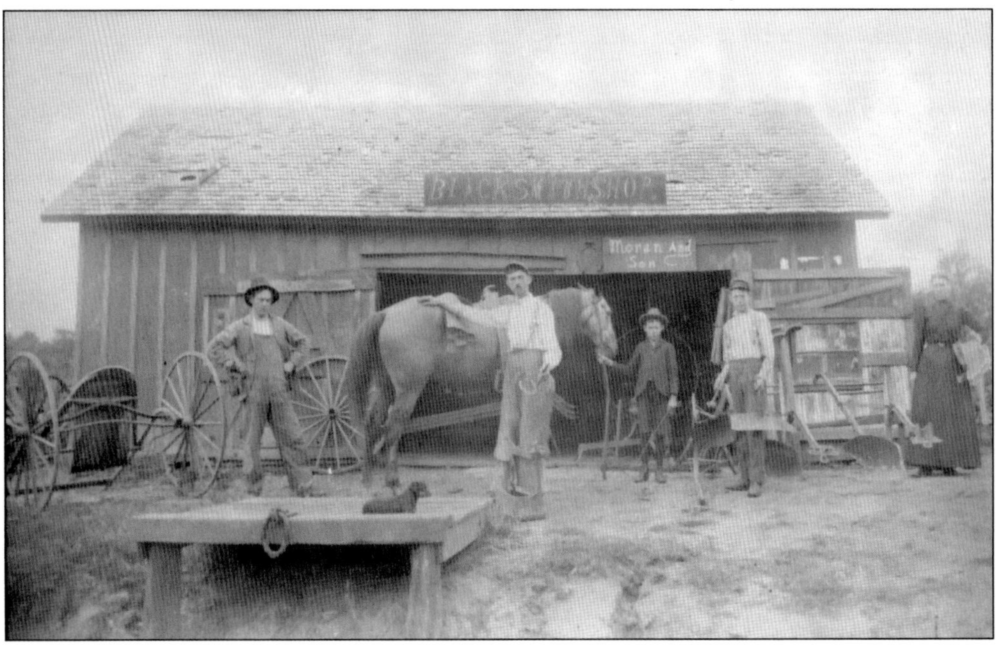

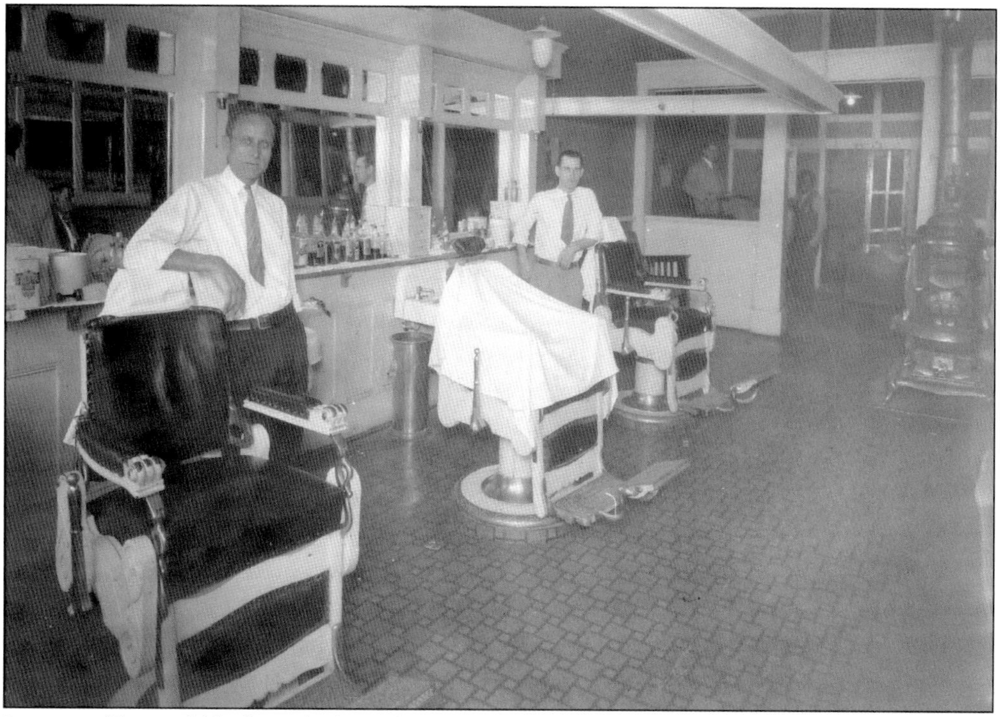

Livery stables and blacksmith shops began to vanish as the horse-drawn era gave way to the automobile age. While men lost two primary neighboring spots, barbershops remained places to talk about sports and solve the world's problems. The photograph above shows Harrington's Barber Shop in Savannah in 1929. Pictured are, from left to right, Frank Harrington, Basil Workman, Grover Cleveland Sparks (in the shoe-shine chair), and King West. In 1916, author Rosalind Richards referenced afternoon tea as a prime opportunity for small-town social interaction; this was especially true for women. The c. 1905 image below shows an Andrew County parlor.

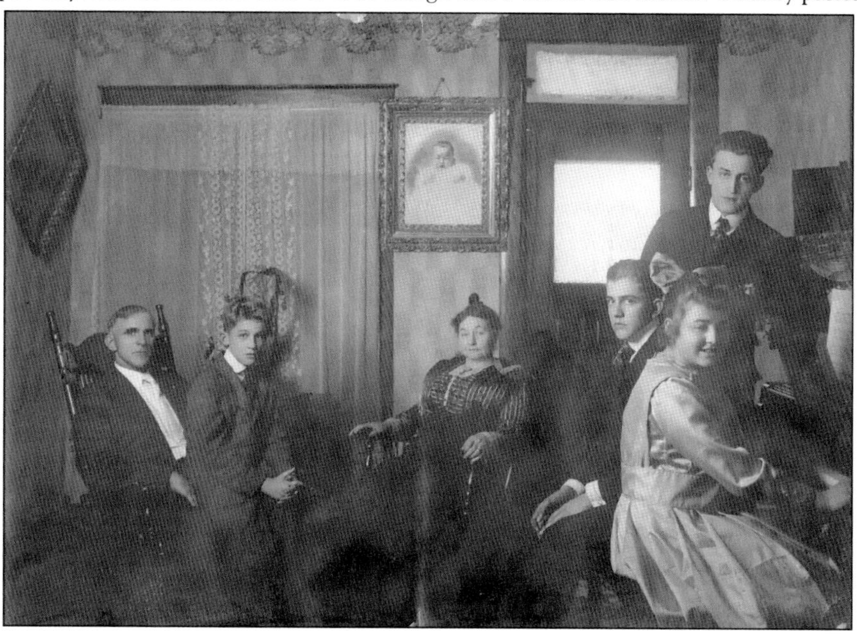

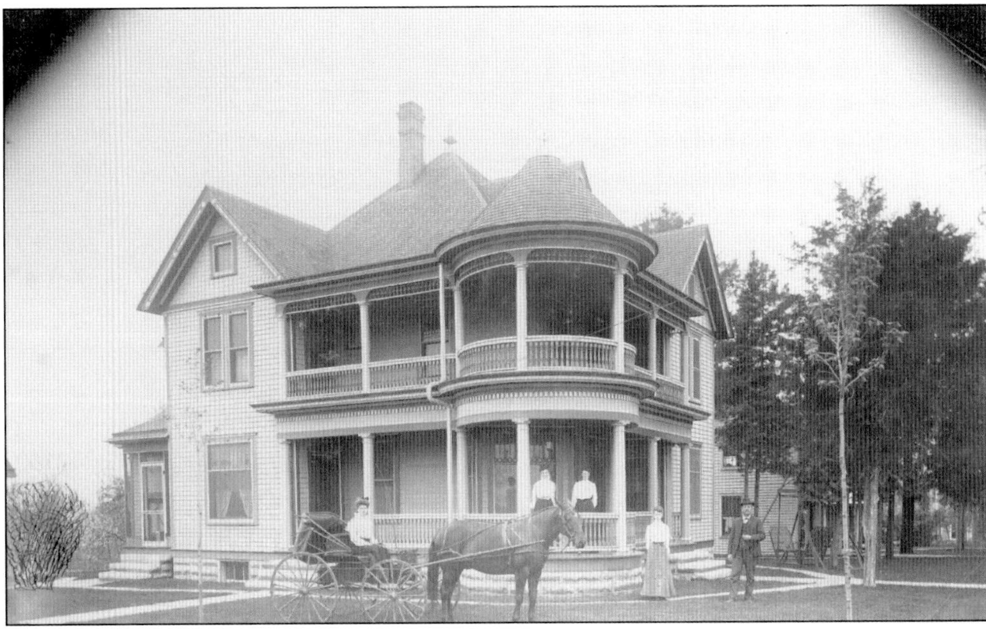

The front porch was an ideal platform for neighboring. Passersby could stop and exchange the latest gossip with porch sitters. The c. 1902 photograph above is of the C.W. Spicer Home in Fillmore. Its size indicates that it was the home of local gentry. In the c. 1910 photograph below, the Townsend family poses on their front lawn. Neighboring spaces could be extended beyond the front porch; people often installed a bench or a swing in front of their homes, creating a comfortable space for conversation.

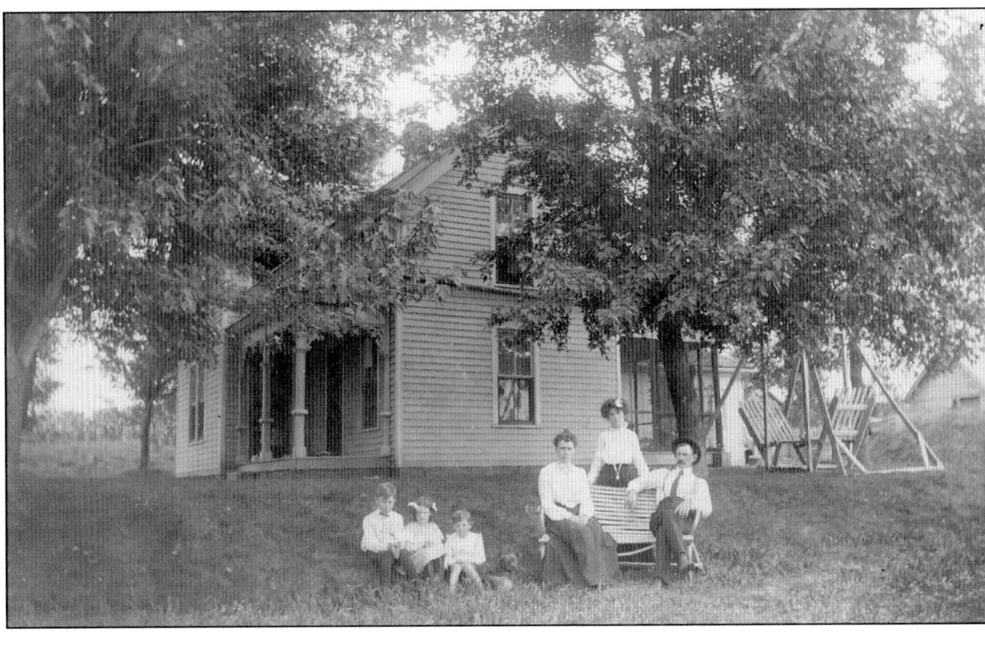

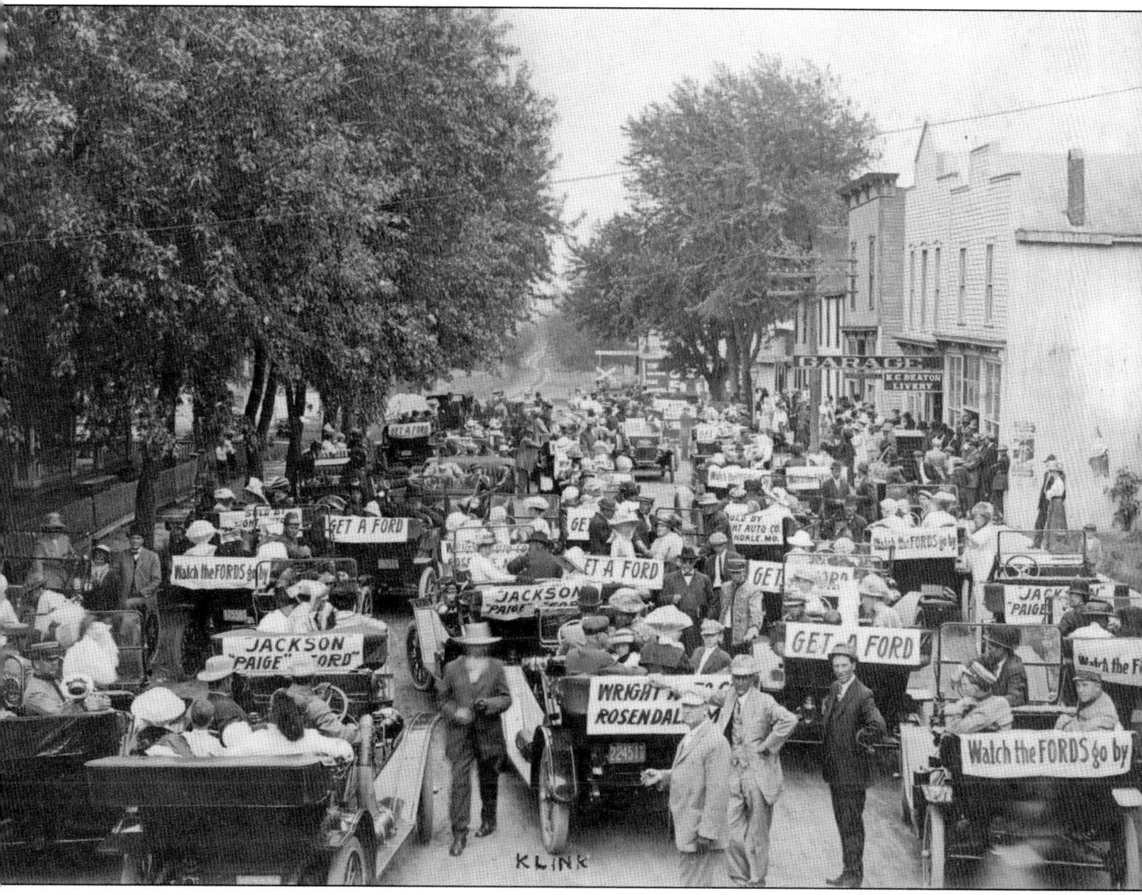

New technologies had the potential to increase neighboring opportunities, including interacting with people beyond one's hometown. This photograph was taken in Rosendale in 1911. Though it promoted the notion that people should "Get a Ford," the event was billed as Wright's Sociability Run. In 1910, the *New York Times* reported that sociability runs held throughout the nation provided evidence of the "widespread interest in pleasure touring and the desire of motorists to flock together." In addition to touring the picturesque countryside, the automobile runs also served a practical purpose. In 1910, about 50 automobiles departed St. Joseph on a 454-mile run in support of improved country roads. Motorists from Savannah drove their cars out to meet the touring party before they rounded the Andrew County Courthouse Square and headed off into the countryside.

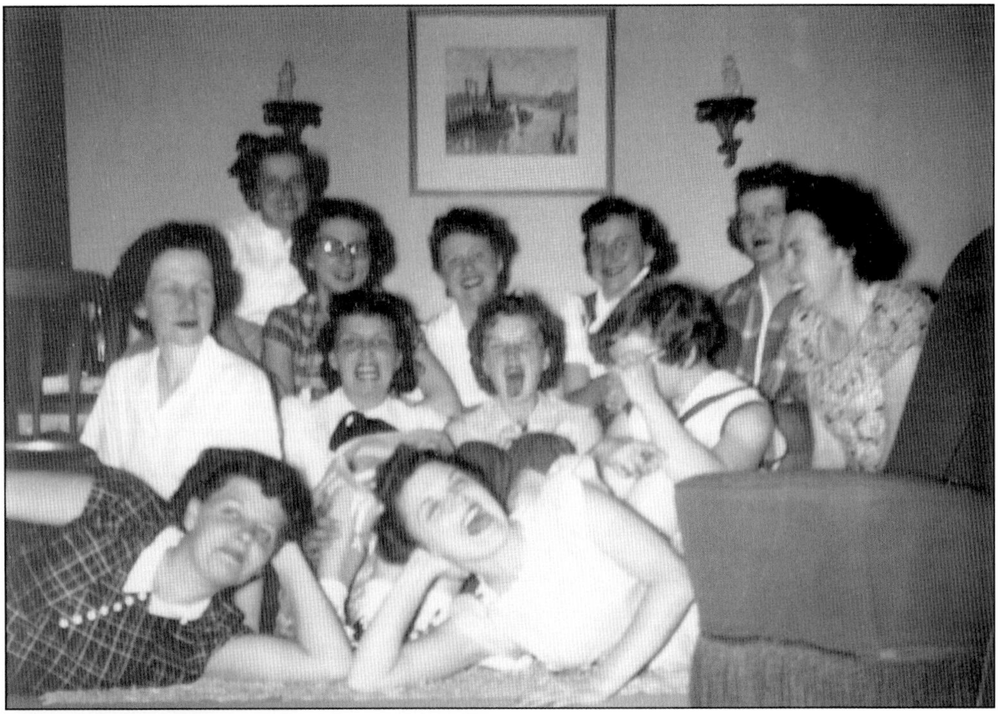

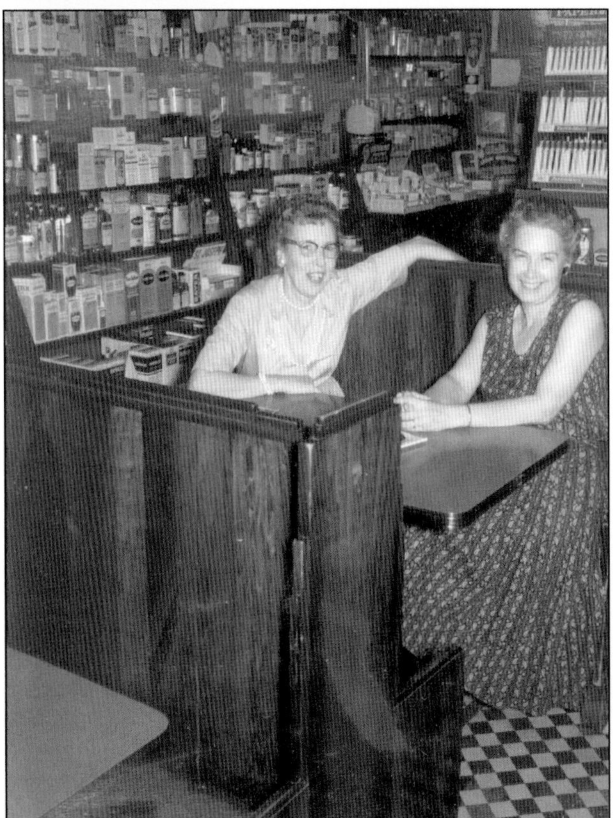

Rural people joined informal groups to provide mutual support and address common issues. The c. 1950 photograph above shows members of the Get Together Club in Savannah. Members were all former war wives whose aim was to "get together and make new friends." From left to right are (front row) Betty Walton and Betty Haldiman; (second row) Helen Brown, Thelma Parsons, Jo Puckett, Bonnie Lee (covering her face), and Bette Maughmer (seated in the arm chair); (third row) Helen Crawford (in glasses), Betty Miller, Eloise Tuck, and Dorothy Hellerick; (fourth row) Patty Vulgamott. The photograph at left shows two women in a booth at the Dray Drugstore in Savannah. The loss of the drugstore counter robbed small-town residents of a primary neighboring space.

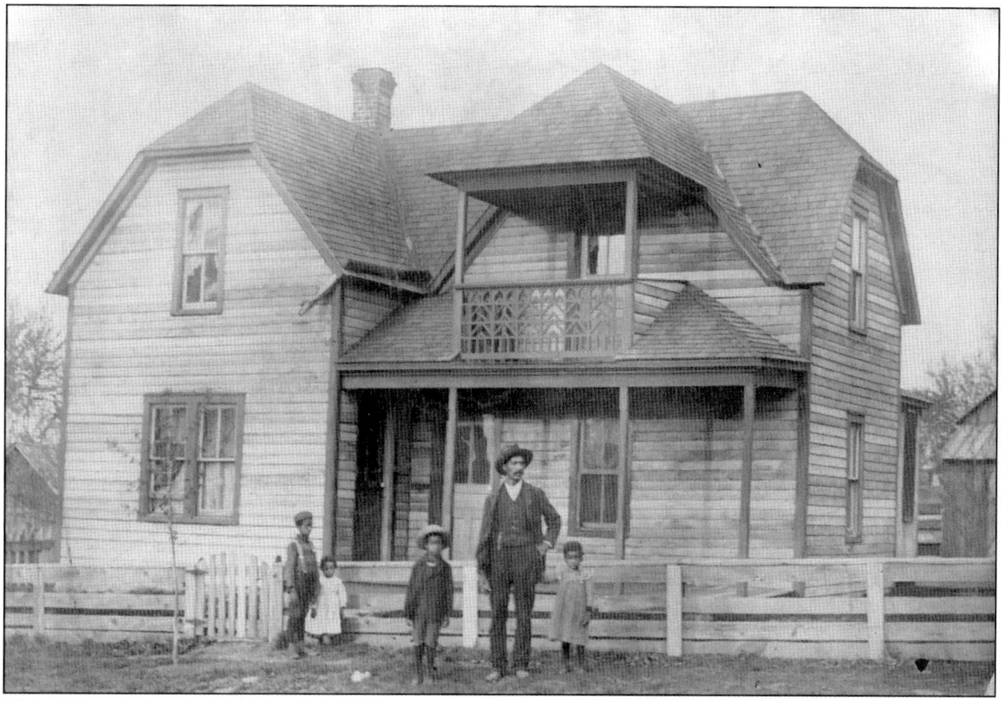

The c. 1910 photograph above depicts an unidentified Savannah family standing in front of their home. Although the house had a typical porch, it was likely that little neighboring occurred with some residents of the city. In the Jim Crow era after the Civil War, racial segregation was the order of the day. After the war, freed slaves formed communities in Savannah and near Fillmore and Flag Springs. The largest, known as "Franklin," was in northwest Savannah. In this area, a grade school and Methodist church provided segregated education and worship. African Americans worked as farmers, carpenters, plasterers, laborers, chauffeurs, domestic helpers, and more. In the 1925 photograph at right, former slave Adeline Warren holds Betty Lee Bryant.

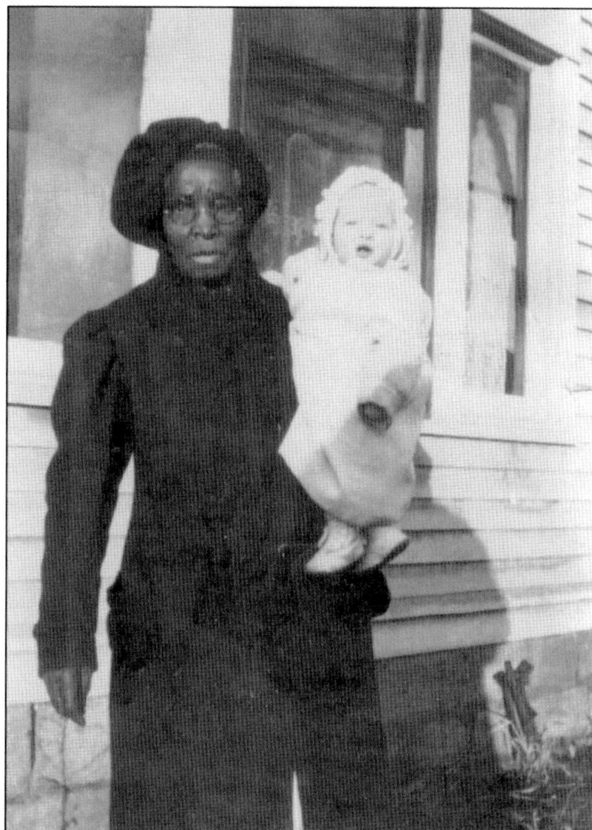

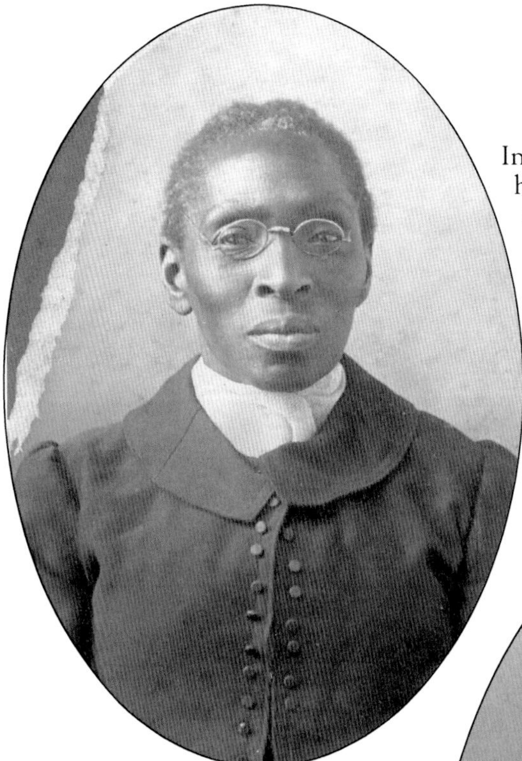

In the late 19th and early 20th centuries, having a professional photographer capture one's likeness was a major event, making these photographs of Andrew County African Americans all the more striking. Hannah Bruce sat for the photograph at left around 1900. The photograph below shows a man in a three-piece suit, identified only as Corine Owen's grandfather, that also dates from around 1900. Photographs like these were a statement of pride and success for family members and acquaintances.

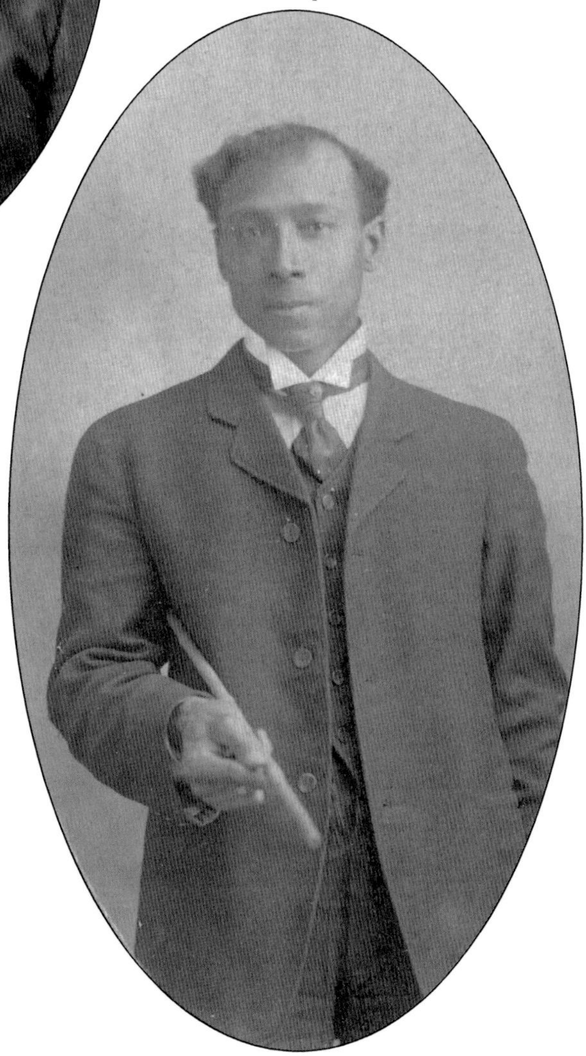

Five

Cycles of Life

In *Our Town* (1938), playwright Thornton Wilder created the character of Charles Webb, the editor of the local newspaper in the fictional town of Grover's Corners. In the first act, Webb utters the lines, "We've got a lot of pleasures of a kind here: we like the sun comin' up over the mountain in the morning, and we all notice a good deal about the birds. And we watch the change of the seasons; yes, everybody knows about them." In fact, Wilder's play revolves around recurring cycles: its three acts focus on daily life, love and marriage, and death and eternity.

Rural areas maintain a special affinity for the cycles of life. Planting and harvest time establish seasonal rhythms that define what chores need to be done on the farm. The daily lives of townspeople and farm families are punctuated by the celebration of a birth or a marriage or the tragedy of a death in the family. In Andrew County, these milestone events traditionally took place in the home. Until the 1940s, most women gave birth at home, assisted by family and midwives or doctors. Into the 20th century, marriage ceremonies took place in front parlors. Death, like birth and marriage, often occurred in the home. After preparing the deceased for burial, friends and neighbors may have sat up all night with the deceased, comforting the mourning family and celebrating the life of the loved one. Death intimately bound families and communities together.

As the 20th century progressed, death became less of a community event. The tasks once performed by family and friends were handed to professional morticians. Children were increasingly born in hospitals, and marriage ceremonies took place in churches. The cycles of life continued, but the ways rural people dealt with them began to change.

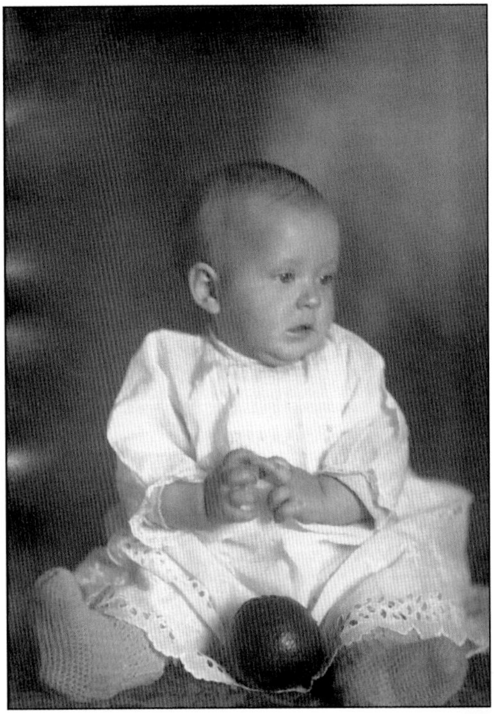

The c. 1916 photograph at left shows Katherine Stanton at 6 months of age. She is wearing an eyelet-trimmed dress and knitted booties. This is a studio portrait, so the infant is outfitted in her best clothes. Similarly, the early-20th-century image below shows cousins Edith and Ruth Fothergill in white, lacy dresses, with each child holding a China doll. These dolls were made of glazed porcelain usually mounted on a wooden, cloth, or leather body. Some dolls had glazed or unglazed legs. The image was turned into a postcard that could be mailed to friends and relatives. In this era, local photographers had the capability to produce small runs of postcards. They could provide clients with cards from family photographs, as well as cards featuring popular local scenes.

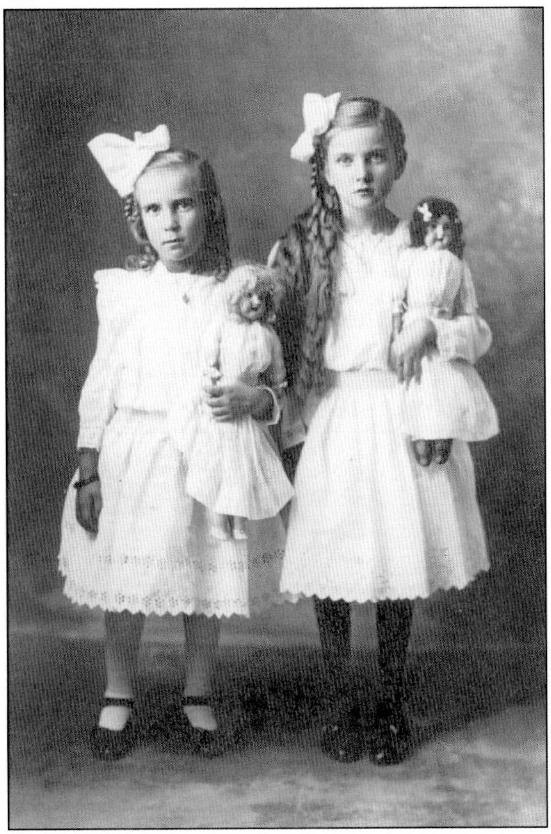

Children's clothing progressed from dresses, cloth diapers, and homemade clothing (in the late 19th and early 20th centuries) to "store-bought" clothing of easy-care fabrics that could be laundered in automatic washers and dryers. The c. 1910 photograph at right shows Fred (left) and George (right) Barnes. Fred wears a suit with knickers and a bow tie, while George, the younger boy, is donning a white shirt and knickers. For boys, the first pair of long pants marked an important step toward adulthood—the Barnes brothers still awaited that step. In the c. 1920 photograph below, Charlene (left), Gwendolyn (center), and Helen VanFossen, dressed up and holding lunch pails, are likely heading to school.

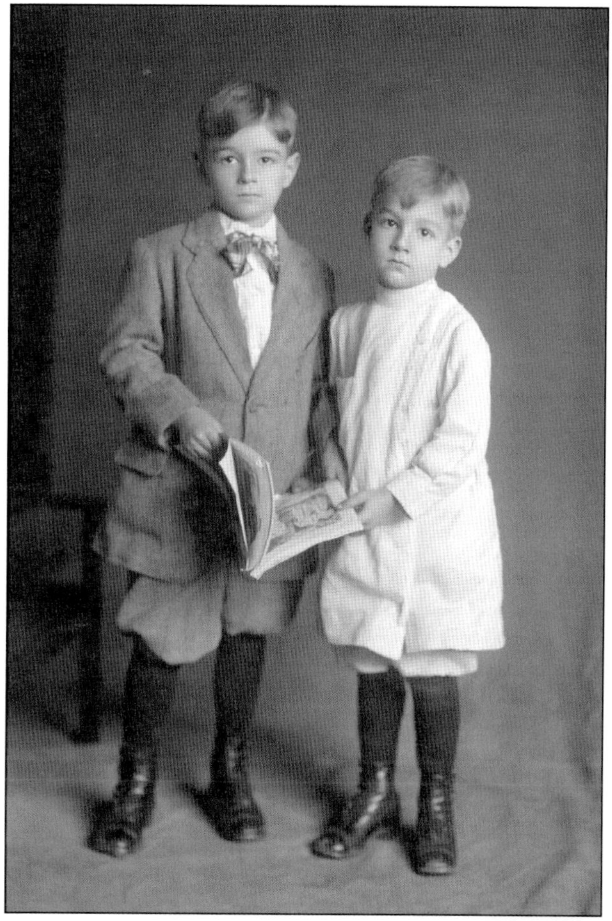

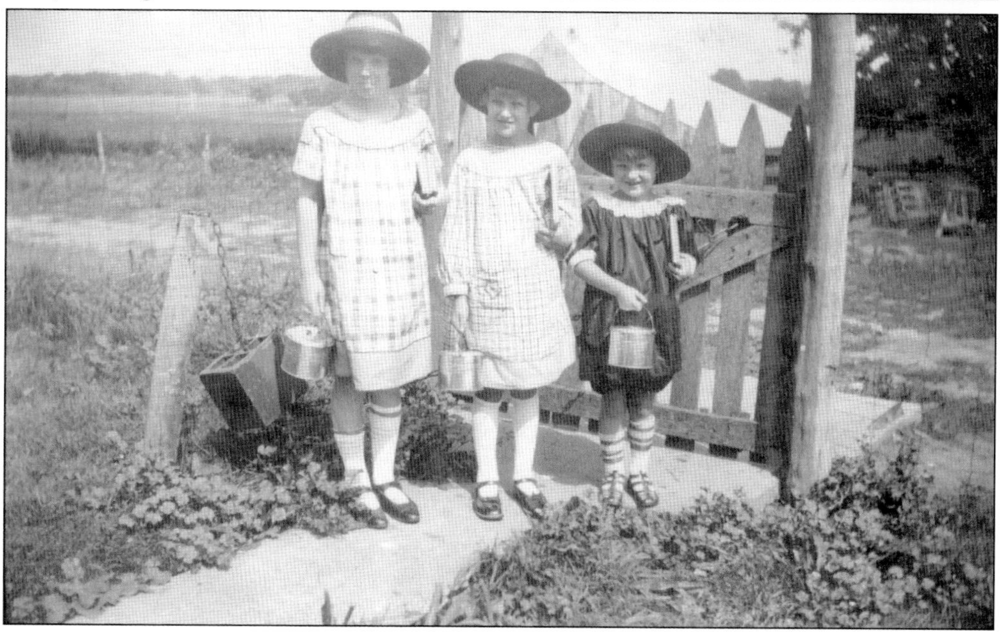

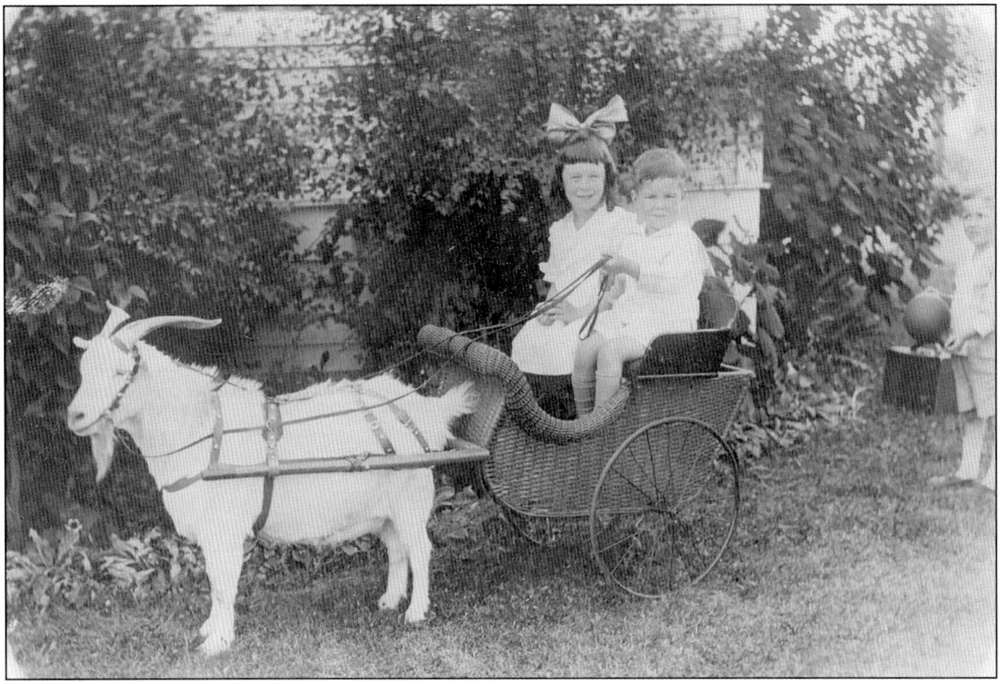

Toys and games evolved from handmade to manufactured items between the 19th and 20th centuries. Some children enjoyed the best of the latter; the c. 1920 photograph above shows two children in a small buggy pulled by a goat. The diminutive vehicle was probably the envy of neighborhood children. The large bow in the girl's hair was not an uncommon sight in Andrew County photographs from this period. The young boy holding the reins wears short pants, and a boy standing behind the buggy holds a ball. The photograph below also dates from the 1920s and features a youngster driving a miniature roadster on the lawn.

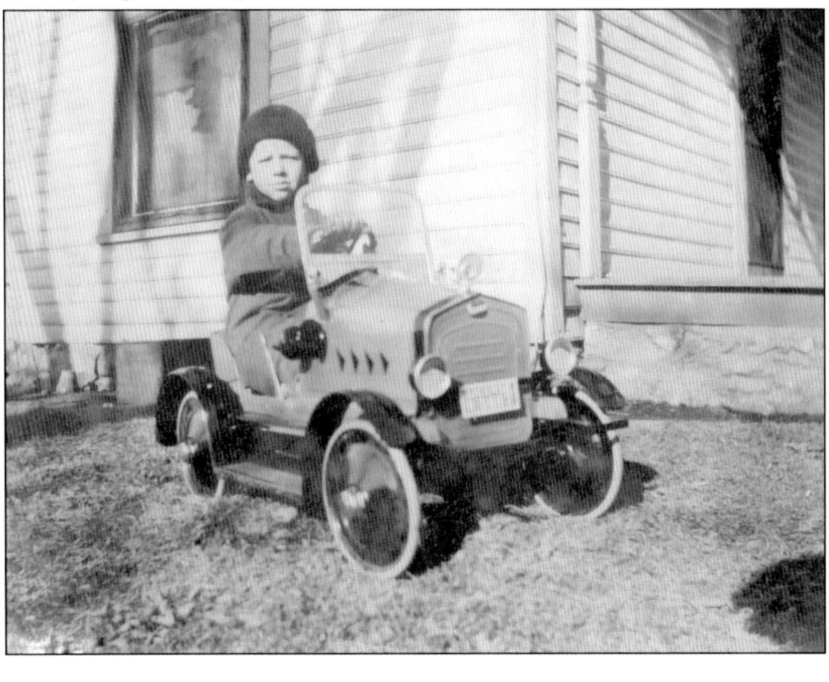

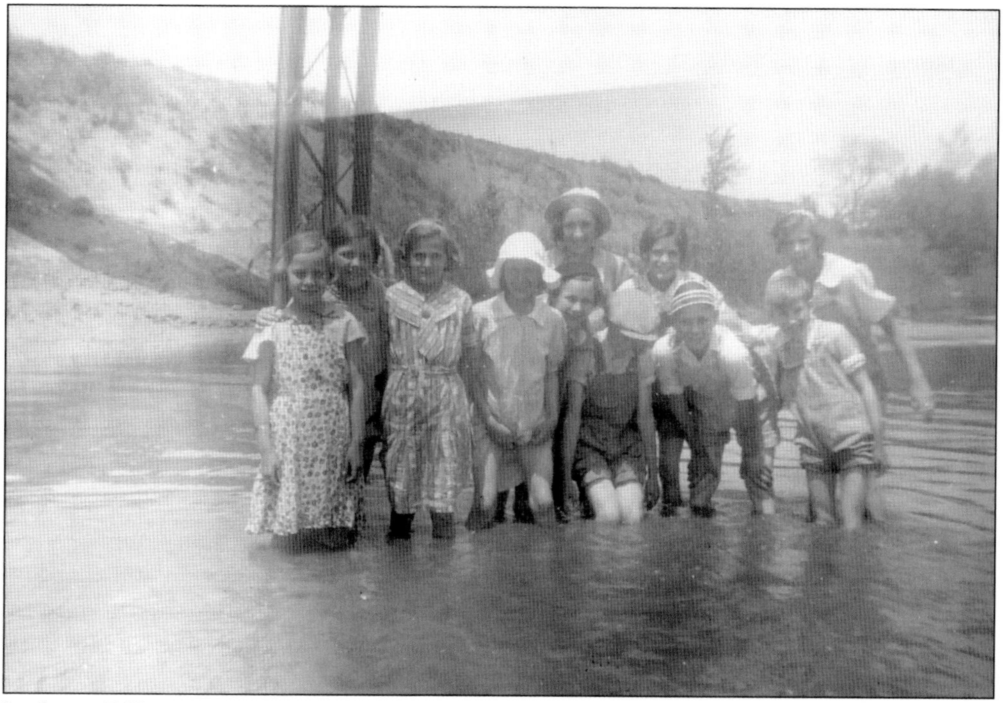

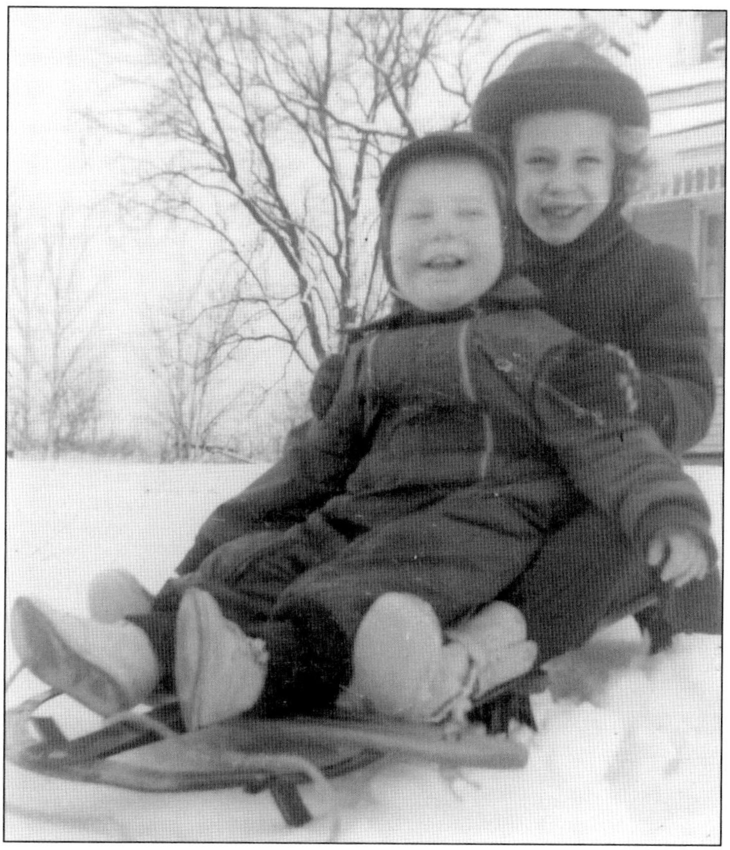

In the c. 1920 image above, a group of young people cools off in a river during the summer. Lewis Atherton observed that freedom from school and access to caves, woods, or swimming holes within walking distance from town gave "the small fry a feverish itch to be about their summer business." In the c. 1940 photograph at right, Wayne Reid Miller and Joyce Miller enjoy sledding in their front yard. Atherton noted that January and February could be cold and raw months, but that did not dim the enthusiasm for outdoor play, especially if it was undertaken in a comfy snowsuit.

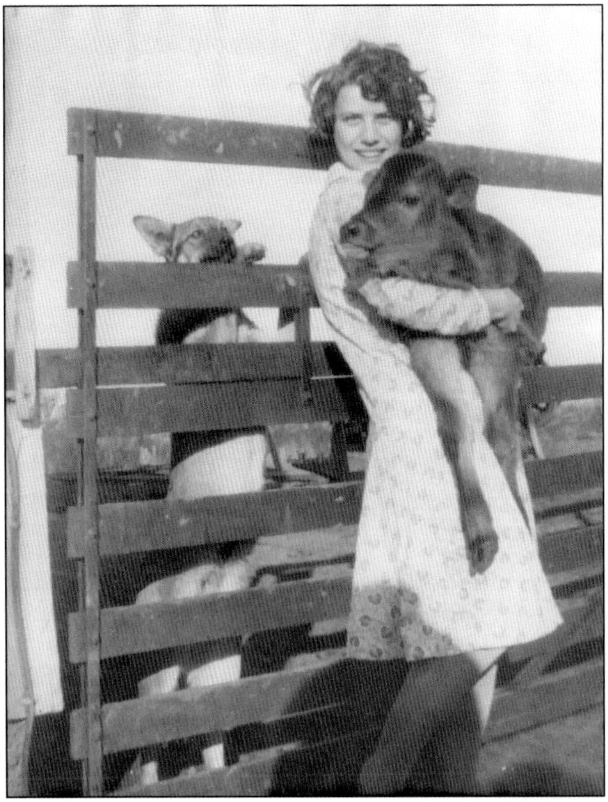

Farm kids understood the cycle of life. They witnessed calves being born and knew that the prize hog they showed at the county fair was destined to become bacon or sausage. In the 1954 photograph at left, Crystal Schweizer holds a heifer headed to market. In the c. 1926 image below, young Tom and Virgil Miller hold a dead possum. Farmers regarded these nocturnal marsupials as major pests. One boy holds a shovel and the other a hoe; presumably, the possum was destined for a decent burial.

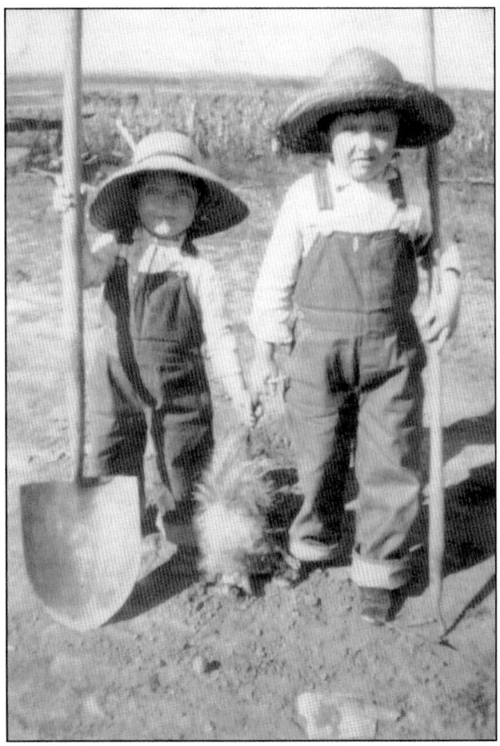

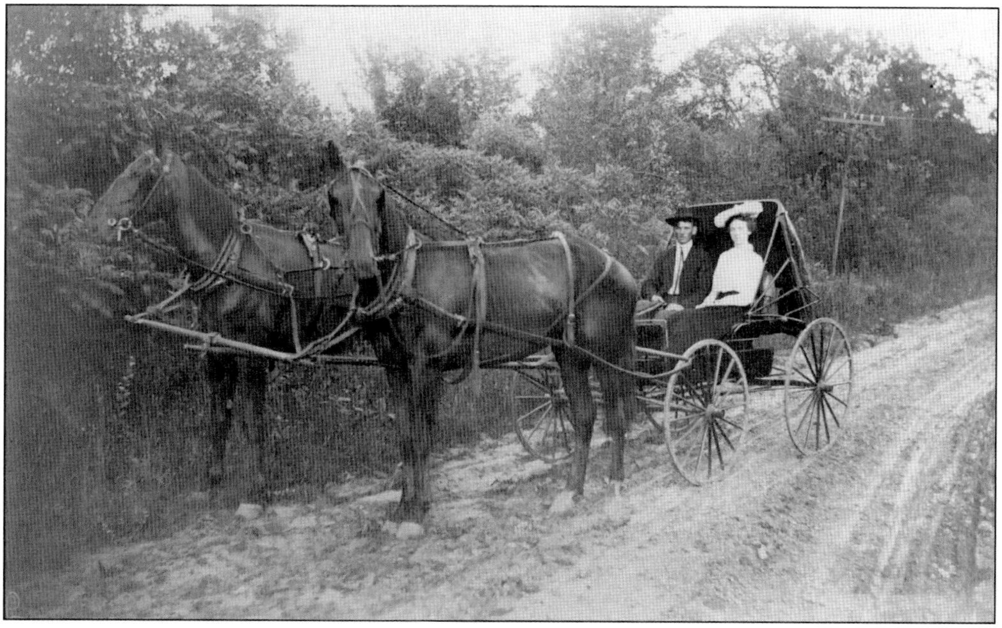

Cultural geographer John Jakle noted how cruising around town became a popular pastime for teenagers in the automobile age as they sought the company of young people of the opposite gender and honked at passing cars filled with friends and acquaintances. In the horse-drawn era, cruising proved more sedate: it was referred to as courting, and the chosen vehicle was a buggy. One definition of courtship describes it as "the act or art of seeking the love of someone with intent to marry." In the c. 1904 image above, Joseph W. Case and Myrtle Beaty are courting on their way "Home from Church," as indicated on the back of the photograph. The c. 1910 photograph below shows a couple that may have been courting on the Savannah Courthouse square.

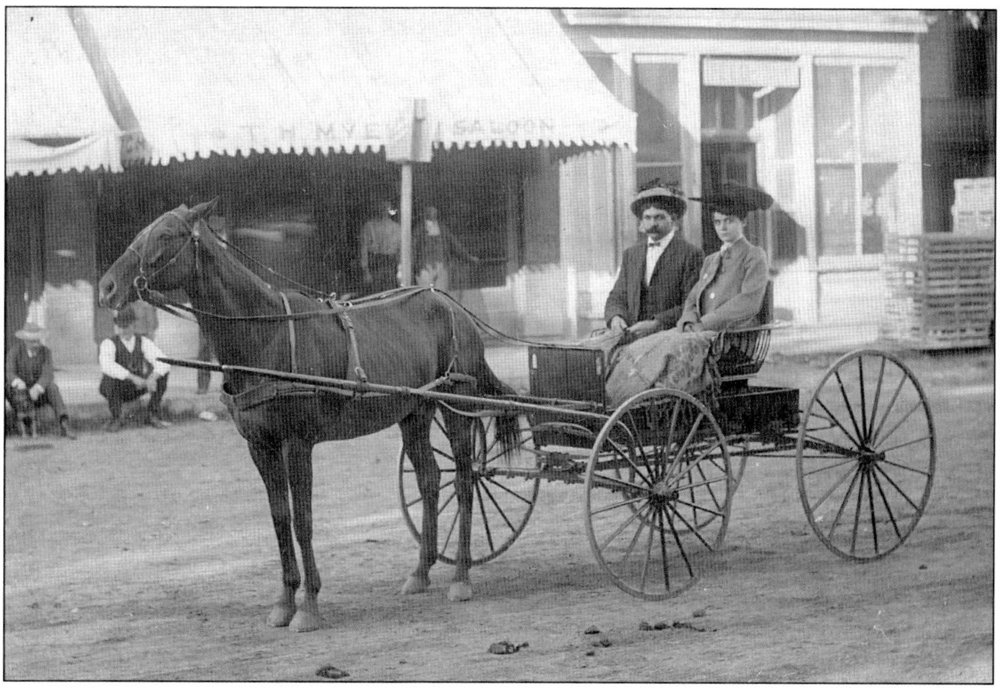

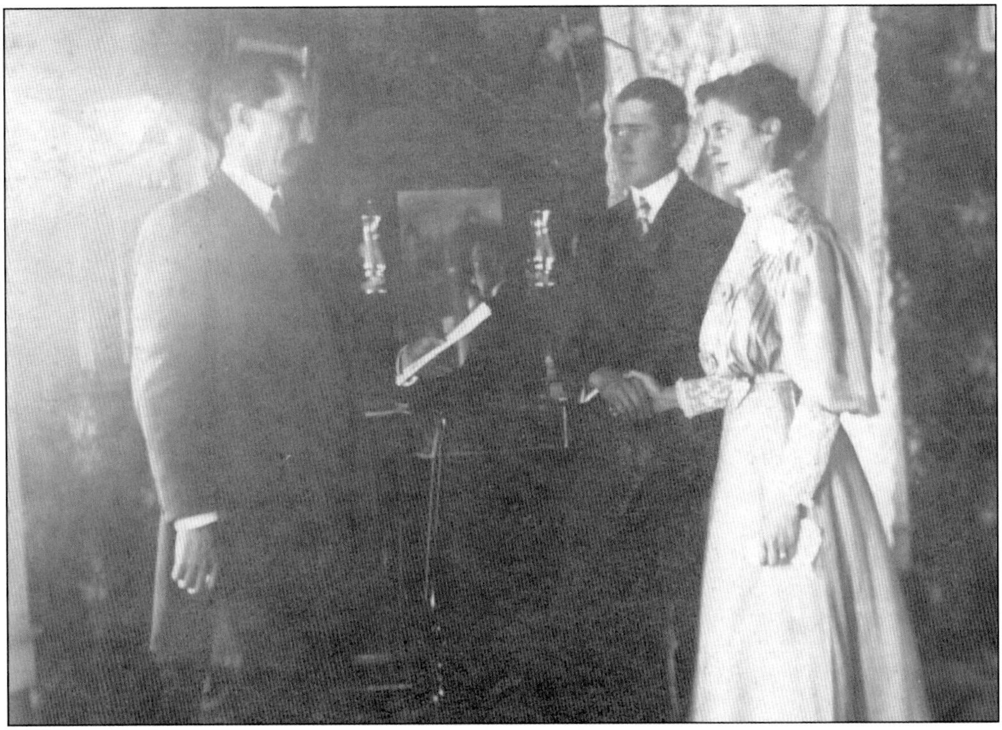

After courtship came marriage. In the 1907 photograph above, Reverend McCall conducts the wedding of Joseph Henry Nuckols and Clara Missouri Breit in a home. The image below shows the wedding reception for Crispin and Annie Helm, which was held at Jack Drydale's home in Bolckow. A short time after being married, a couple was "treated" to a shivaree. Friends and neighbors banged on pans, fired shotguns, and created noise and confusion until the newlyweds "bought them off" with candy and cigars. This boisterous community fun faded away when church weddings became customary. Instead of a shivaree, the couple would be showered with rice or birdseed as they left the church.

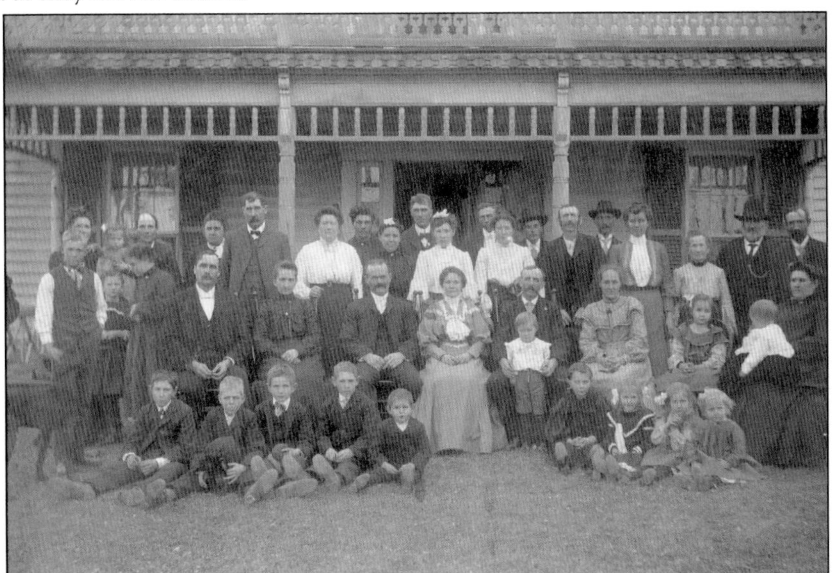

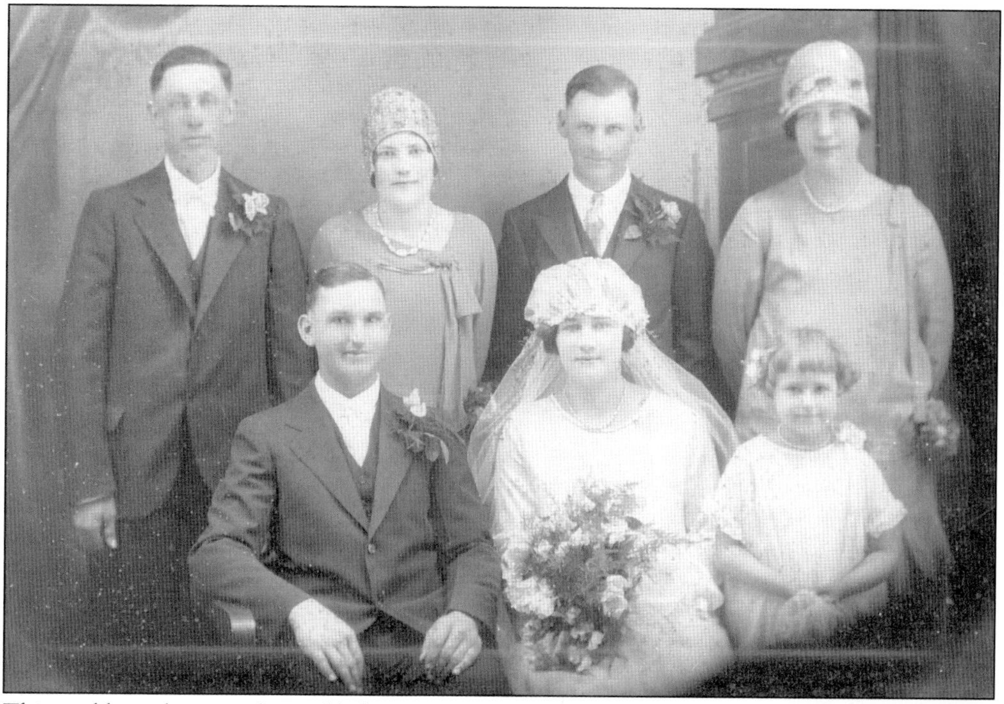

This wedding photograph was likely taken by a professional photographer in a studio around 1920. The group is carefully posed and probably constituted the immediate wedding party. The groom (along with all of the men pictured) wears a three-piece suit and sports a flower in his left lapel. The bride, holding a bouquet, wears a white dress, a mop cap, and a pearl necklace.

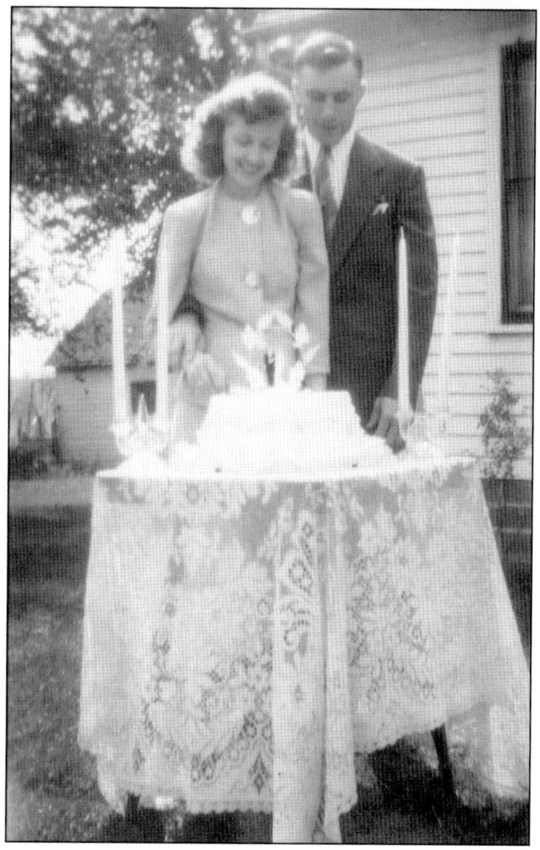

In this 1946 image, Vesta Clayton Holt and Wayne Holt cut their wedding cake on a small, lace-draped table. The photograph illustrates that the tradition of home weddings and/or receptions lasted well into the 1940s in Andrew County. This cake cutting occurred at the home of Vesta's parents, located six miles north of Savannah.

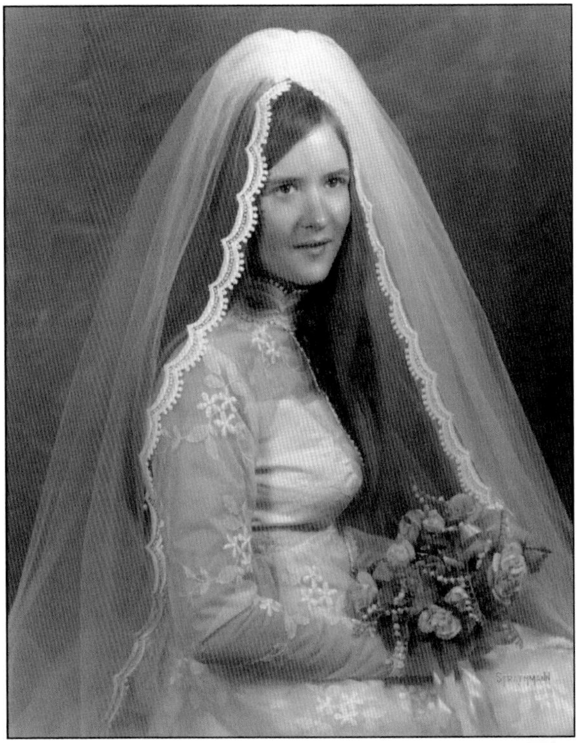

Debbie Bonham wore this dress for her 1973 wedding at the First Baptist Church in Savannah.

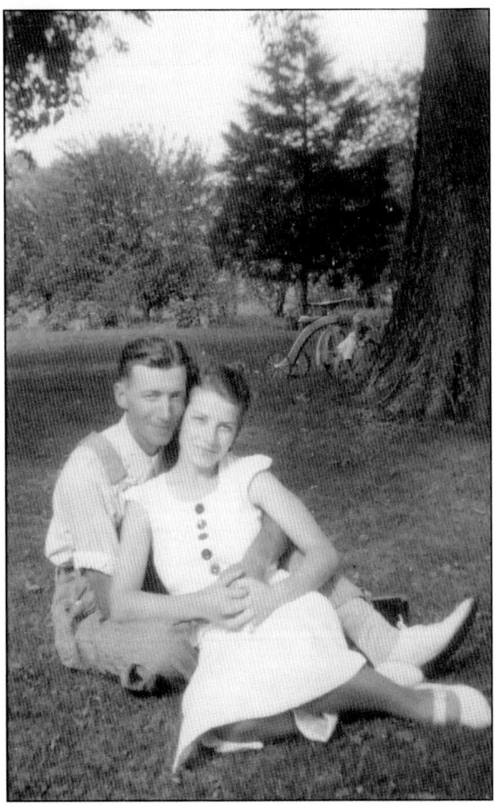

The art of courtship apparently lingered for Estella and Harold Miller, pictured shortly after they were married in 1937 at Estella's parents' farm near Savannah.

Even as early as the 1840s, not every marriage lasted. In one of the earliest Andrew County court cases, Sarah Tracy Duncan petitioned to divorce James Duncan for desertion. On the opposite end of the spectrum, long-lasting relationships were celebrated. This photograph shows the 50th anniversary party for Albert and Mary Messick Trapp (seated to the left of the hostess in the foreground).

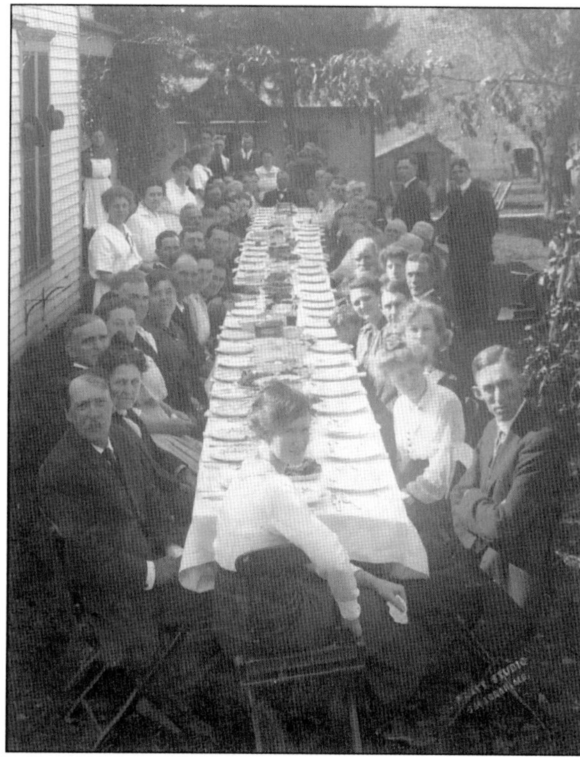

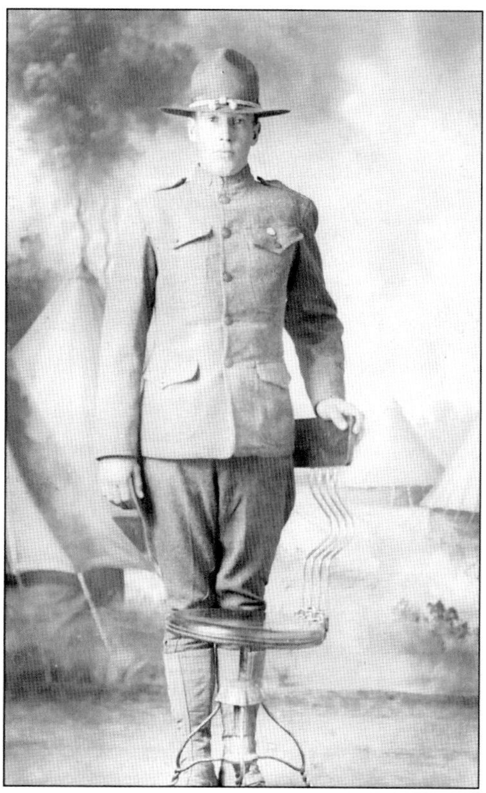

From the time of the Civil War, professional photographers took formal portraits of soldiers in uniform. This c. 1917 photographic postcard shows Harry W. Field, who served in Company A, 356th Infantry, 89th Division during World War I. For young men from rural areas, military service provided an opportunity to gain a larger perspective of the world.

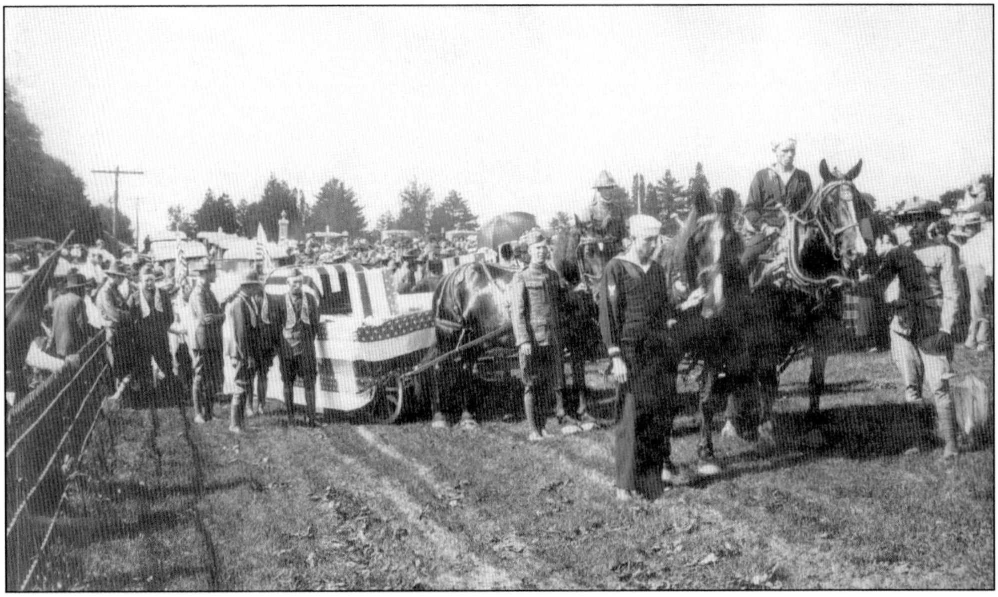

The photograph above shows the funeral procession of Pvt. Rueben Horton on its way to the Savannah Cemetery in 1918. Private Horton died serving in World War I. The loss of young men in the Great War affected many small-town residents, but the passing of any community member was noted. In the 1980s, Henry Bunse recalled, "Before the telephone, someone went to the parsonage, and the minister would toll the bell to let the people know that someone had died." Cemeteries served as memorials to console the living. In 1993, Ewing Mink fondly remembered his spouse, "I reckon the saddest time was when my wife died. She was a good cook. I couldn't have wanted nothing more." The photograph below shows Andrew County pioneer Joseph Walker's grave marker.

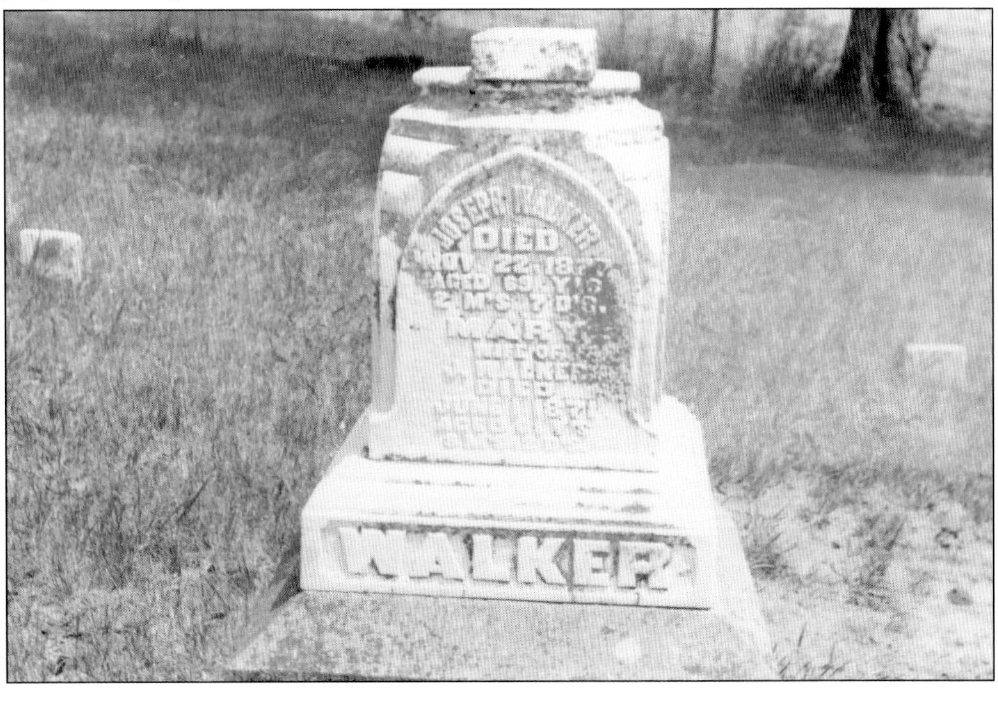

Six

THE PUBLIC WELFARE

In her remembrance of rural life in *A Northern Countryside*, Rosalind Richards observed that city dwellers might merely look on if a neighbor died or went bankrupt. In the country, Richards insisted, "We *must* help, whether we will or no! We cannot get away from duties that are so imperative. Our neighbor's necessities are inescapable, and a certain soldierly quality comes to us in that we cannot *choose*."

Such mutual helpfulness might have involved a neighbor rushing to summon a local doctor. Lewis Atherton observed that the idealized image of the old-fashioned country doctor still retains its appeal. Doctors once lived directly in the communities they served, and people also remember when a doctor personally knew his patients, spent long hours at bedsides, and charged modestly for his services. In 1976, Gladys Popplewell Sanders recalled, "Dr. E.C. Jefferies settled in Whitesville in 1888 and practiced medicine there for 49 years. Those were horse and buggy days for house calls. Dr. Jefferies carried a bull's-eye lantern on his buggy for night calls; a light was necessary on the country roads. He did not fail to respond."

Atherton points out that in actuality, the picture was not so idyllic. In the absence of telephones, country people had to ride to town to summon a physician, who could lose hours before reaching a patient. In town, a person suffering from injury or illness might wait an equally long time if the doctor was away on a country call. In addition, diagnostic tools and available medications were limited. People remember the country doctor fondly because he served as a confidant and friend rather than as a skilled, perhaps emotionally and literally distant, specialist.

In 1912, Savannah did attract a specialist, as Dr. Perry Nichols began to build a sanatorium for cancer treatment. His secret escharotic agent was popular with many patients, and the sanatorium became one of the largest employers in Andrew County. Professionally criticized at the time, research conducted almost a century later revealed that the treatment did have limited merit.

Today, rural areas face difficulties in attracting physicians, whether general practitioners or specialists. Andrew County is fortunate to have a modern health clinic in Savannah.

Individual help alone could not address some issues regarding public welfare. Infrastructure development required considerable public and private investment. No town could be up to date without water and sewer service, paved streets, and electricity.

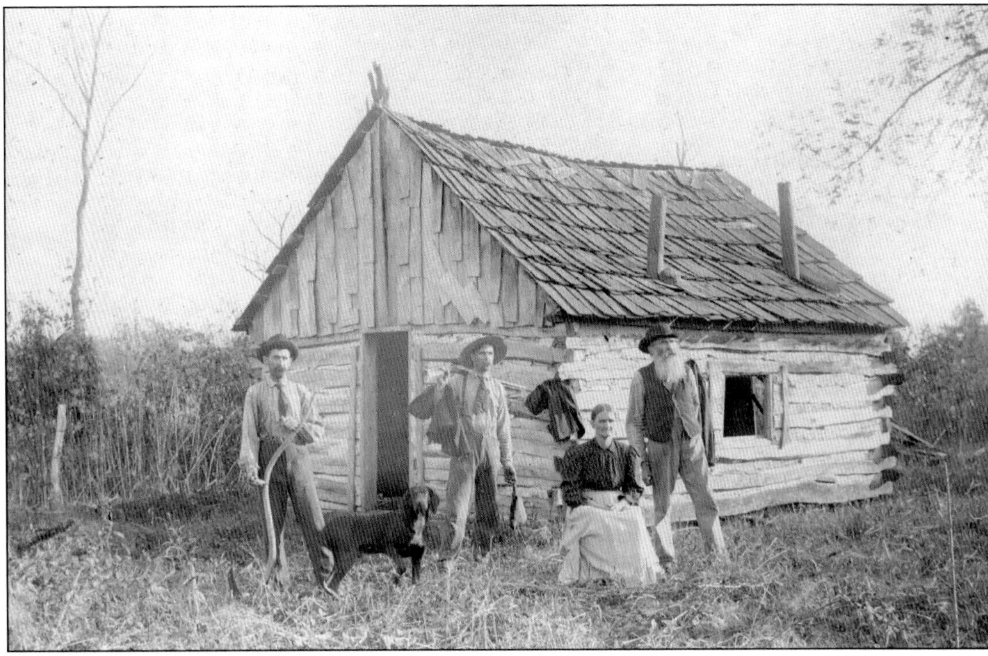

For Andrew County pioneer families into the early 20th century, mutual helpfulness proved essential among neighbors. This was true for the family above, posing before a log house, as well as the Miller family, pictured below in front of their clapboard home around 1910. Infrastructure development was nonexistent for rural families, and into the early 20th century medical assistance was not close at hand. Even picking up the mail required a trip to town.

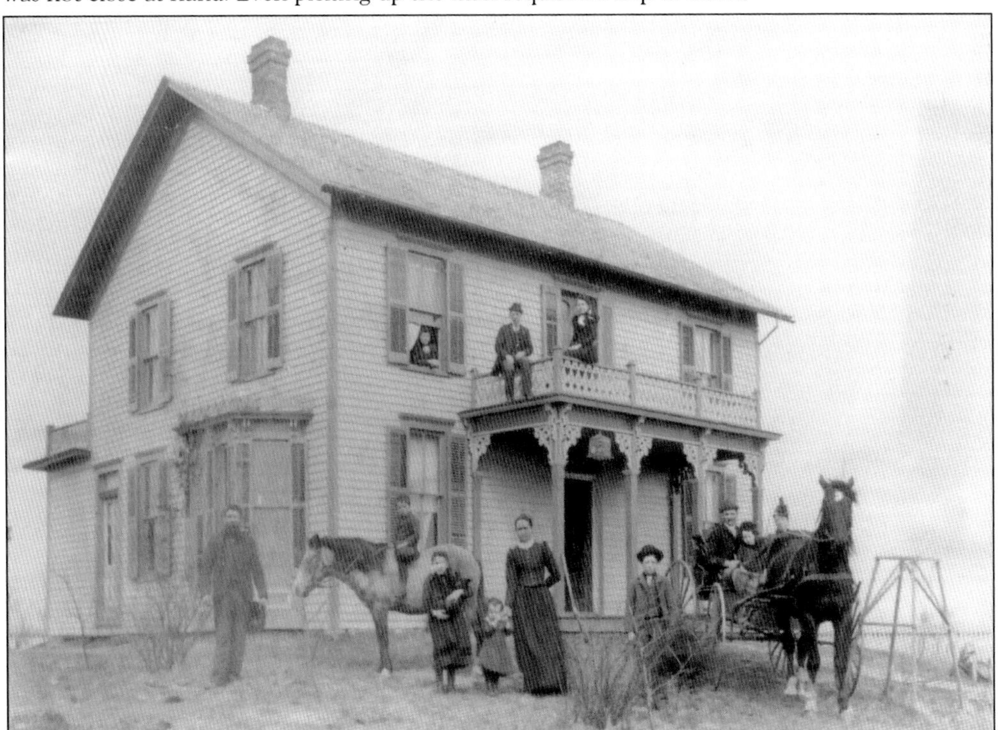

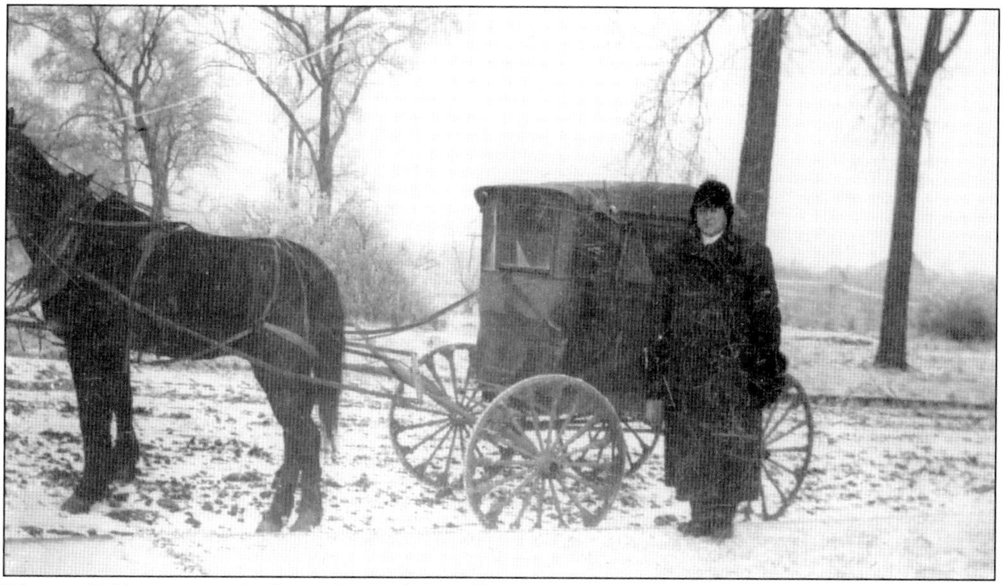

This c. 1914 photograph shows Dr. Ralph Kelley in front of his house in Savannah next to the horse and buggy he used to make house calls. In addition to their limited medical equipment, in wintertime doctors carried scoop shovels, axes, wire cutters, and lanterns on country calls in order to get through snow-blocked roads.

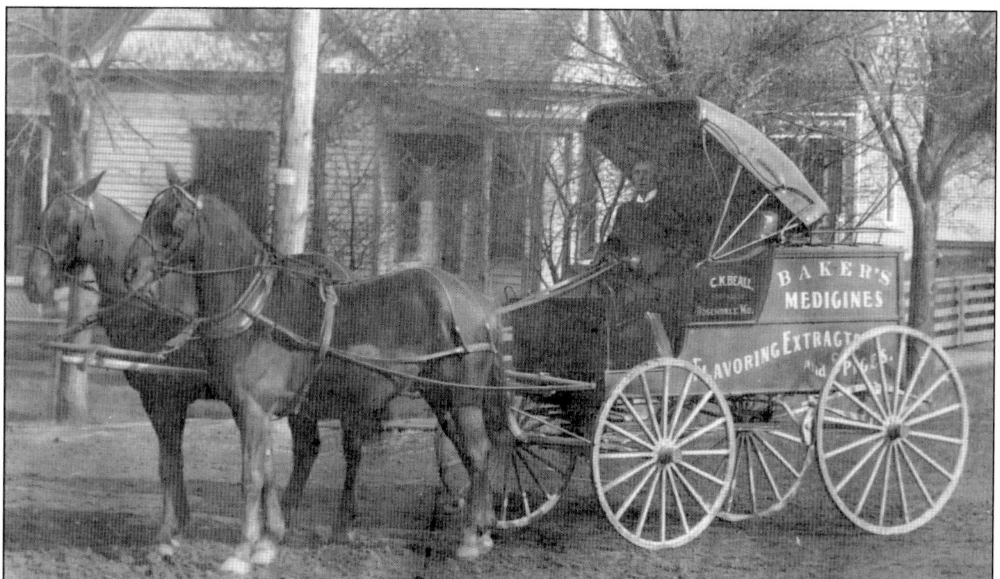

The lettering on the side of this wagon proclaims, "Baker's Medicines, Flavorings, Extracts, and Spices." A smaller sign identifies "C.K. Beall, Rosendale, MO." Medicine men trumpeted extravagant claims of miraculous cures as they traveled along country roads. Some followed the same circuit of towns for decades.

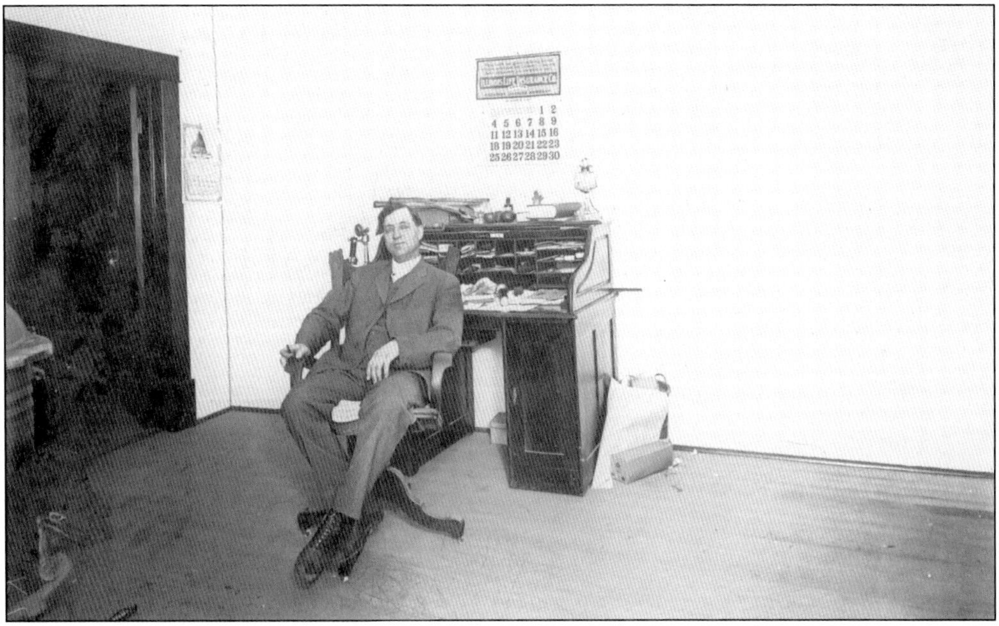

The c. 1910 photograph above shows Dr. J.C. Hosher, while the image below from around the same time captures the building in Rosendale that bore the name "J.C. Hosher, Druggist." In small towns, it was not unusual for a local doctor to also operate a pharmacy. In 1994, Carl Rudolph remembered that Old Doc Bever had a drugstore and office in Amazonia. He recalled, "My older brother drove to town there in a buggy and had his tonsils taken out right there." For country doctors, a drugstore had the advantage of operating largely on a cash basis. For medical services, patients often paid in kind. In the 1990s, Ivan Hewitt Jr. noted, "I can remember the doctor saying how many different things he had brought to him, old hens or eggs or corn or what-have-you, to pay the bill."

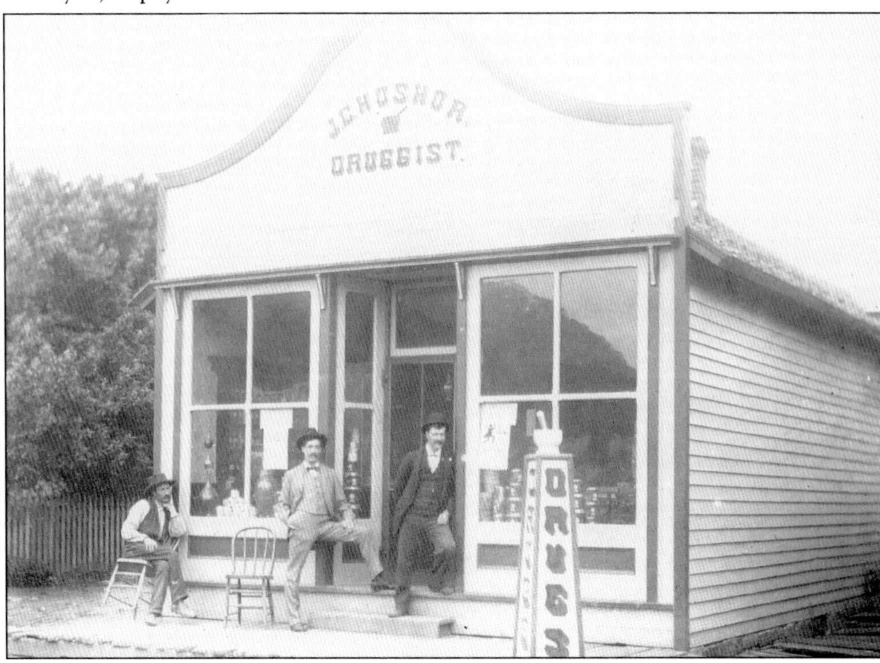

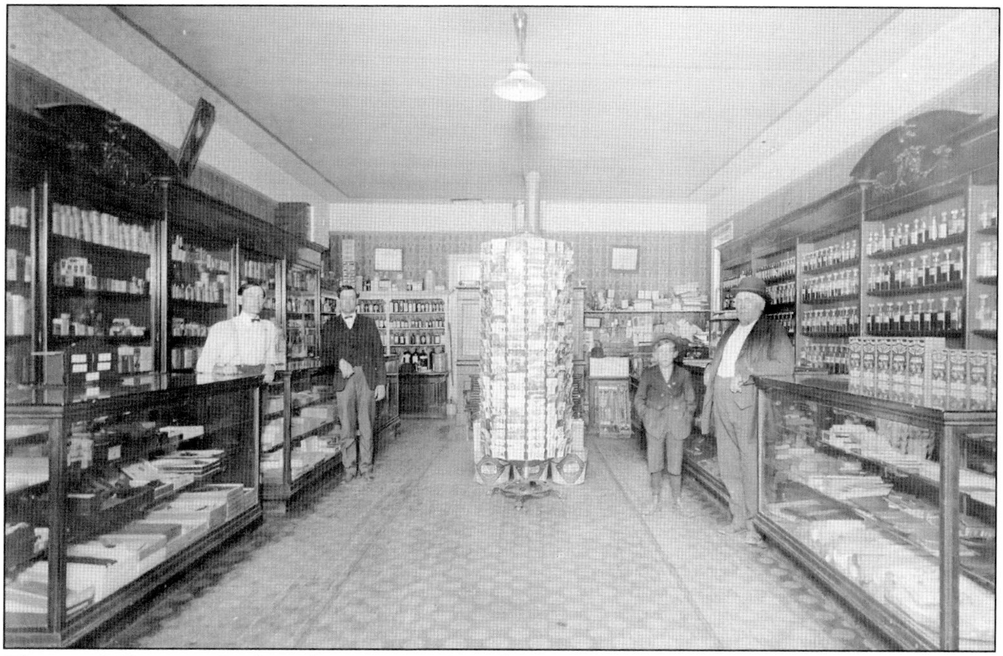

This c. 1915 image displays the interior of Hosher's Drugstore in Rosendale. The products on the shelves illustrate that the store sold more than prescription drugs. In the 19th and early 20th centuries, numerous patent medicines were promoted; these nostrums were sometimes of questionable effectiveness. Some brands, however, live on today, including Luden's Cough Drops and Fletcher's Castoria.

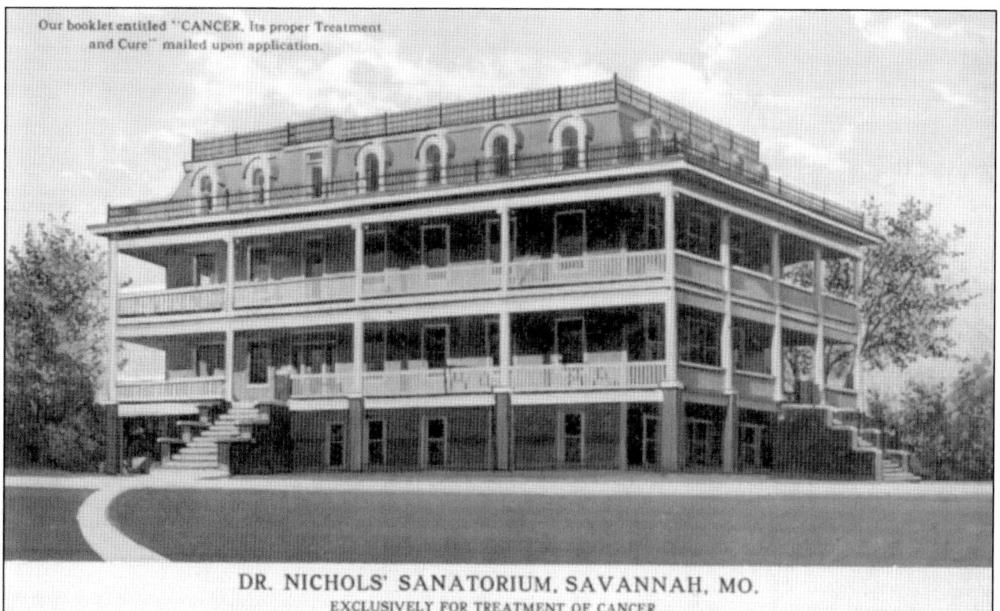

In 1912, cancer specialist Dr. Perry Nichols purchased 30 acres of land in Savannah on which to build a sanatorium. Wood-framed Building No. 1 was constructed in 1915. The current brick structure was added in 1924. The facility operated through 1956. Approximately 70,000 patients received treatment at the clinic.

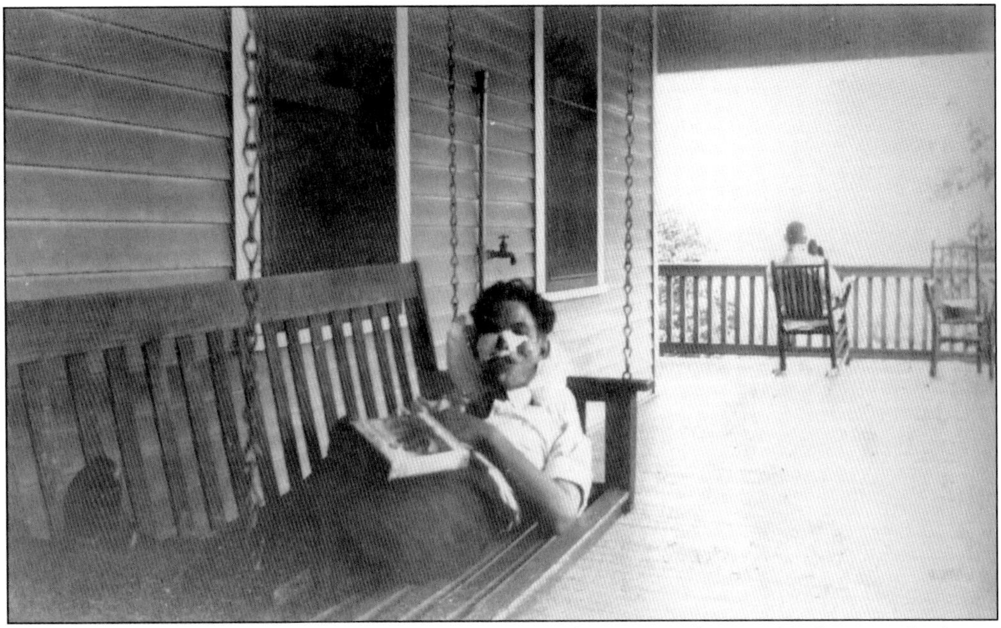

A patient at the Nichols Sanatorium reclines on a porch swing in the c. 1920 photograph above. Older Andrew County residents recall seeing bandaged patients in downtown Savannah. The image below shows the dining area in the sanatorium facility, opened in the mid-1920s, where employees took their meals. Dr. Perry Nichols insisted on training the nurses himself. The jobs necessitated by the opening of the sanatorium provided work opportunities for locals.

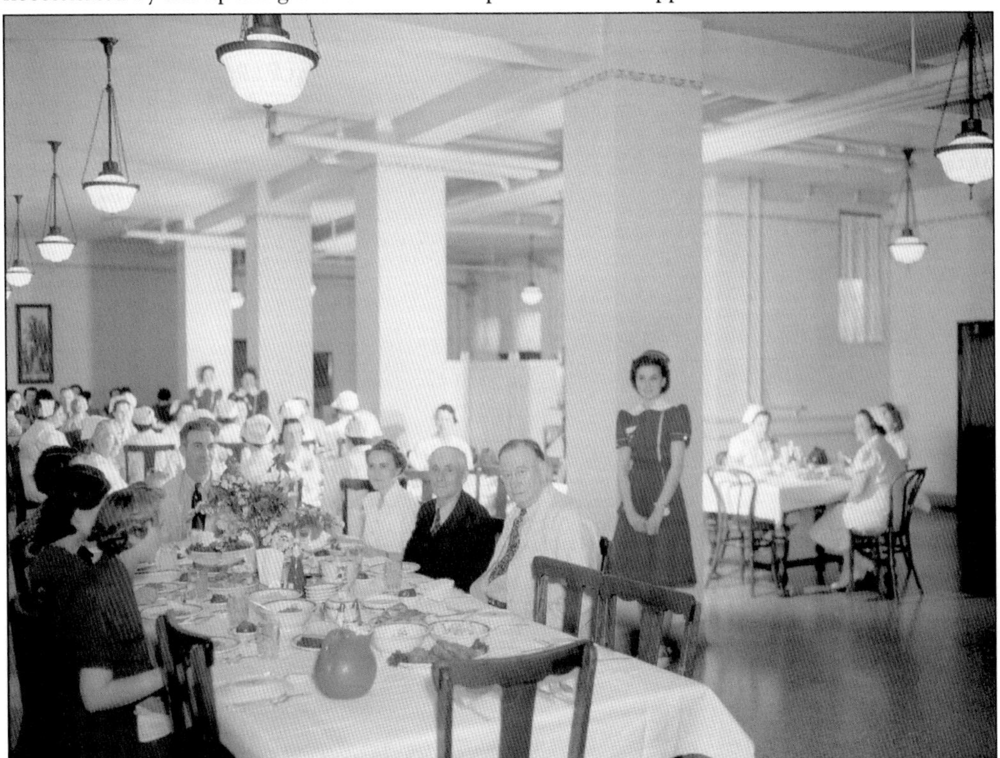

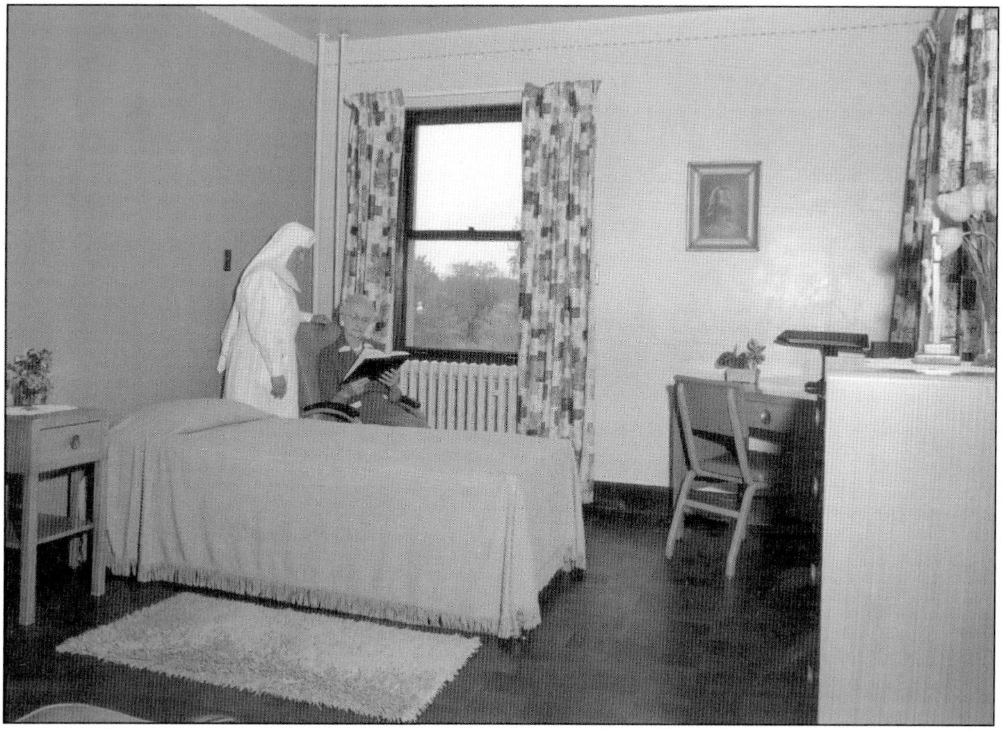

In 1956, the Sisters of St. Francis purchased the sanatorium building to start a retirement home for ladies, naming it LaVerna Heights. Elderly and ill women who needed extra care lived here. Although it was operated by Catholic nuns, women of all denominations were welcome as residents. The photograph above displays the accommodations provided in a LaVerna resident's room in 1957. The image below, of residents gathered around a television set, dates from the same period. Many Andrew County residents associate the sanatorium building with LaVerna Heights as opposed to the cancer treatment center.

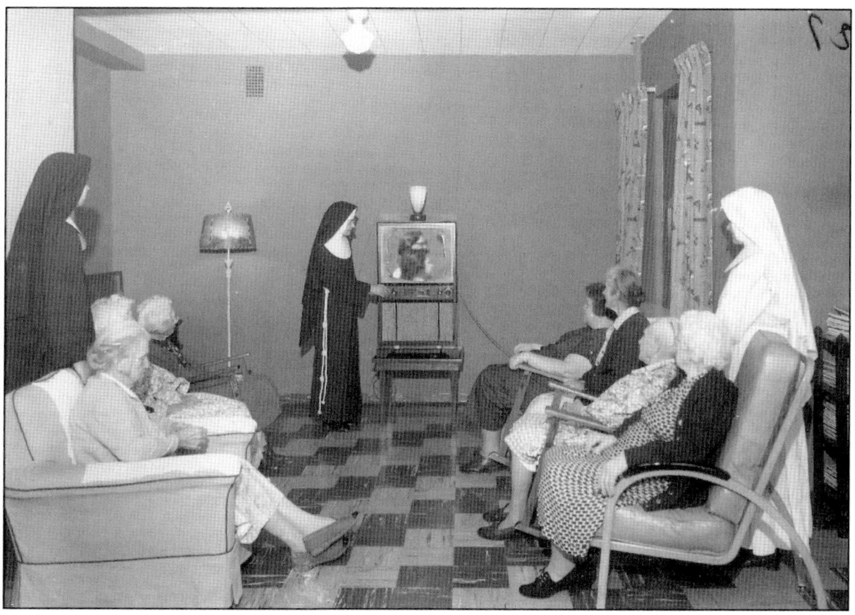

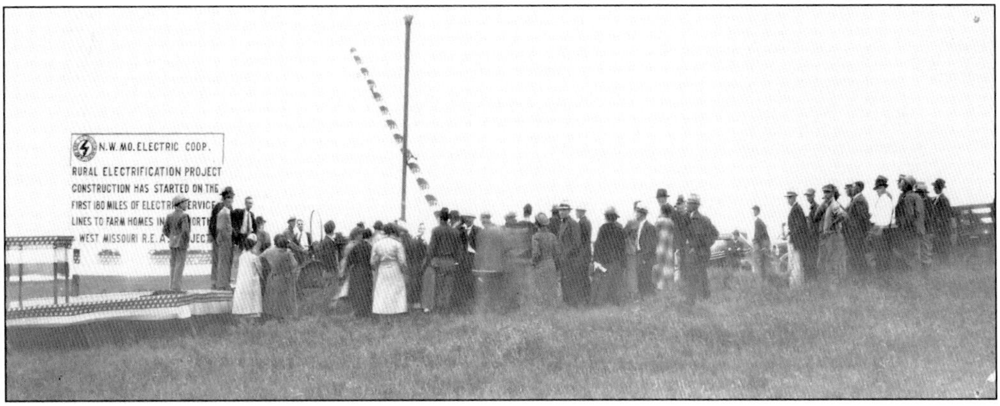

In 1938, this crowd gathered in Savannah to witness the erection of the first utility pole in a rural electricification system. The size of the gathering testified to the importance of the utility to people in Andrew County. The Northwest Missouri Electric Cooperative was incorporated in 1936, with 18 farmers as the original incorporators. The first section constructed by the cooperative included 150 miles of power lines in the county.

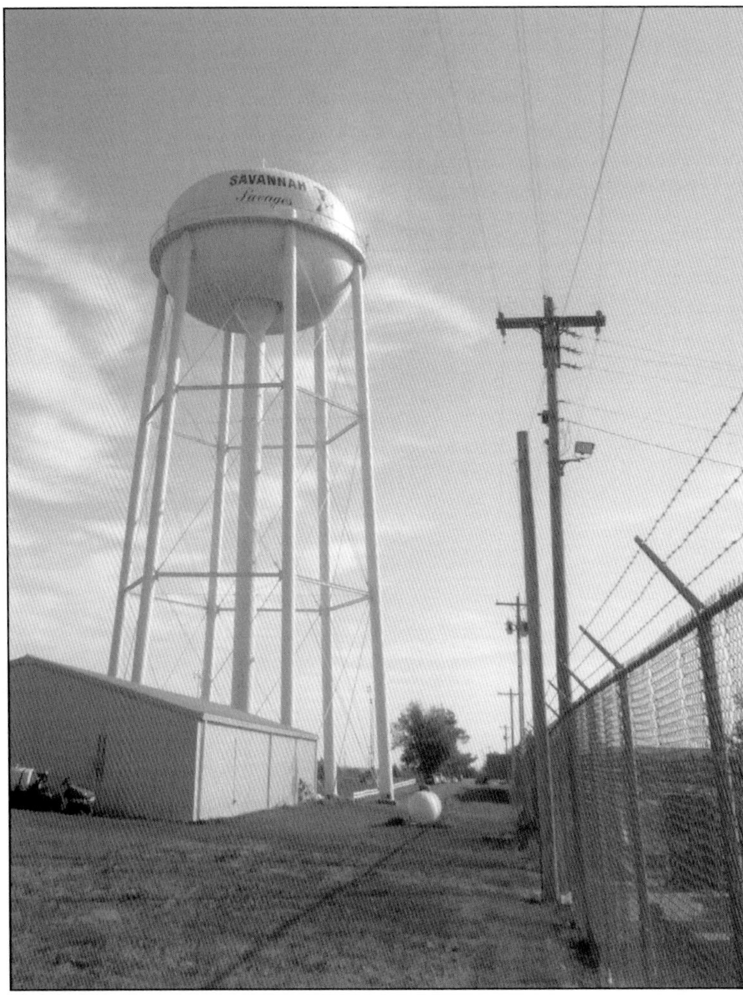

Savannah now proudly boasts two water towers. These structures often bore the names of a town and signified that a place was a "progressive" community. In *West of the Water Tower* (1923), northwest Missouri novelist Homer Croy identified a local water tower as a "town character." Young boys climbed its ladder "as high as courage lasted," and picnic parties often gathered at its base.

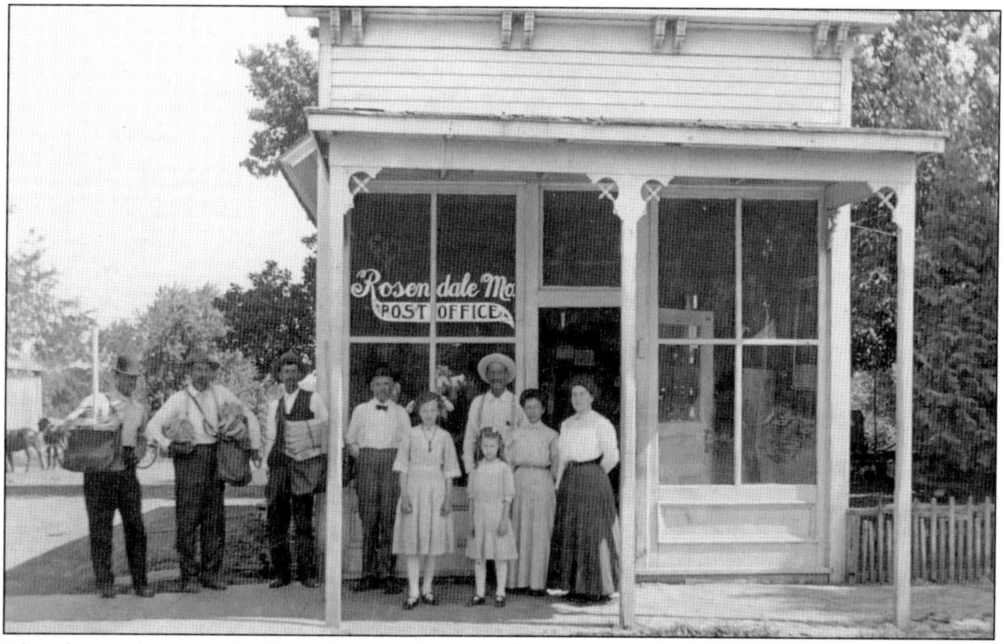

The above photograph of the Rosendale post office dates from around 1920, while the image below shows Aaron Odie Kellogg on his rural mail route around 1915. Rural free delivery (RFD) became available in Andrew County in 1903. Before RFD, farmers had to travel to the nearest town to pick up their mail. With the introduction of rural routes, the volume of mail handled at local post offices dramatically increased. By May 1903, the Savannah Post Office reported handling 50,000 pieces of mail each week. For farm families, RFD was transformative, since the postal service now connected them to the outside world almost every day.

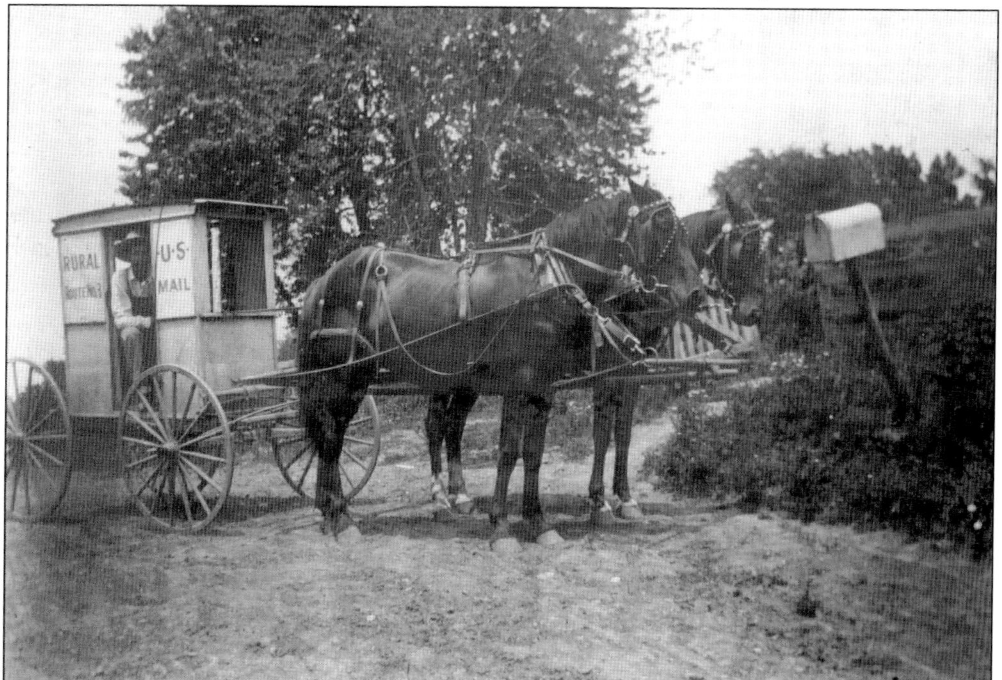

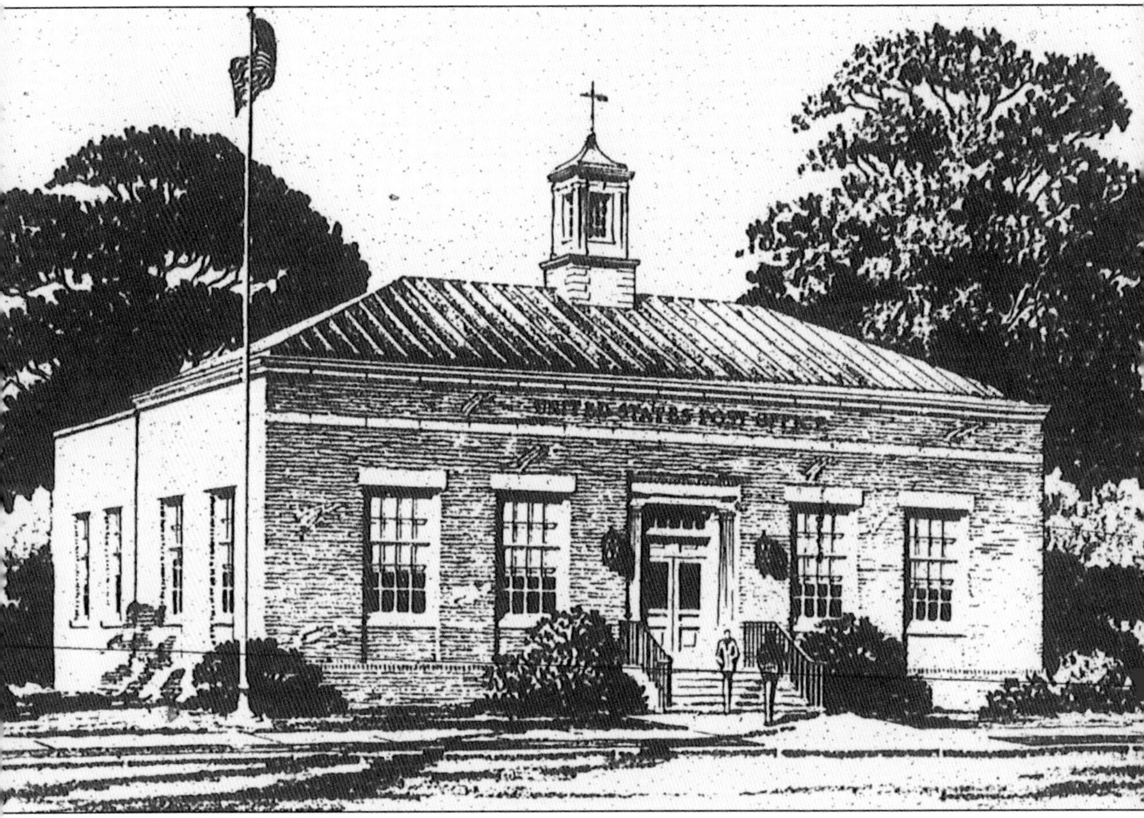

This architect's drawing of the Savannah Post Office appeared in the local newspaper in 1939 on the occasion of the laying of its cornerstone; a crowd of 2,000 gathered for the ceremony. The high school band played and the local Masonic lodge helped make the arrangements. As in many small towns, the post office was referred to as the federal building since offices for public agencies were located in the basement. Appropriately, Missouri senator Harry S. Truman participated in the cornerstone-laying ceremony. On the occasion, merchants took out an advertisement in the local newspaper that read, in part, "In its stateliness, usefulness and magnificence, this new federal building will stand as a mark of advancement and progress in the county." The building continues to serve as the local post office.

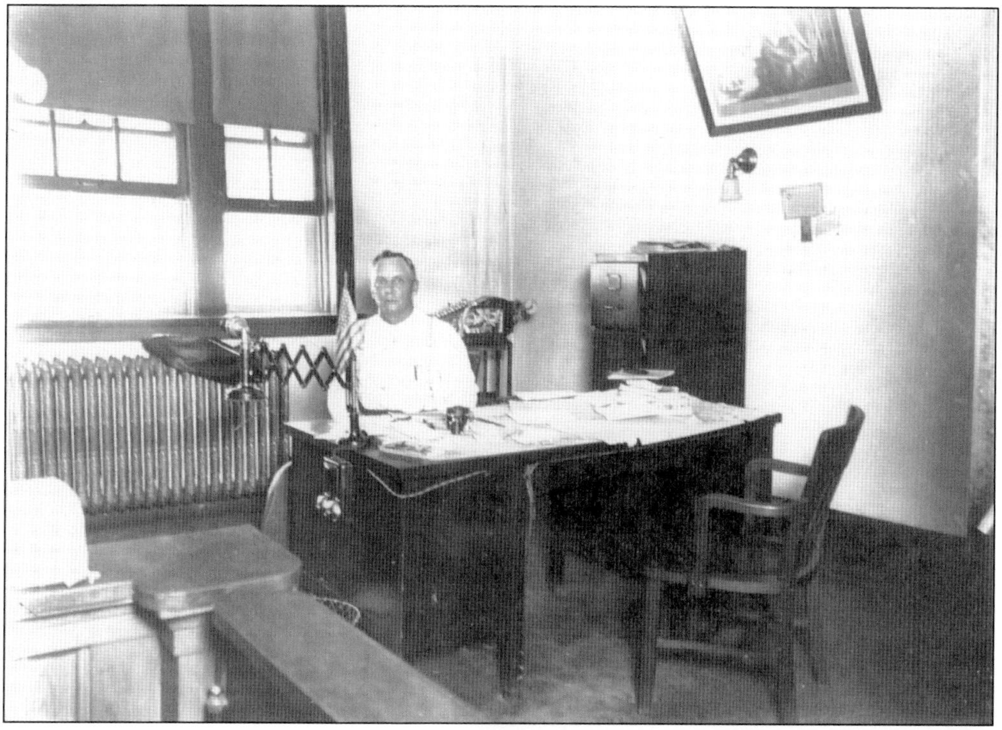

The c. 1920 photograph above shows O.V. Sells Sr. sitting at his Mutual Telephone Company desk in Savannah. At right, switchboard operator Nellie Mullinex Bentley Dungan sits at the switchboard in her home in Flag Springs. Her daughter Marjorie remembered that being a switchboard operator brought in extra money, recalling that "it was not hard work but very confining. Someone had to be in the house at all times." Switchboard operators like Dungan also expanded a town's neighboring network.

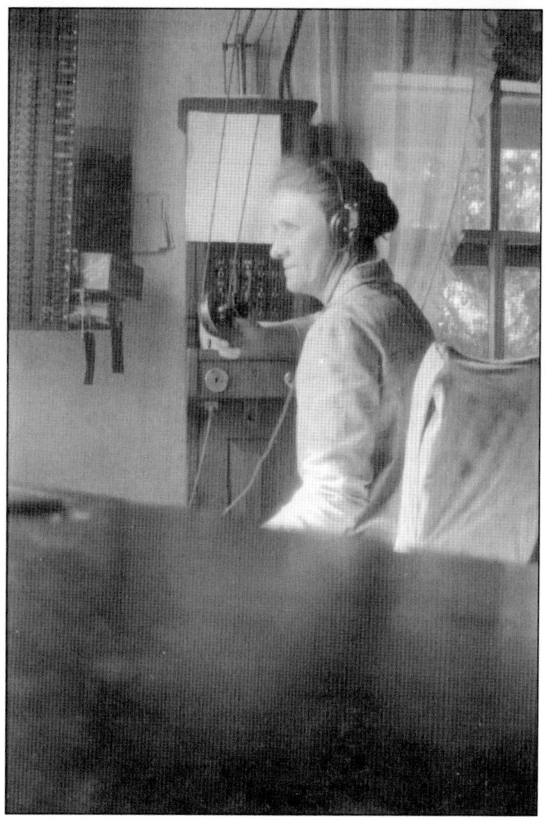

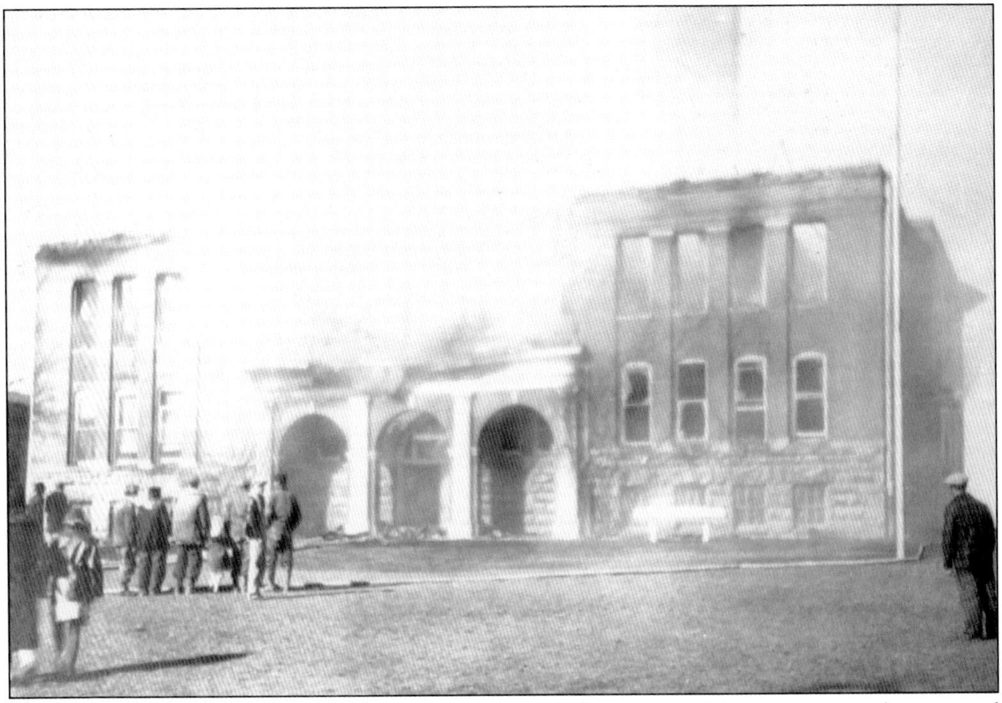

Nearly every town at some point experienced a disaster that struck without warning; these served as important landmarks in a place's history. More importantly, a big fire, flood, or tornado often proved an important turning point in a town's development. A town that pooled its resources as a community usually came back stronger than before. Fire proved to be the most frequent form of disaster in small towns. As shown in the above photograph, the Savannah Public School building that housed all 12 grades burned in 1932; the building was quickly replaced. The photograph below recorded a flood in or near Rosendale around 1915.

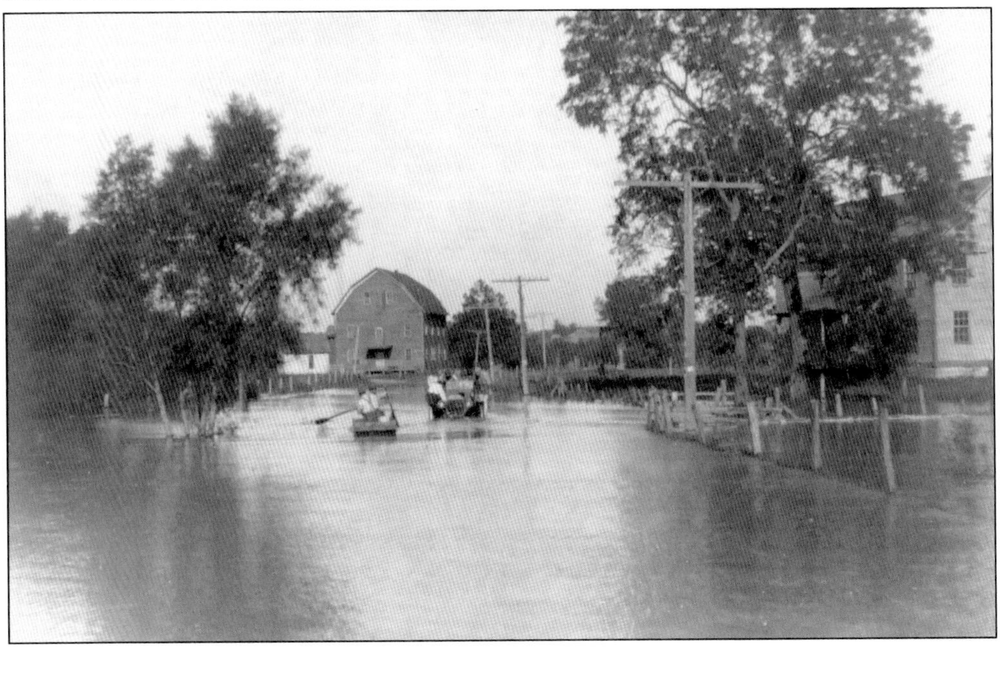

Seven

Manufacturing and Movement

Mills operated for a century in Andrew County, grinding grain, sawing lumber, and carding wool. Before the Depression, flour mills produced the Crown Jewel brand in Savannah and Belle of Andrew in Whitesville, but competition from Gold Medal and other big-name producers put the county's last mills out of business in the 1930s.

In the 1900s, the Commercial Club in Savannah aggressively sought to lure industries to the area. Armed with subsidies, it attracted such companies as Novelty Stove, Star Disc Company, and Empire Cigar. Schuyler Manufacturing relocated to Savannah to utilize castings made by Howard Stove.

With the exception of Schuyler Manufacturing (1907–1920), most industries were short-lived. The Schuyler factory produced washing machines, funnels, and other products. Since manufacturing never flourished in Andrew County, few of these types of businesses remained after 1920.

Compared to manufacturing, transportation technology exerted a long-term impact on the Andrew County economy. Railroads, and later trucks traveling along improved highways, carried the products of farms to market and increased mobility for people. Steamboats also facilitated travel. Away from the river and railroad lines, however, transportation proceeded on foot or with the aid of horses.

The extension of railroad lines to many small towns after the Civil War allowed faster movement of people and freight. In 1911, the interurban gave Savannah residents a convenient, time-saving rail connection to larger towns.

In the 20th century, vehicles and improved roads lessened travel time. By 1950, farm families no longer needed nearby towns to provide goods and services, as automobile travel increased mobility and expanded shopping opportunities. With the building of interstate highways in the 1960s, travel to larger towns and cities became even more convenient.

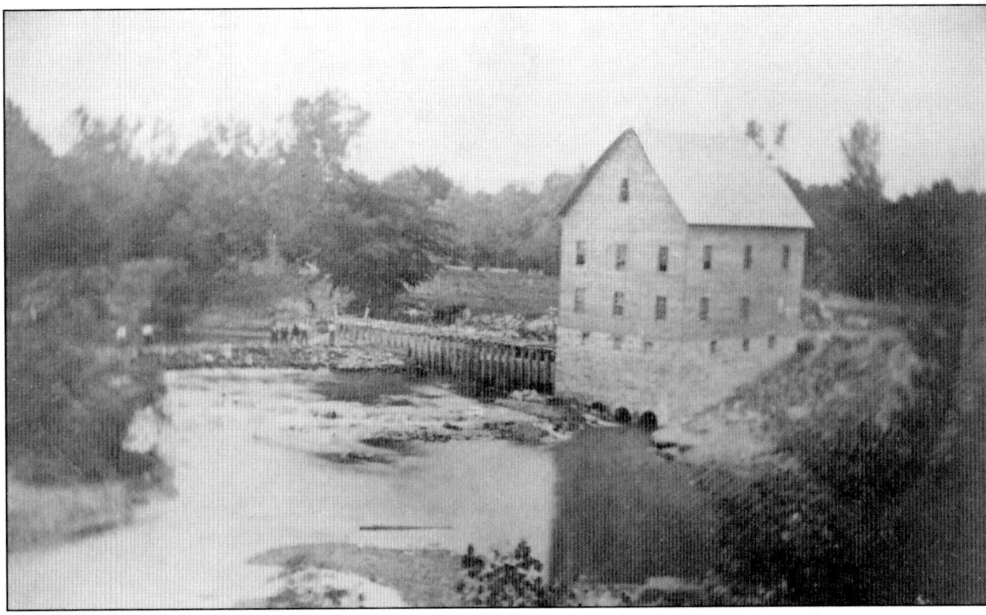

The image above shows the Whitesville Mill in 1892. The photograph below of Ogle's Mill in Rosendale dates from about 1900. Along streams and rivers in rural America, such mills performed basic functions for farmers. Powered by water or steam, they sawed lumber or ground grain into flour. In 1950, Emma Egger Rudolph recalled, "The farmers would take a load of wheat and corn to Rosendale and to Rochester. They had a mill wheel that was turned by water and the grain was made into flour and [corn] meal for the winter's supply."

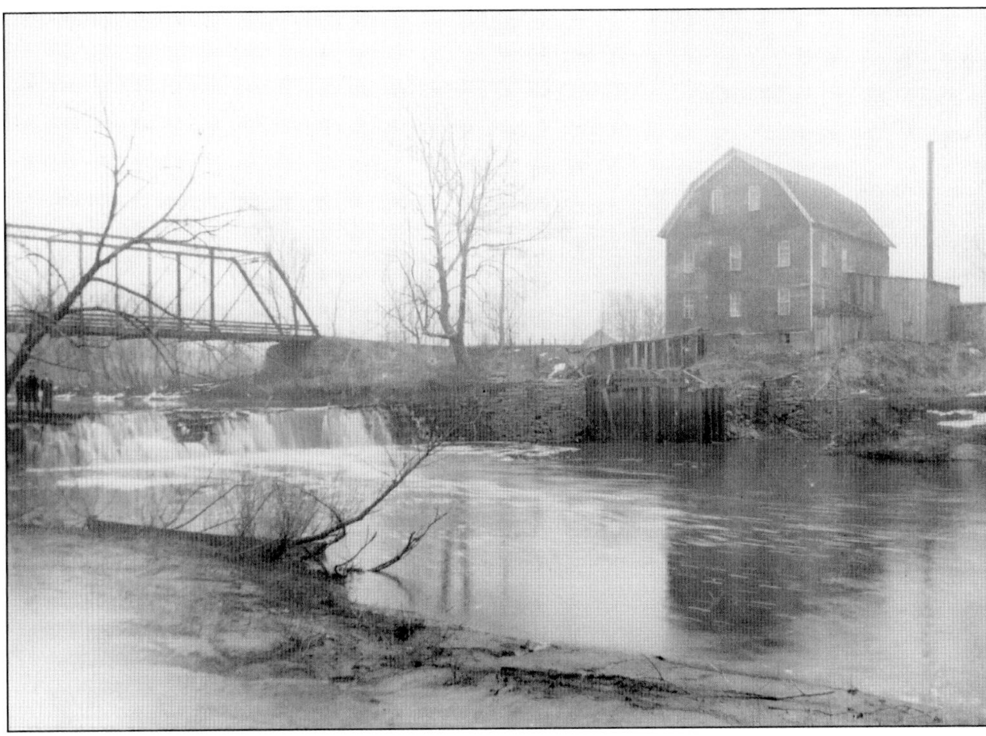

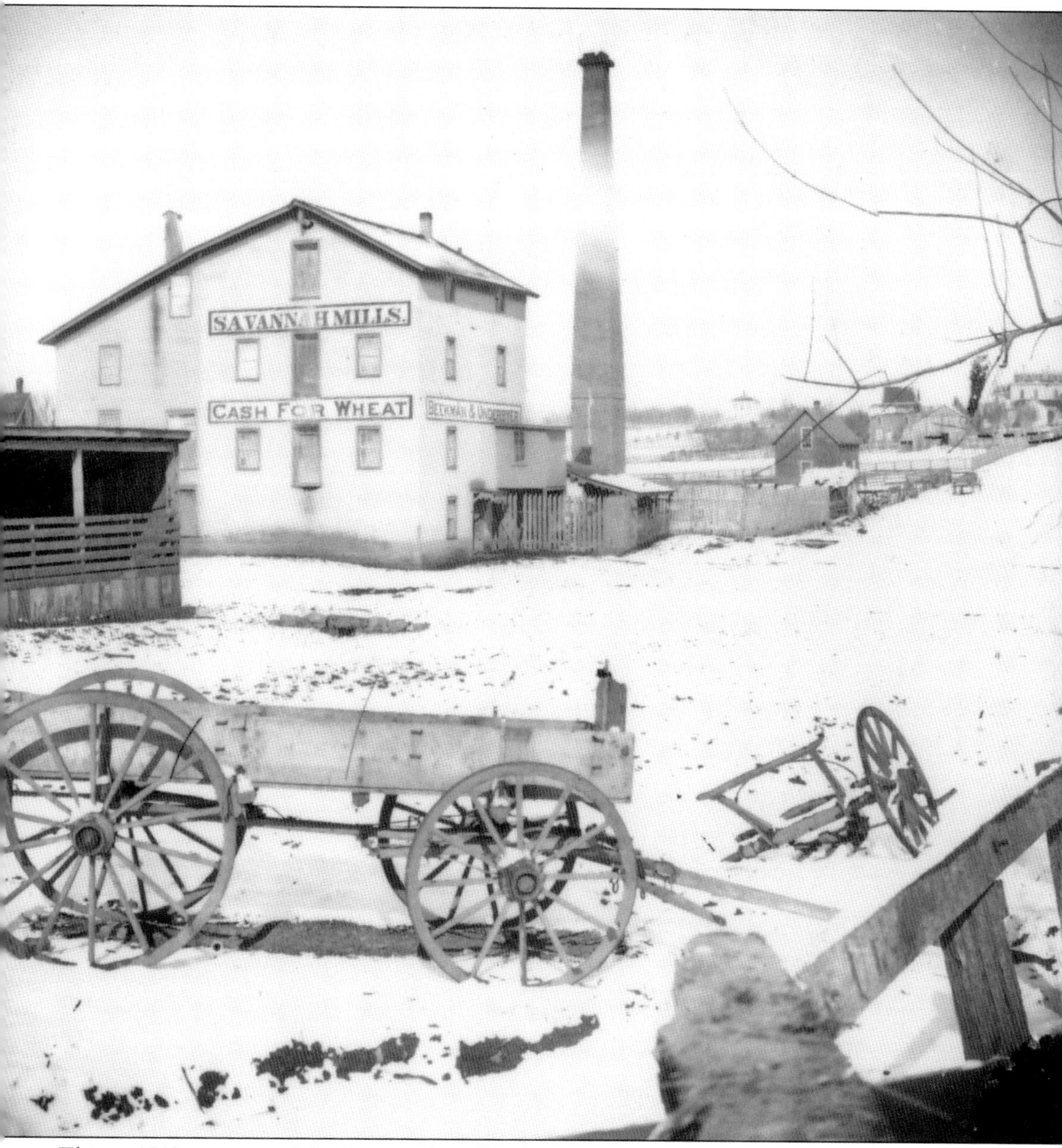

This c. 1910 image is of the Savannah Mill, where the miller offered "Cash for Wheat." The smokestack suggests that the mill was steam powered. If waterpower proved inadequate or unreliable, mills utilized stationary steam engines to turn saws or millstones. Even the smallest local mill represented a technological accomplishment. A skilled millwright was needed to design the building and its equipment. A poorly designed mill could shake itself apart once its power source was engaged. Local operations like the Savannah Mill eventually lost out to larger competitors. In 1977, Harold A. Modlin remembered that his father looked for a way to generate income in 1919. He recalled, "Dad was seeking a remunerative investment and somehow wound up buying the old abandoned grist mill on the Platte River in Rochester. He tried to compete with some of the big flour mills in St. Joe and Kansas City and they undercut their prices so much that Dad could not compete in the market nor support the operation of the mill."

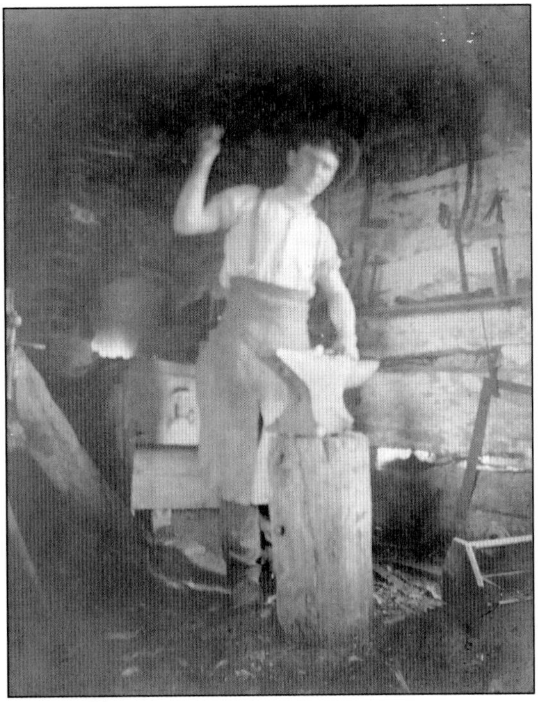

The photograph at left of a local blacksmith was taken around 1895. The image below of a construction crew building a church likely dates from around 1910. These images represent how working people were depicted in photographs in the late 19th and early 20th centuries. The blacksmith, an independent artisan, is seen in his workspace with the tools of his trade. The construction crew is at the work site, with the workers dominating the picture space. Later in the 20th century, huge machines often defined an image, with workers included to provide a sense of scale.

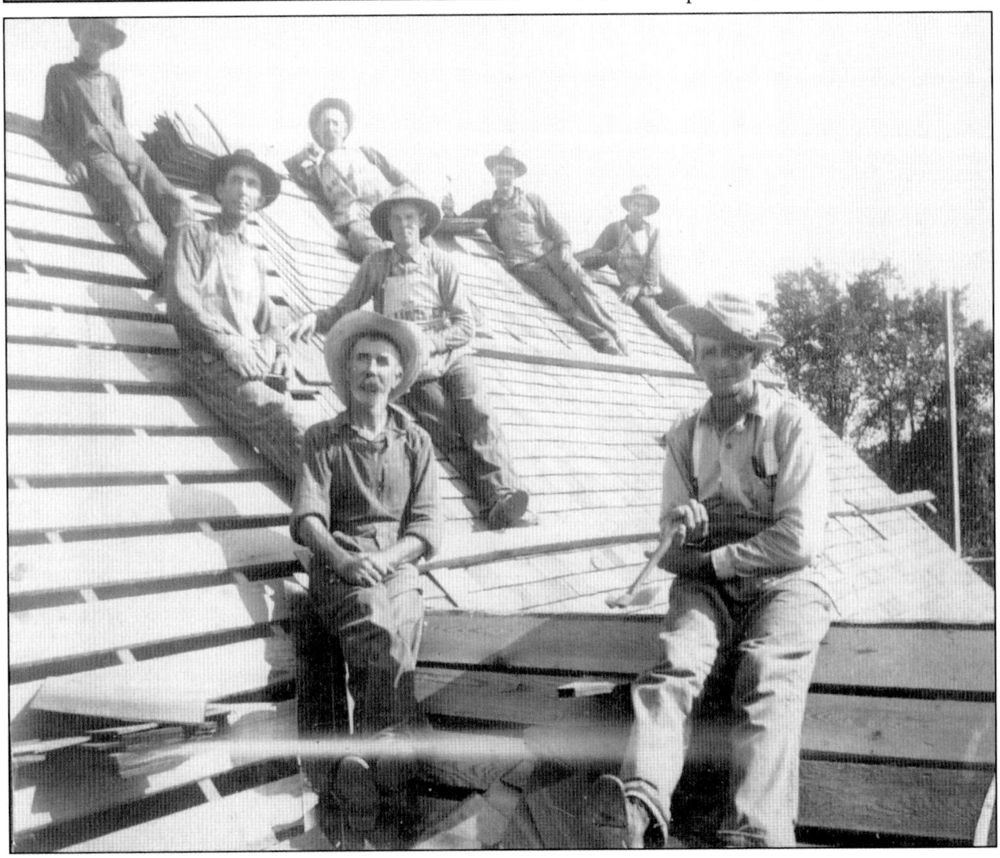

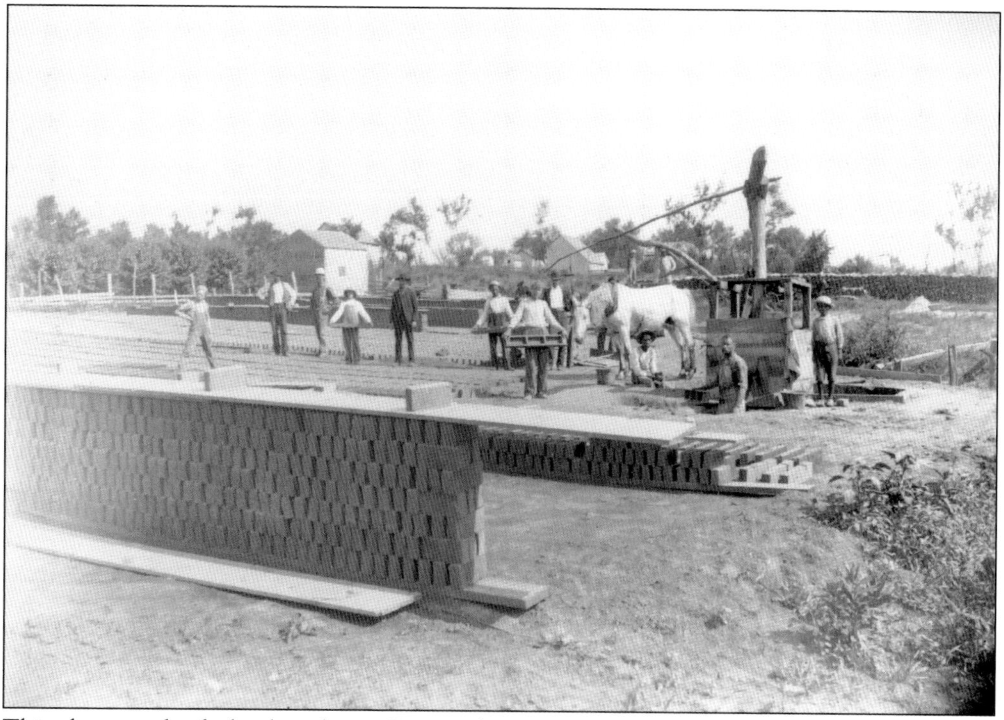

This photograph of a brickyard near Savannah dates from around 1890. In small towns, bricks were often produced locally. They could be of uneven quality depending on the skill of the brick maker and the quality of available materials. In the post–Civil War era, brick making provided one of the few job opportunities for African Americans in Andrew County.

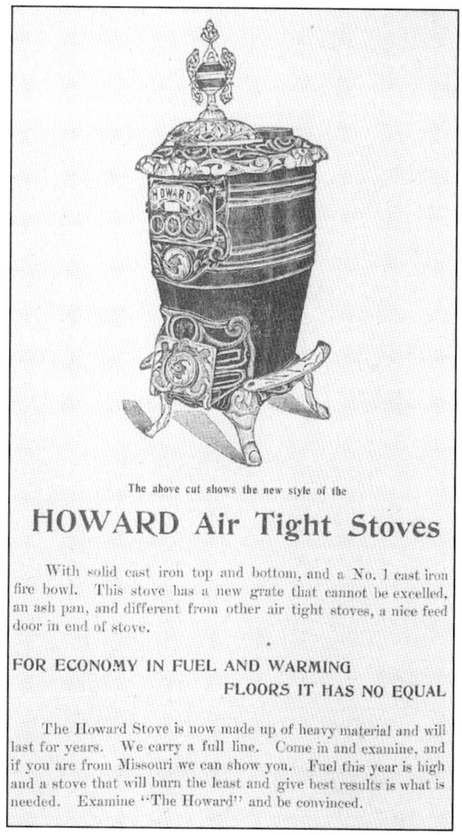

The Howard Stove Company was the brainchild of Methodist minister Lincoln Howard. In the 1890s, he thought that an inverted conical base on a heating stove would circulate heat downward, thus improving a stove's efficiency. Howard stoves were manufactured in Savannah until around 1911.

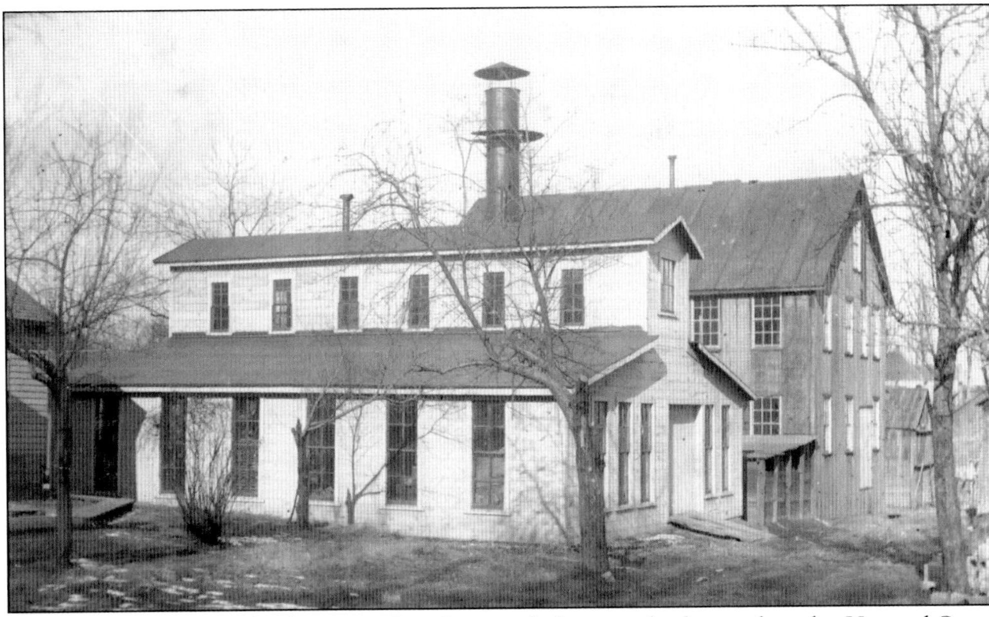

Around 1905, W.S. Schuyler arrived in Savannah because he knew that the Howard Stove Company made castings as well as stoves. The c. 1910 photograph above shows the Schuyler Manufacturing Company, which produced numerous products, including a combination washing machine and vacuum cleaner. The 1915 photograph below is of the "Funnel Gang." During World War I, Schuyler's filter-funnels were used to filter gasoline for aircraft. Oil companies across the United States also purchased funnels. The company also produced metal supports for running boards on Model T Fords.

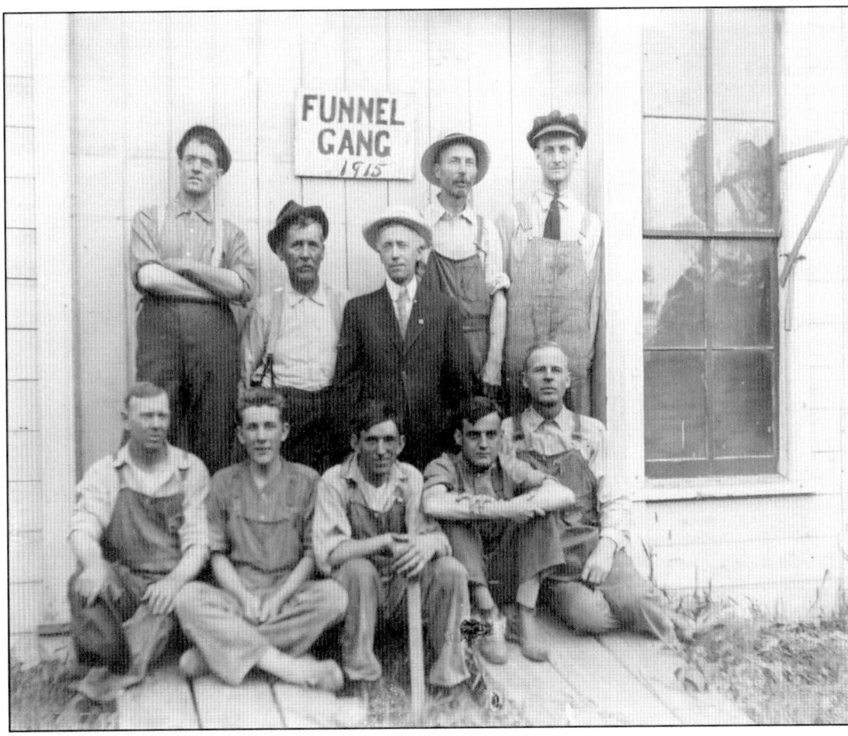

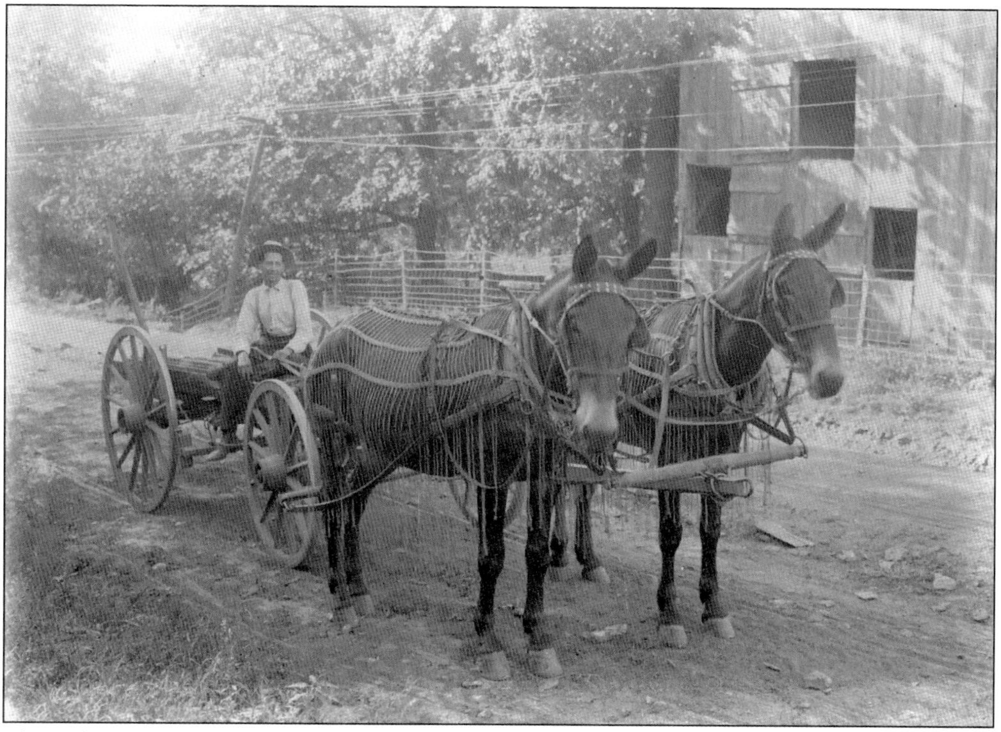

Throughout the 19th and early 20th centuries, transportation in Andrew County was powered by horses and mules. This photograph was taken around 1910.

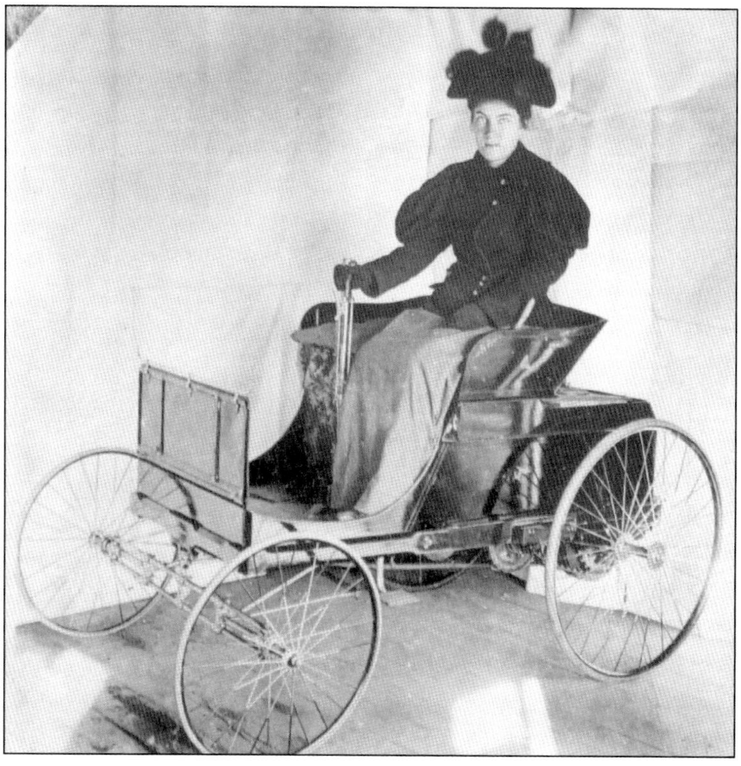

The first automobile in a small town often created a sensation. The information on the back of this picture reads, "Horseless carriage called automobile, built by John L. Glazier, Savannah, MO in 1898. His daughter, Julia A. Glazier in seat." At the time, few people likely imagined the impact the horseless carriage would have on rural life in Andrew County.

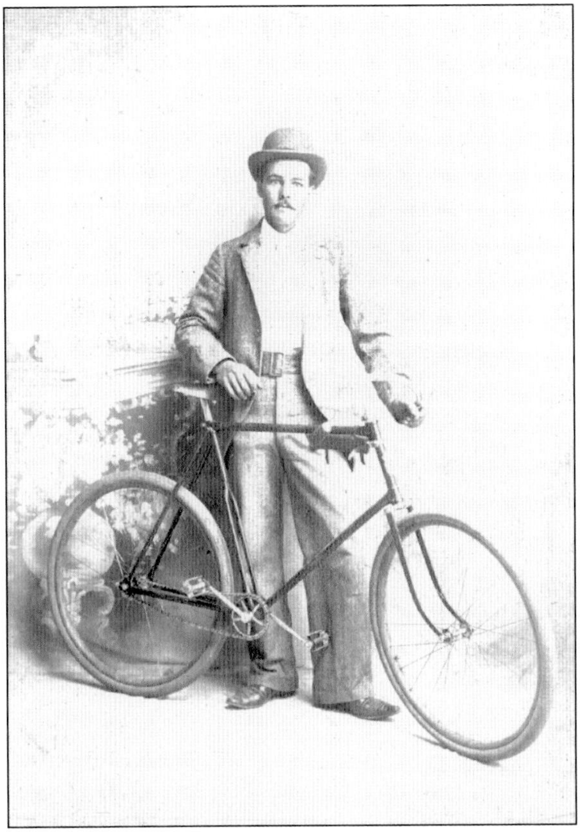

The photograph at left shows a young man and his "safety bicycle." This type of cycle featured pneumatic tires and reliable brakes. It was a vast improvement over the earlier, high-wheeled "bone shakers." Rural people used bicycles for both recreation and basic transportation. An even better form of transportation was a motorcycle. The photograph below is a postcard of Clarence Eisiminger and George Riddle on an Indian motorcycle in 1920. In the *Savannah Reporter*, Harley-Davidson and other manufacturers promoted motorcycles as an affordable means of motorized transportation. Given the demeanor captured in this image, Eisiminger and Riddle regarded the Indian as something more than just a practical way to get around.

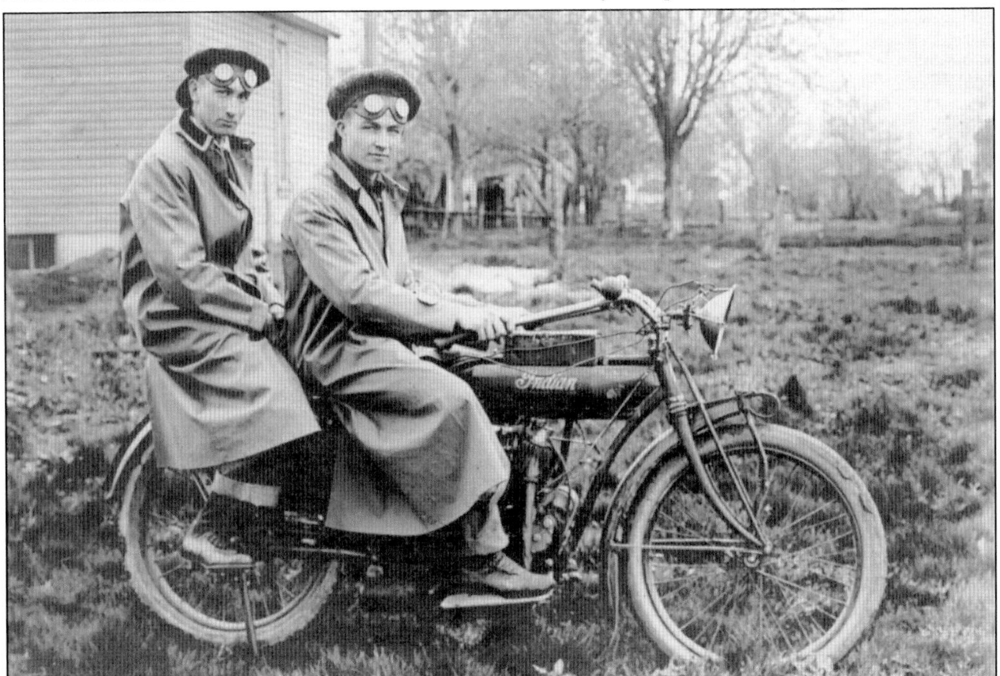

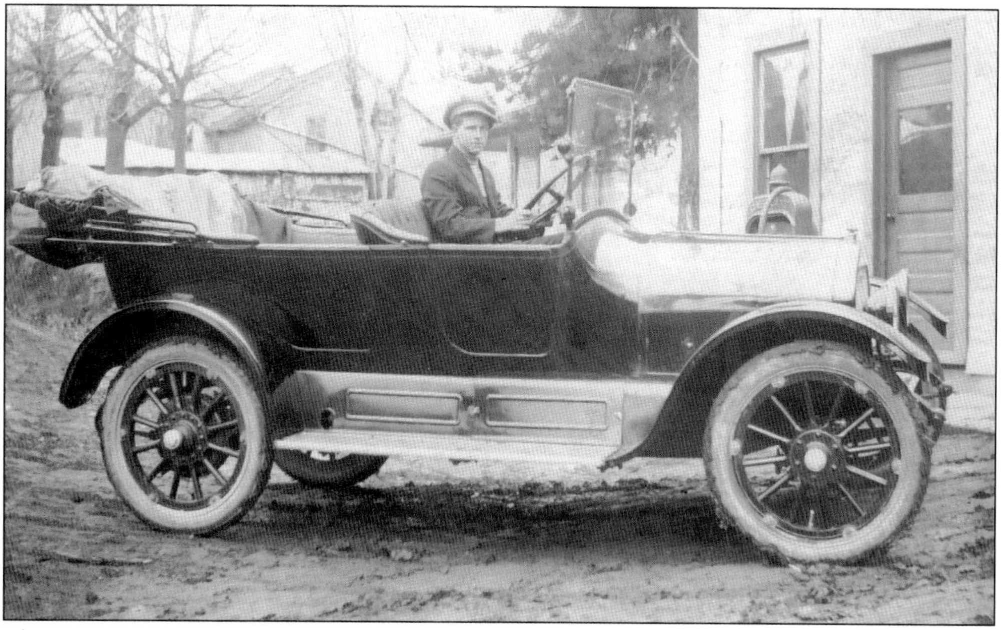

The c. 1920 image above shows a young man at the wheel of a touring car. Automobiles dramatically reduced the time required to visit a town. Trips that could take an entire day with a horse-drawn wagon had travel time reduced to a few hours. The popularity of the automobile led to the demise of the livery stable. In their place, garages—like the one in the c. 1920 photograph below—appeared. Like the livery stable, a garage could function as a neighboring space for men. Lewis Atherton pointed out that the livery's distinctive odor of liniment and horse manure was displaced by the smell of grease and gasoline.

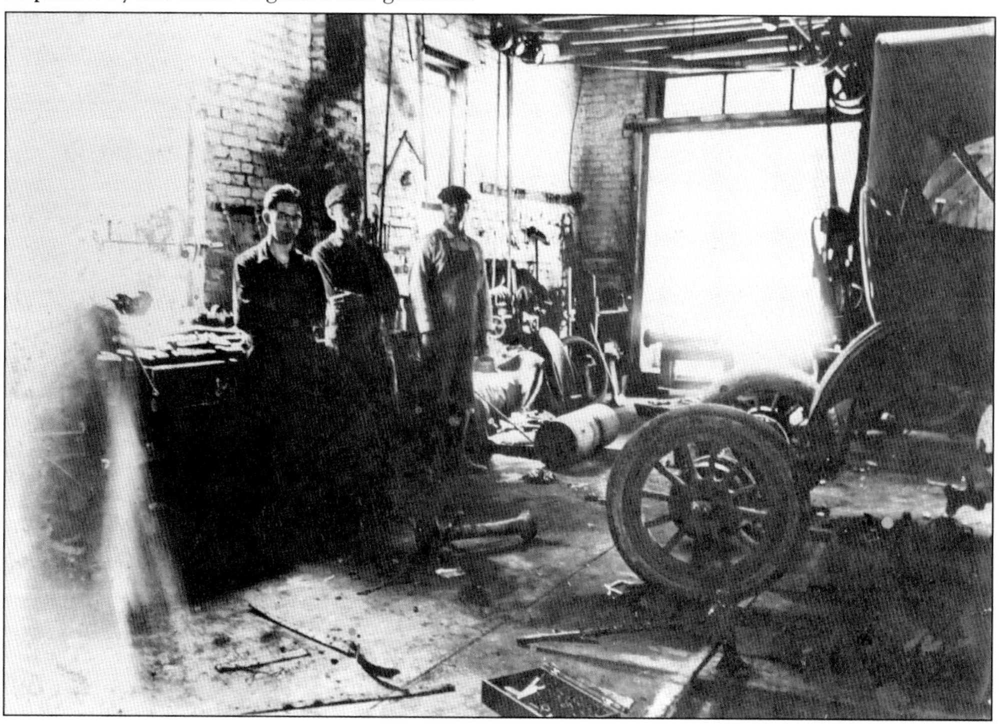

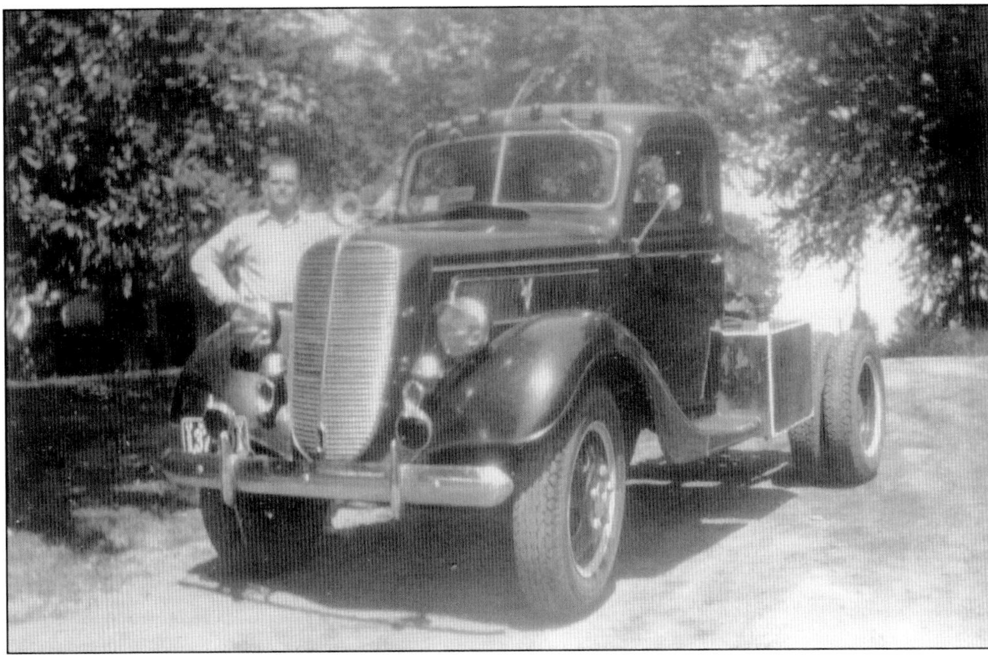

As much as the automobile replaced the horse and buggy, work trucks took the place of farm wagons. In the photograph above, Bill Herman stands beside a new truck purchased for his hauling business in 1936. The truck was built to haul trailers. In the below image, Jerry Dishman (left) and either Quentin or Vernon Dishman stand next to their truck in Cosby. The truck, a self-unloading lime spreader, was manufactured in the 1930s.

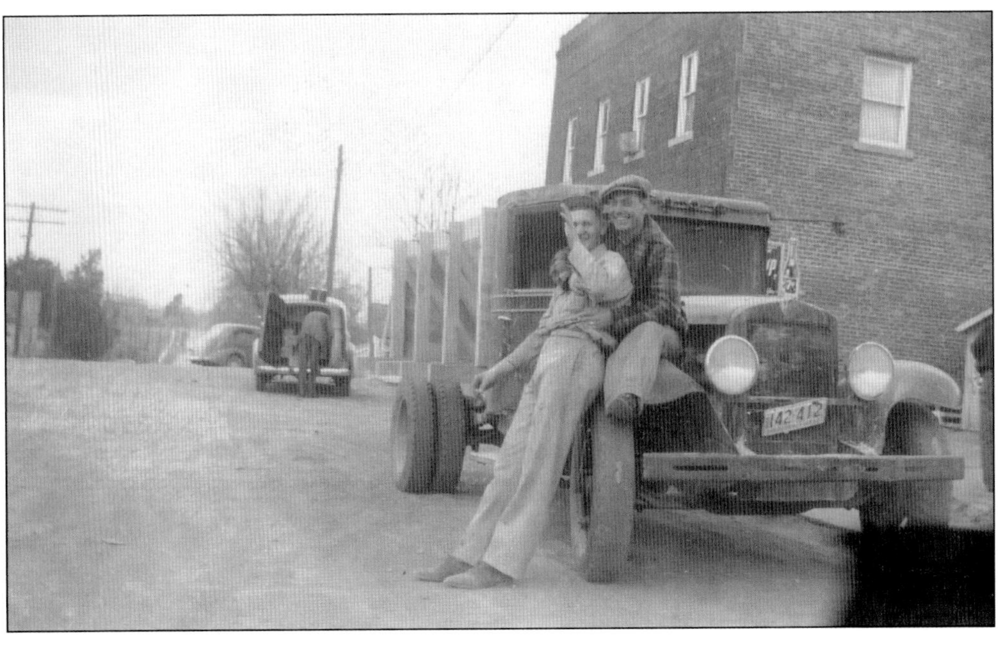

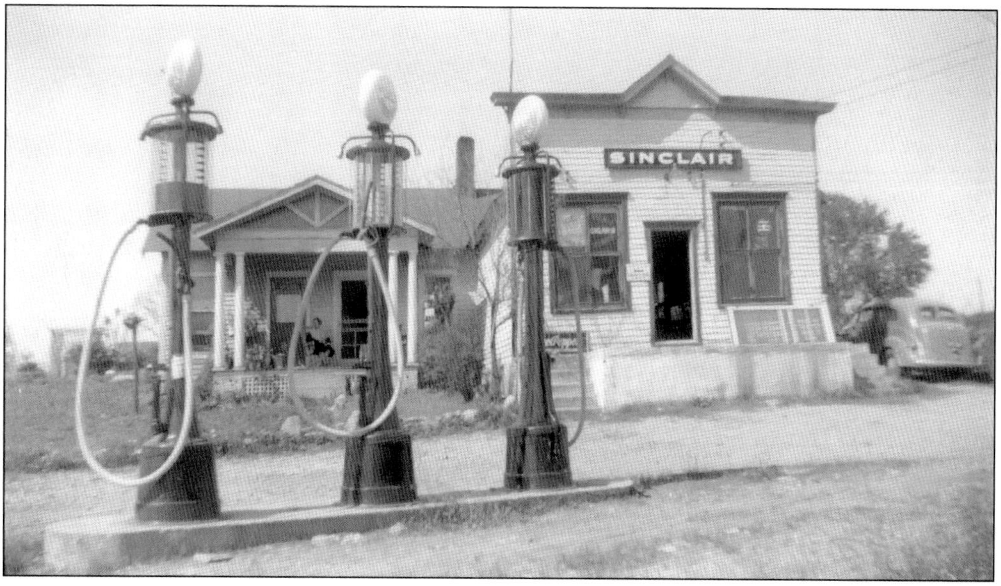

The Sinclair Gas Station and Convenience Store is pictured above in 1935. The Shop & Hop near Bolckow is seen below in 1999. The automobile altered business patterns and brought fundamental change to the rural economy. Before the automobile age, country people operated within two separate and simultaneous economic systems: a money economy and a subsistence economy. The town doctor kept a garden and perhaps raised chickens. He was equipped to accept farm goods as bartered items for his services. New cars, however, cost hard cash and hastened the shift toward a money economy. Mutual helpfulness seemed greater when it cost a person work or goods rather than money. The gas station and convenience store reflected the shift toward cash transactions—there is no "Barter & Hop" along Route 71.

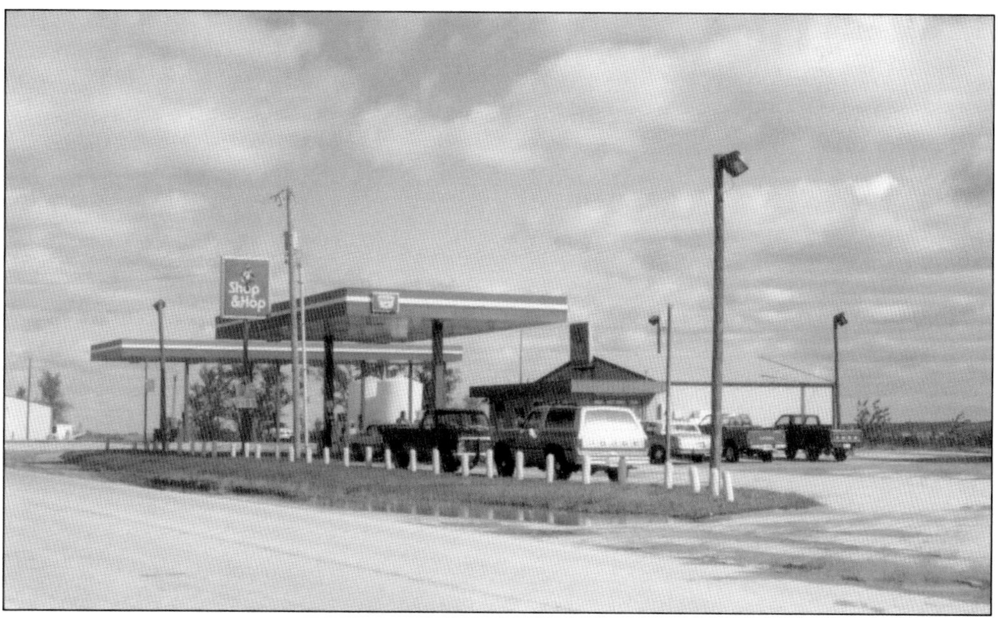

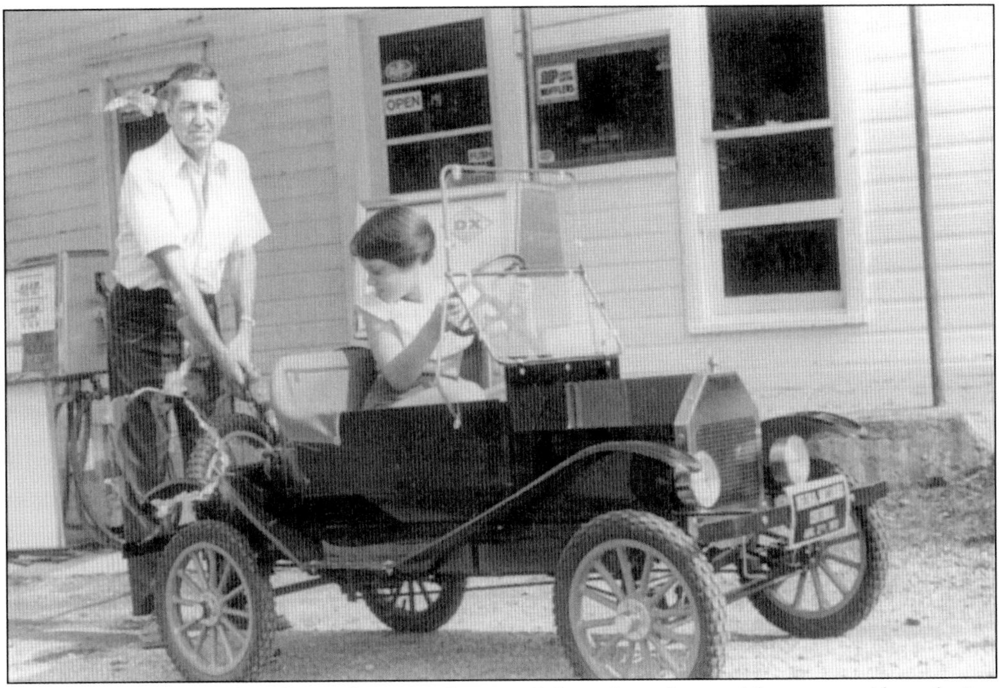

The economic and cultural significance of automobile and truck travel became evident during civic celebrations. In the above image, the daughter of John and Joan Hickman sits in a miniature antique car before participating in the Helena centennial celebration. George Clark is fueling up the vehicle. In the photograph below, a pickup truck converted into a parade float sits in front of the Amble Inn filling station.

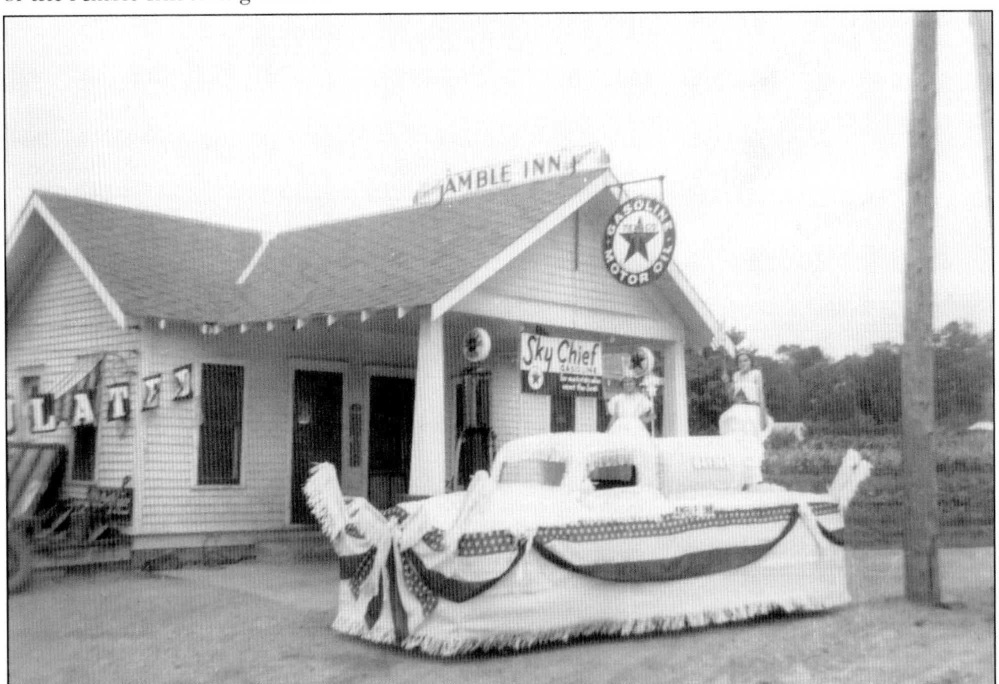

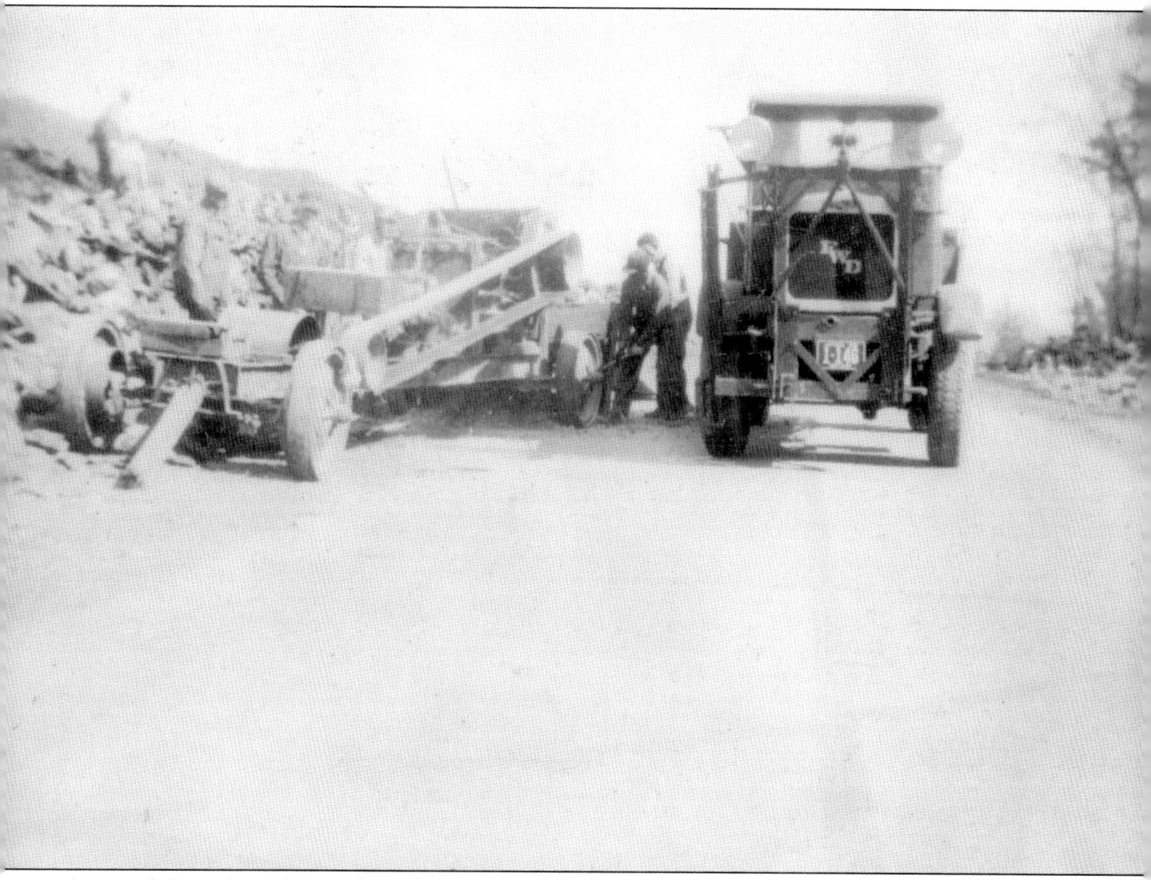

Automobile and truck travel accelerated the impact of the "good roads movement," which was launched by bicyclists in the 19th century. They argued that improved rural roads both enhanced the pleasures of cycling and provided an economic benefit to farmers. Country roads could turn into muddy bogs after rain, making travel and the transportation of farm goods difficult. In 1953, Lola Spohn Nielson recalled, "When spring came, and all the ice and frost went out of the ground, the mud was deep. The roads seemed bottomless." In the early 20th century, the Savannah newspaper ran regular features championing the goal of creating good roads. Here, highway workers with a rock crusher are improving Highway 59 around 1920.

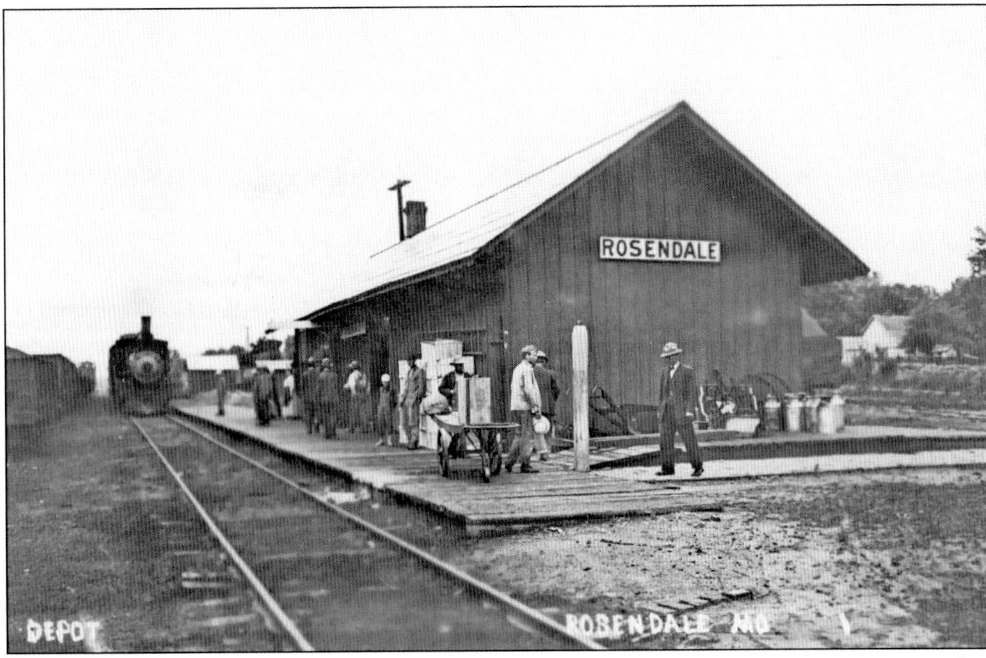

By the late 19th century, railroads were the lifeline of Andrew County, and almost every town had its own depot. The importance of depots was indicated by how often they show up on postcards. The c. 1910 postcard image above is of the Rosendale Depot. The photograph of the Nodaway Depot below is likely from the same period. A depot was a principal interface with the outside world, with both products and travelers arriving at and departing from town. The cycles of life could often be viewed on its platform. School groups took trips to the city, newlyweds left on honeymoons, and young men went to war. Most depots also contained a telegraph office, which held the instrument that one historian has dubbed the "Victorian Internet."

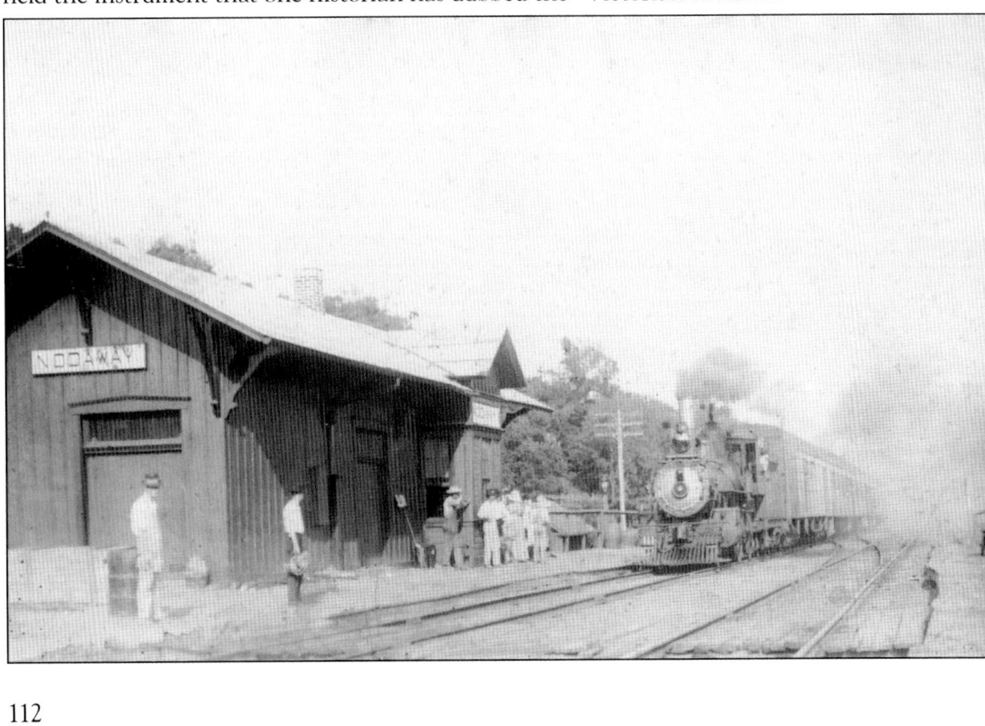

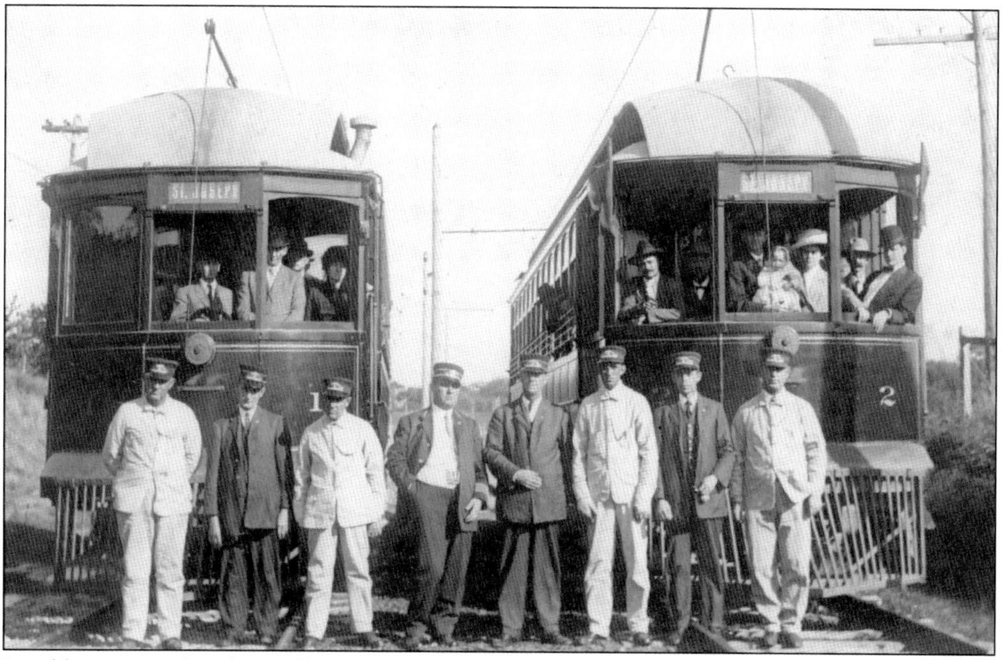

In addition to railroads, small towns were linked to larger towns and cities via interurban lines. The 1911 photograph above shows two interurban cars, and the workers who maintained them and served as conductors, shortly after trolley service began between Savannah and nearby St. Joseph. The image below is of an interurban car in the 1930s shortly before trolley service stopped in 1939. The automobiles parked along Main Street were evidence of one reason for the demise of interurban lines: people could drive the 15 miles to St. Joseph. In addition, many lines experienced financial difficulties during the Great Depression.

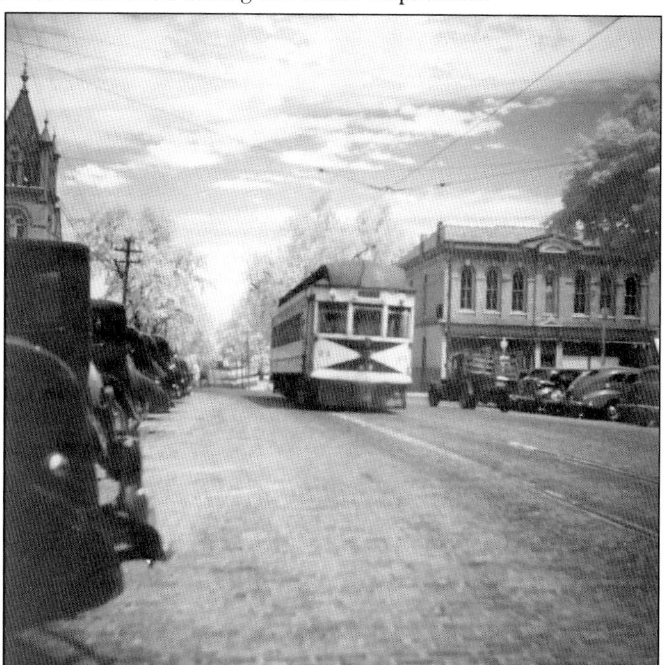

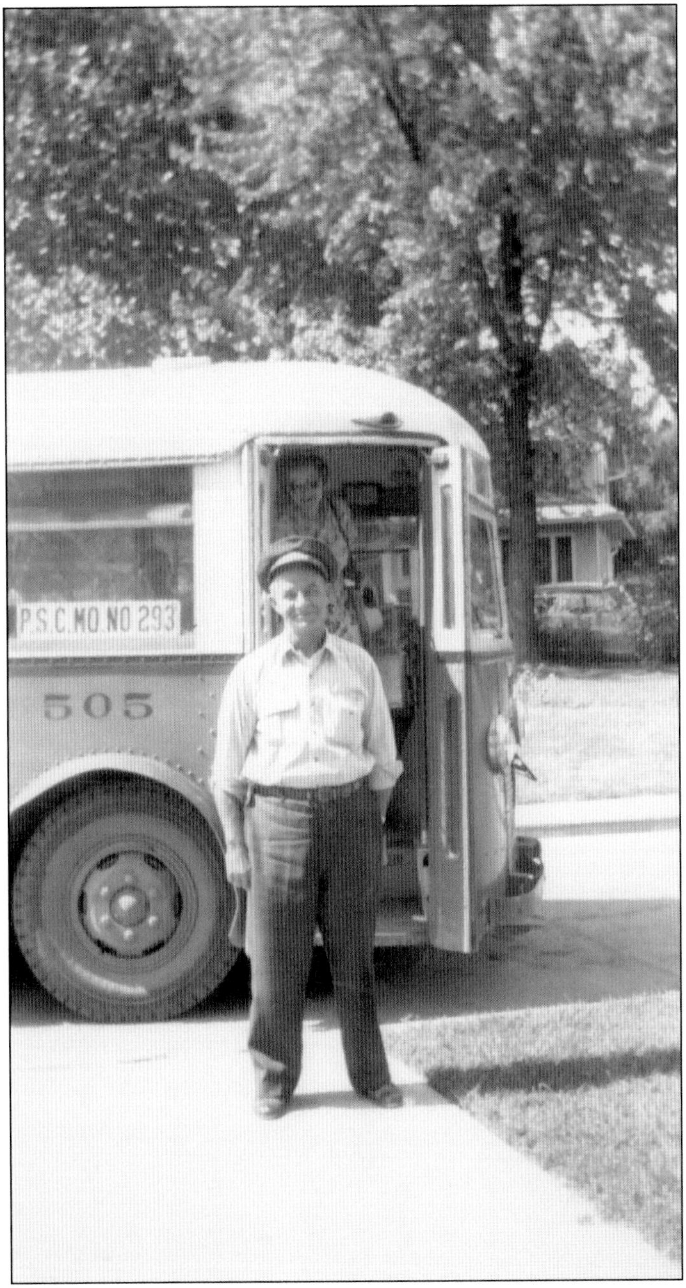

The loss of interurban service cannot be solely traced to economic hard times in the 1930s. Improved roads encouraged the replacement of trolley lines with buses. Bus service between Savannah and St. Joseph was inaugurated in 1940. This photograph of a bus driver in his uniform and cap likely dates from roughly that period. Some trolley conductors simply switched to being bus drivers. The dismantling of the interurban line in Andrew County occurred with remarkable rapidity. Tracks were torn up and bridges dismantled within months of the discontinuance of service. Ironically, regularly scheduled bus service between Savannah and St. Joseph has now gone the way of the interurbans. In the first decades of the 21st century, no public transit system has existed in Savannah. It proved easier to get from place to place 100 years ago via a trolley.

Eight

Big Times in Small Towns

Rural people enjoyed two types of entertainment: homegrown and commercially produced. Regarding the former, in 1983, Henry Bunse recalled, "We did not have radio, TV, or telephone, so for pastime we would play checkers or dominoes and read and reread the few books we had and church papers. Often in the evenings I would hold a hank of yarn while mother would wind it into a ball for knitting." Almost every town had a band, and sports teams bolstered local pride, especially when they defeated a competitor from a nearby rival community. Church suppers and pancake breakfasts at the American Legion remain staples of social life in Andrew County even in the present day.

As mentioned in the introduction, small-town audiences were not passive recipients of urban-based popular culture. Their preferences influenced the development of mass entertainment. Savannah, Fillmore, and other towns were on the Redpath-Vawter Chautauqua circuit. In 1904, impresario Keith Vawter launched his first Chautauqua circuit out of Cedar Rapids, Iowa. On the circuit, he grouped a number of nearby small towns together and offered a weeklong program of entertainment and intellectual treats. Each day's performers would rotate from town to town, presenting the same program. Local committees needed to guarantee a certain amount of ticket sales. In exchange, their community had access to a range of entertainment that they could never assemble and afford alone.

The term "Chautauqua" took its name from a summer community in upstate New York that originally served as a training ground for Sunday school teachers. It eventually broadened its appeal to the general public by offering lectures, concerts, and a range of classes in the arts. Vawter took the original concept and made it mobile. It was not surprising that his operation was sometimes labeled the "Sunday School circuit." His programs conformed to the sensibilities of his rural audiences. This chapter explores how Andrew County people enjoyed themselves with simple pleasures and also both devoured and exerted an influence on new forms of mass entertainment such as radio and television.

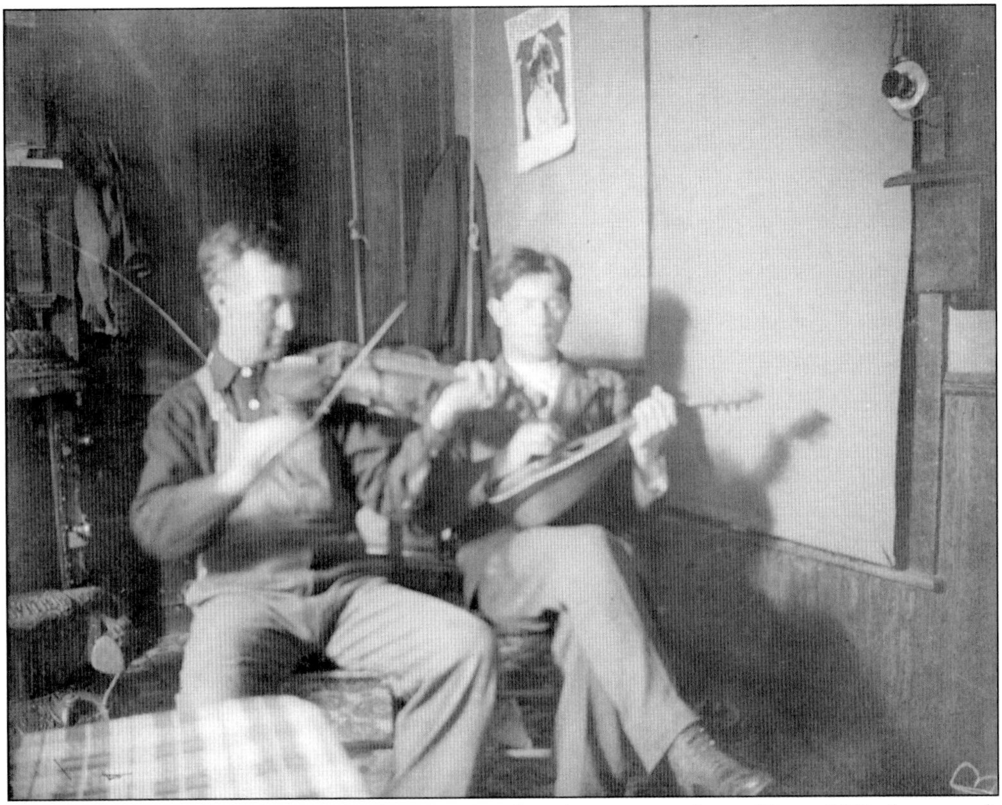

Rural people take their pleasures both indoors and in the great outdoors. The c. 1910 photograph above shows two young musicians practicing the fiddle and mandolin. They likely impressed young ladies during parlor performances. The photograph below of a group of young people on a picnic was taken around roughly the same time. In rural areas, such outings proved popular because they allowed youth to escape the prying eyes and supervision of adults.

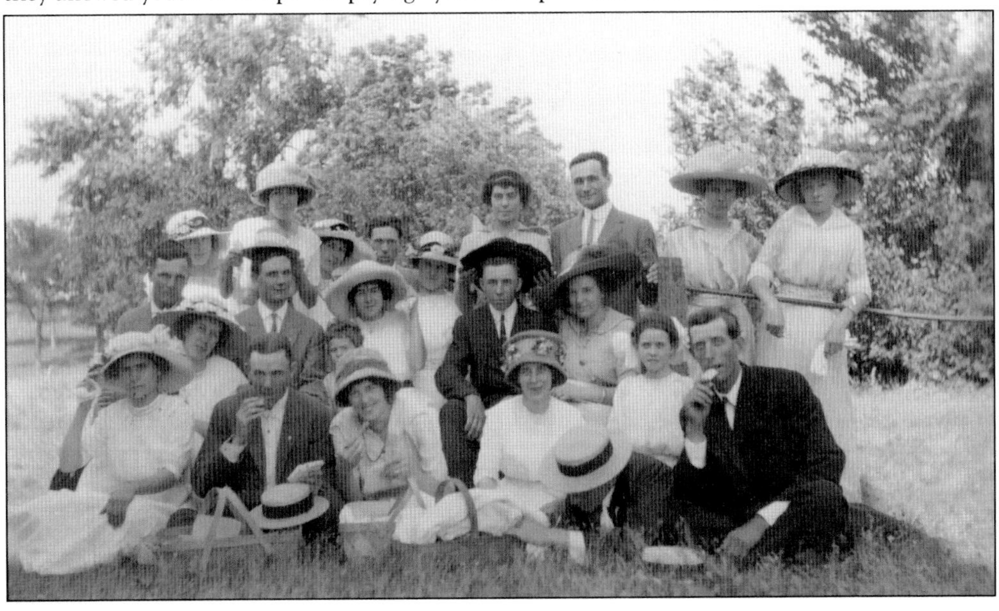

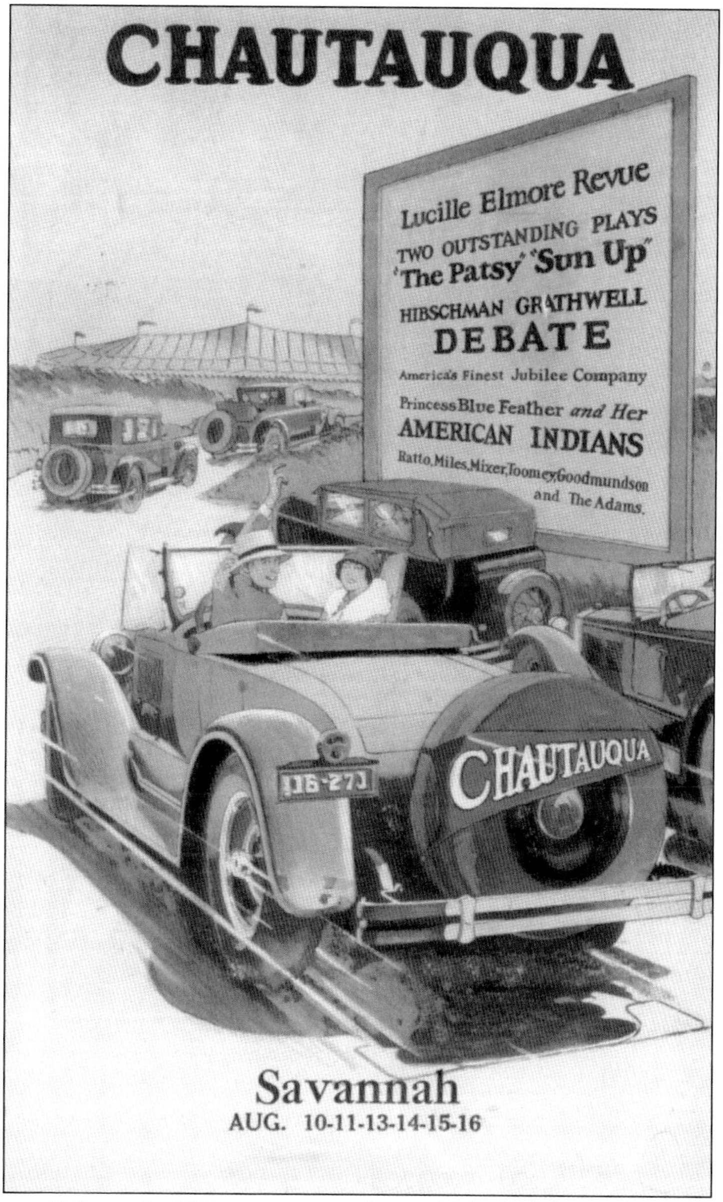

In the summers of the early 20th century, rural people looked forward to the arrival of the Chautauqua circuit. The program drew both praise and condemnation from social commentators. Supporters viewed it as a source of self-improvement in all faculties, while critics sneered that circuit organizers just sold canned culture to small-town audiences. In truth, a weeklong Chautauqua program was tremendously diverse, providing the possibility for both. According to this brochure, under the big tent at the Savannah program in 1920 the "versatile, talented young ladies" in the Columbia Players presented a "delightful mélange of melody and mirth." During the rest of the week, attendees took in lectures such as "The Great American Home" and "America's Tomorrow." They also were entertained by "one of America's greatest bands" and well-known vaudevillians. For some Chautauqua-goers, the highlight of the week might have been the Powerful Katrinka, who swallowed swords, ate fire, and was a fortune teller to boot. Spectators were assured that one of the acts presented the "most wholesome fun seen on the stage in several seasons."

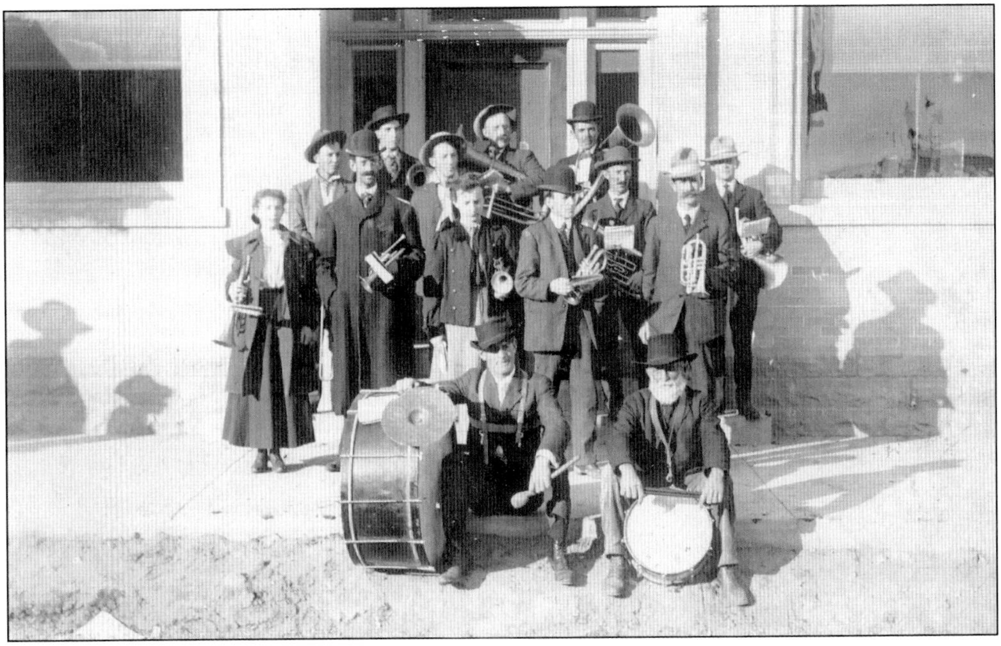

According to Lewis Atherton, the local band outranked all other musical organizations in any town. Bands furnished concerts and played at important civic events, and they performed at Fourth of July celebrations and Memorial Day processions. The c. 1908 postcard image above shows the Whitesville band, while the c. 1924 picture below is of the Rosendale band. Sometimes these homegrown musicians intersected with commercial popular culture. When the New Globe Theatre opened in 1938 and offered free showings of a movie program, a crowd estimated at 2,000 gathered on the courthouse square in Savannah. As people waited for the next showing, they were serenaded by a local band.

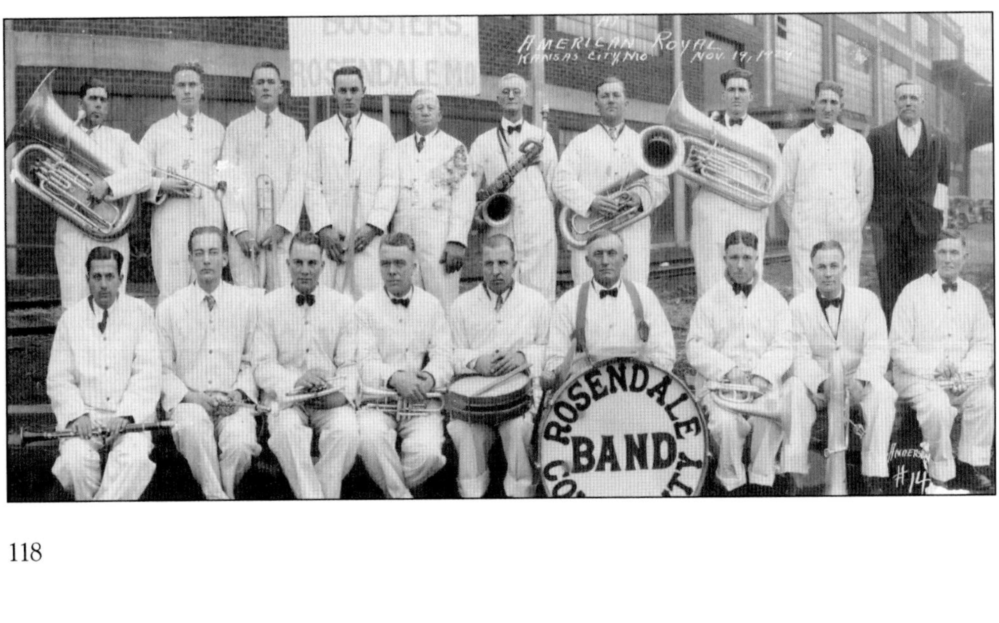

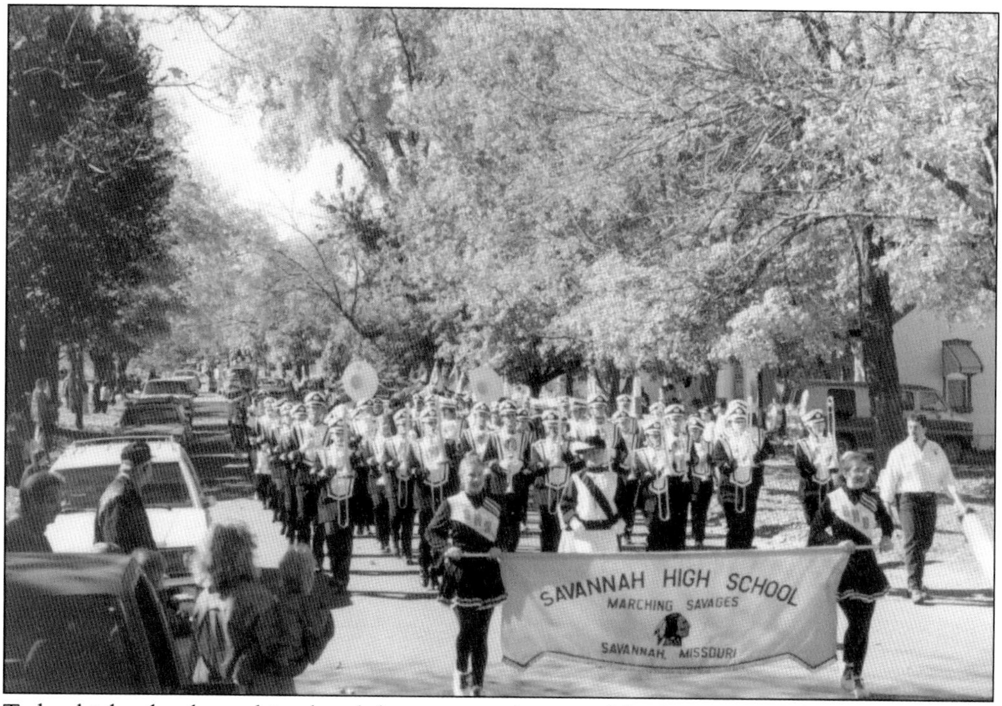

Today, high school marching bands have assumed many of the functions of the old-town bands. The Savannah High School Marching Band is pictured on Main Street during the homecoming parade in 1998. The local football team's flags still fly around the courthouse square on home-game days.

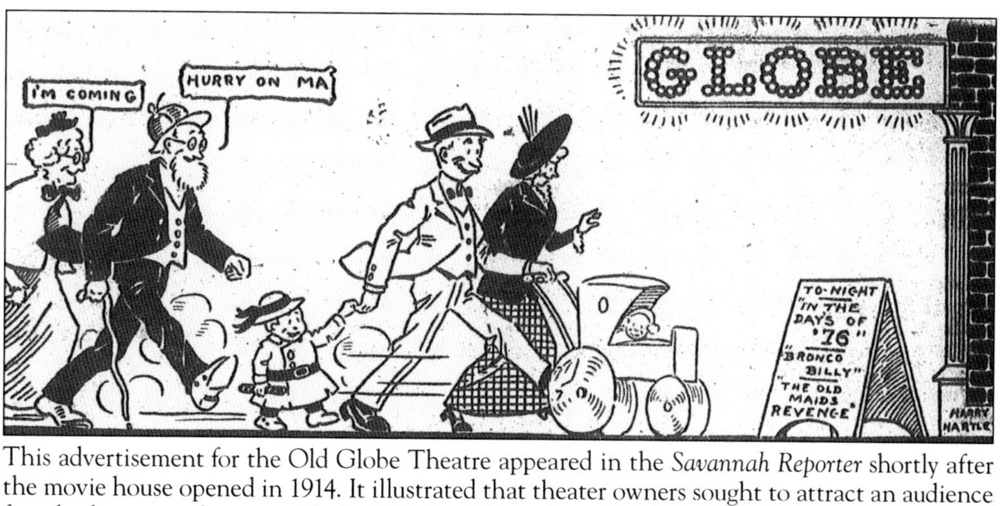

This advertisement for the Old Globe Theatre appeared in the *Savannah Reporter* shortly after the movie house opened in 1914. It illustrated that theater owners sought to attract an audience from both town and countryside. In 1976, Ina Wachtel recalled that theater manager Fred Hartley converted a store into the Globe, adding an inclined floor and a piano so that a player could "fit the mood" of the silent pictures.

November Calendar

New Globe Theatre

NEWS
Fri. & Sat.
Sun. & Mon.

No Advance in Prices Like Everything Else
Admission Still 10-20¢

MATINEES
2 o'clock
Sat. & Sun.

Owl Show 11:45, Sat.	31	"Torpedo Boat"	with	Richard Arlen Jean Parker	plus	Col. Cartoon
Sun. & Mon.,	1-2	"Footlight Serenade"	with	Betty Grable Victor Mature	plus	Cartoon-News Band Act
Tues.-Wed.-Thurs.,	3-4-5	"Eagle Squadron"		D. Barrymore Robt. Stack	plus	Merrie Melody
Fri. & Sat.,	6-7	"Drums of the Congo"	with	Stnart Irwin Ann Gwynne	plus	3 Stooges Serial-News
Sun. & Mon.,	8-9	"Talk of the Town"	with	Cary Grant Jean Arthur	plus	Looney Tune MGM News
Tues.-Wed.-Thurs.,	10-11-12	"Rio Rita"	with	Abbott and Costello	plus	Col. Cartoon Air Raid Warden
Fri. & Sat.,	13-14	"Twilight on the Trail"	with	Hopalong Cussidy Andy Clyde	plus	Col. Cartoon Comedy
Sun. & Mon.,	15-16	"Joan of Ozark"	with	Judy Canova Joe E. Brown	plus	Special in color Midway Battle
Tues. & Wed.,	17-18	"Tarzan's N.Y. Adventure"	with	M. O'Sullivan J. Weissmuller	plus	Merrie Melody Ed. Kennedy
Thursday,	19	"One Born Every Minute"	and	"Kid Glove Killer"		
Fri. & Sat.,	20-21	"A Hunting We Will Go"	with	Laurel and Hardy	plus	Donald Duck Serial & News
Sun. & Mon.,	22-23	"Sweater Girl"	with	Eddie Brecken June Preisser	plus	Band Act MGM News
Tues.-Wed.-Thurs.,	24-25-26	"Tortilla Flat"	with	Spencer Tracy Hedy Lamar	plus	Col. Cartoon
Fri. & Sat.,	27-28	"Men of Texas"	with	Robert Stack Jackie Cooper	plus	Looney Tune Serial & News
Sun. & Mon.,	29-30	"Take a Letter, Darling"	with	Rosalind Russell Fred MacMurray	plus	Col. Cartoon MGM News

COMING

"Cardboard Lover"
"In Old Kentucky"
"Sunset on Desert"
"Beyond Blue Horizon"

"Iceland"
"My Sister Eileen"
"Orchestra Wives"

"West of Tombstone"
"Are Husbands Necessary"
"Springtime in the Rockies"
"Holiday Inn"

See All The Pictures Before They Ration Gasoline

The New Globe Theatre opened in 1938. A modern movie house equipped to show talkies and color films, the New Globe carried on the tradition of attracting a broad rural audience. This flyer dates from the early 1940s based on the mention of wartime gasoline rationing. Promotional materials like this were distributed through the postal service's rural free delivery. The flyer also illustrates that theaters offered a full movie program. In addition to a feature film, theatergoers saw a newsreel, a short serial, and a cartoon.

In 1952, Joyce Miller, with her hair in rollers and wrapped in a scarf, and Wayne Reid Miller sit in front of a television. In 1994, Leola Holt Nicholas recalled when television came to Savannah, "I remember every Saturday afternoon we put out chairs around our living room here and the kids would bring popcorn and apples, and they would sit for about an hour and watch test patterns."

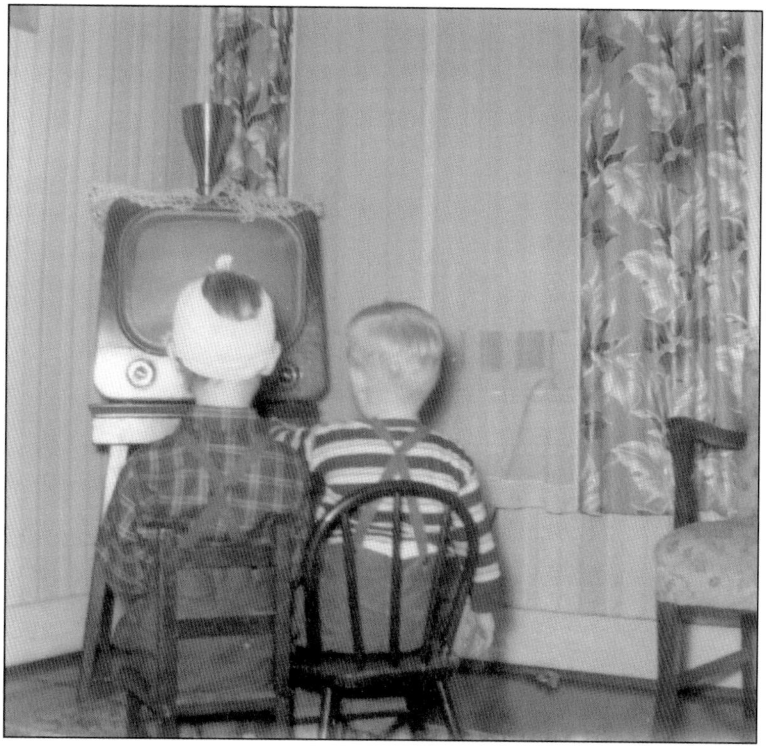

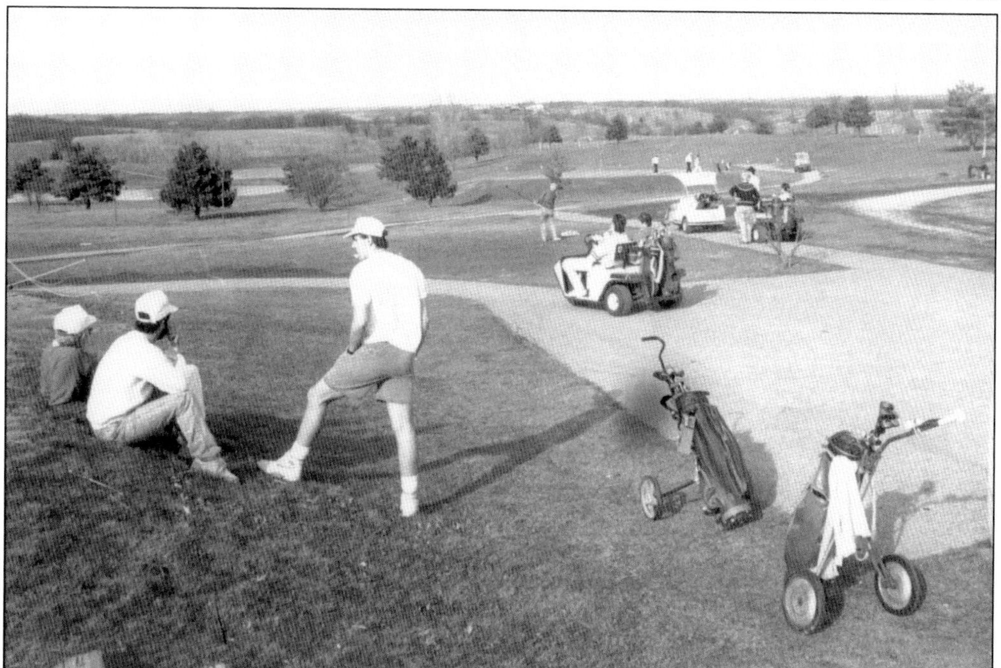

These golfers play on the public course in Savannah's Harry F. Duncan Memorial Park around 1990. Golf is among the activities that sports historians describe as becoming "democratized" over time. Originally enjoyed by those who could afford a country club membership, the building of public golf courses vastly increased the availability of the sport to average Americans.

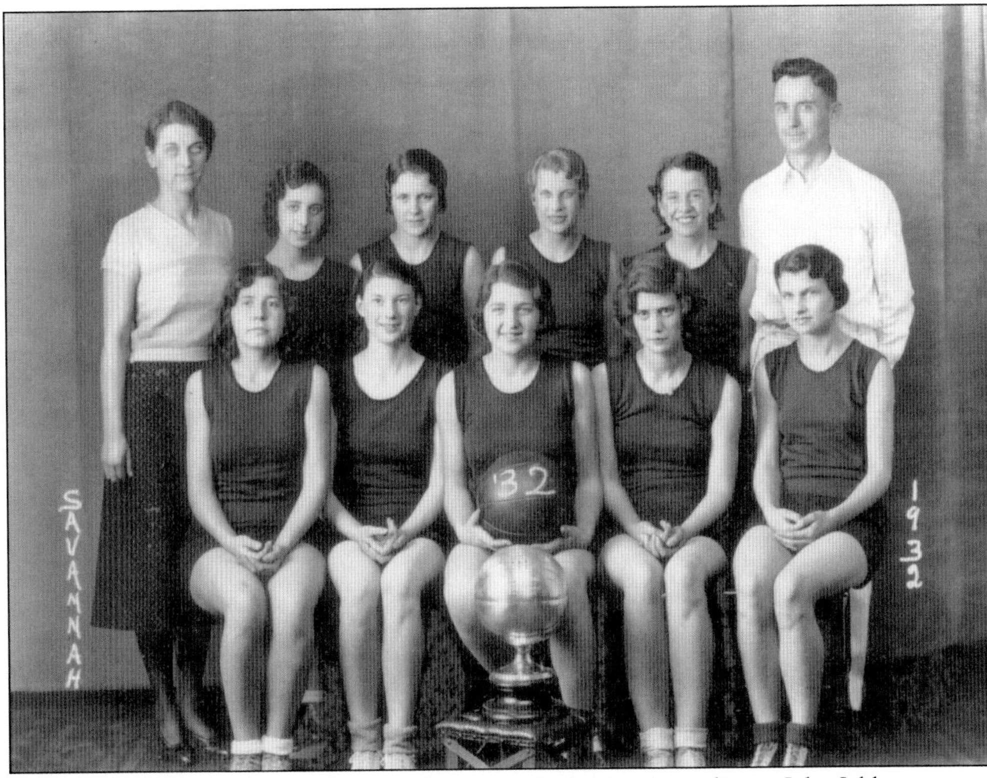

Today, public schools still contribute much to a town's identity. According to John Jakle, organized sports at the high school level "pitted small-town teams against one another in an exercise of pride." The above photograph shows the 1932 Savannah High School girls' basketball team. It might surprise modern readers to learn that images of young female athletes from small towns were not uncommon in the first half of the 20th century. Locals took pride in the accomplishments of all their offspring. The photograph below shows a women's lacrosse team around 1920.

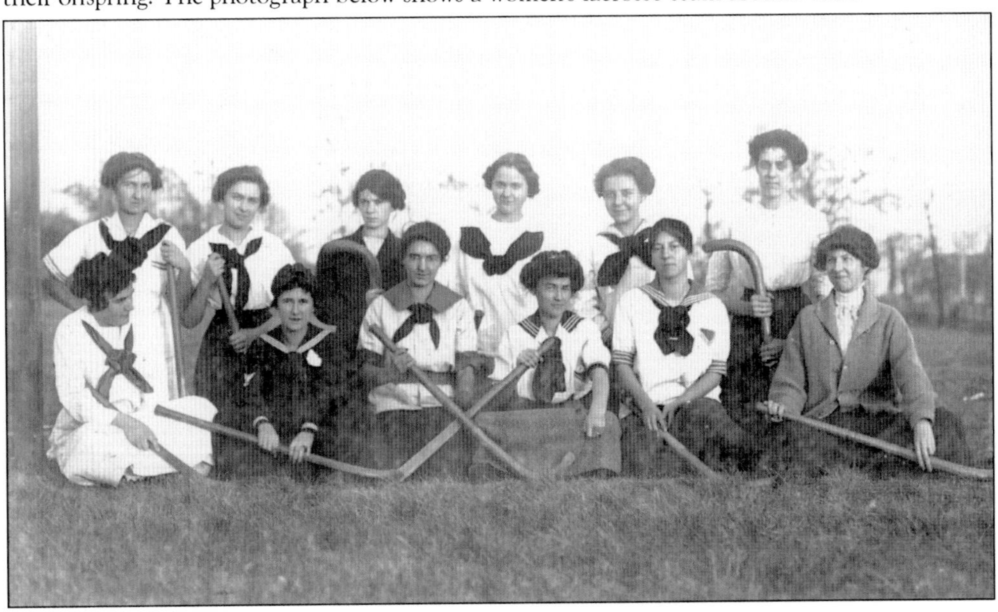

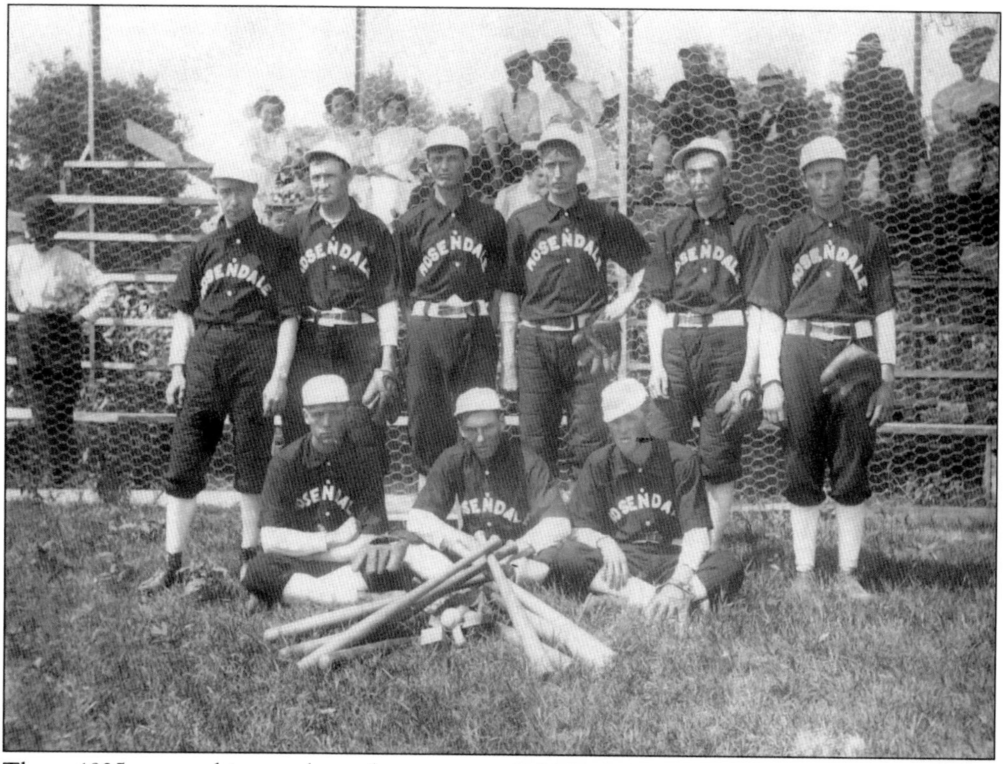

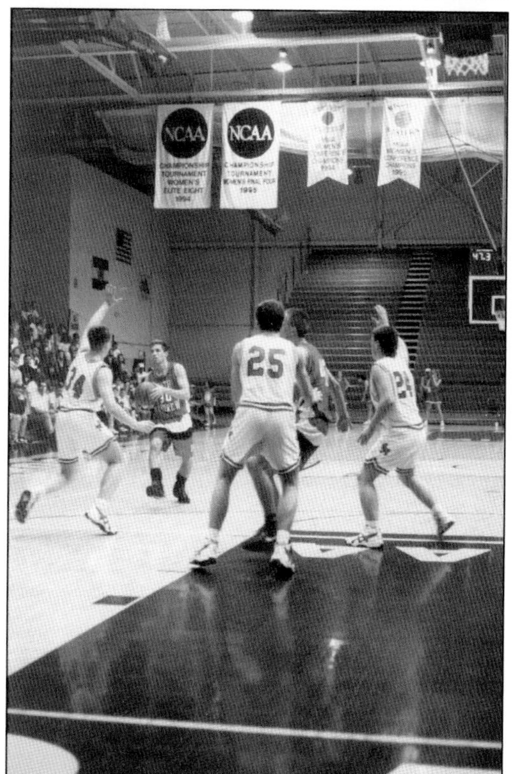

The c. 1925 postcard image above shows the Rosendale baseball team. Baseball was a big hit in Andrew County by the late 19th century, inciting competition between towns for decades. Softball fervor took over in the late 1940s, when Helena organized teams for both men and women. In the 1970s, Savannah's junior boys clinched national championships, and Fillmore's Nan Carter built Turner Field for her trophy-winning women's fast-pitch softball team. The photograph at right shows the North Andrew basketball team playing Stewartsville for the regional championship in 1997.

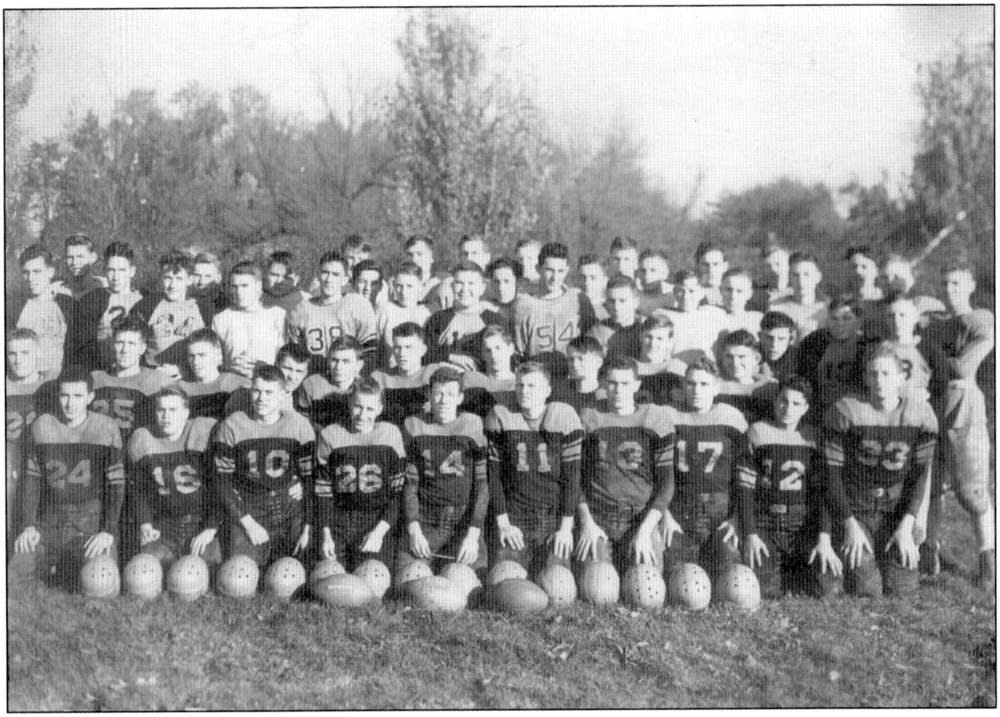

In the 1910s, football rose to prominence based on the popularity of the college game. Harry Duncan remembered, "We played a lot of football in the field in back of the school." Across the United States, town spirit became increasingly measured by support of its high school football team. This photograph shows the Savannah High team in 1946.

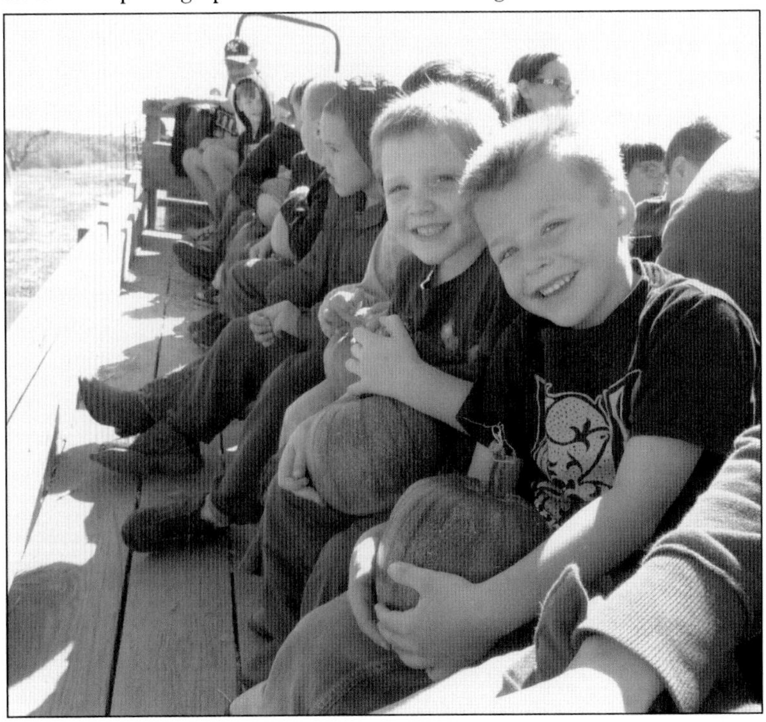

Hunt Orchard has a retail operation in Andrew County. Its popularity among residents of nearby large towns and cities testifies to continuing interest in rural lifestyles. Among the attractions are hayrides and the opportunity to pick pumpkins. In 2011, these two delighted in their take from the pumpkin patch.

Nine

City and Town

Among her observations about rural life in the early 20th century, Rosalind Richards addressed the issue of young people leaving the countryside and going to the cities. She wrote, "The drain to the cities, which robs all small places of part of their life's blood, touches us nearly; the young wings must be tried, the young feet take the road." She also recognized that the accomplishments of former hometown boys and girls were a "source of pride and strength." In the cities, they became "torch-bearers, and their light shines back to us." Their small-town experiences and values infused the "arterial system of the whole country."

Richards's perceptions are instructive. In the 20th century, urban growth was fueled from two sources: the first was emigration from outside the United States, and the second was a stream of country people migrating to the cities. Like immigrants, the latter carried cultural baggage with them from their point of origin.

Harry F. Duncan (1899–1992) never forgot his roots. When someone asked where he was from, he replied, "I'm from Savannah, Missouri." Duncan made his fortune selling bags full of small hamburgers and good cups of coffee through his chain of Little Tavern Restaurants that operated in the Washington, DC, area. He later became a benefactor for many Savannah institutions, including the Andrew County Museum.

Coming from a small town, Richards enjoyed losing herself in the anonymity of an urban crowd. By contrast, Duncan brought something of the small town to the city. In *Fast Food* (1999), historian Keith Sculle remembered his experience in Chicago "hamburger joints" while growing up. He recalled, "The eateries of my childhood were small places. Chicago had always loomed too big and dizzyingly hectic to be possible of comprehension but felt somehow accessible on a human scale in these restaurants." Duncan invited urbanites into a Little Tavern where even the hamburgers were small. He brought the human scale of Main Street into the city while shining a light back toward Savannah through his philanthropy.

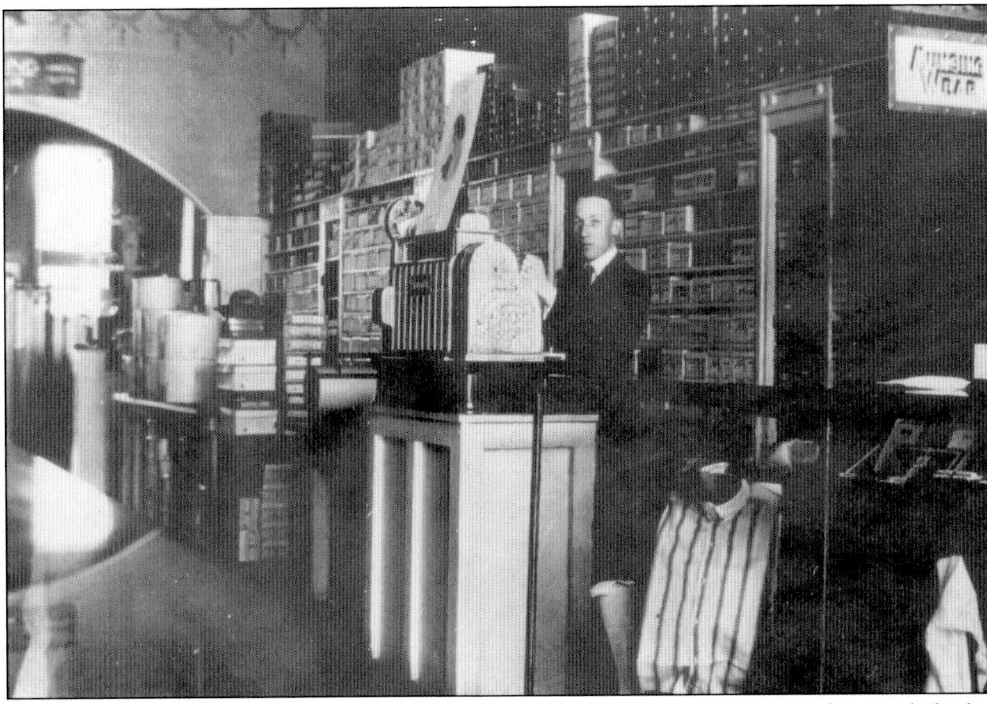

After graduating from Savannah High School in 1918, Harry Duncan started to work for his uncle Fred Becker in the Quality Shop, a men's clothing store on the Andrew County Courthouse square. He remembered, "Saturday nights everybody came to town, and that was when you were busy. On Saturday night, we would stay open as long as there was anyone on the street. I got very tired working there." A young Harry Duncan is pictured above behind the cash register at the Quality Shop. Haberdashery was not to his liking, but Duncan blossomed as a restaurateur. He poses below holding a hamburger and a trademark cup of his good coffee next to a model of one of his Little Tavern restaurants.

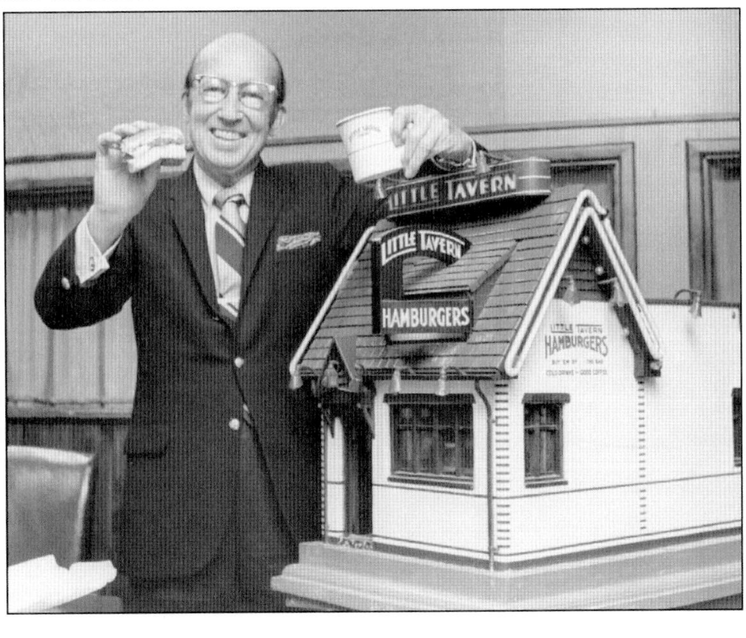

About the Organization

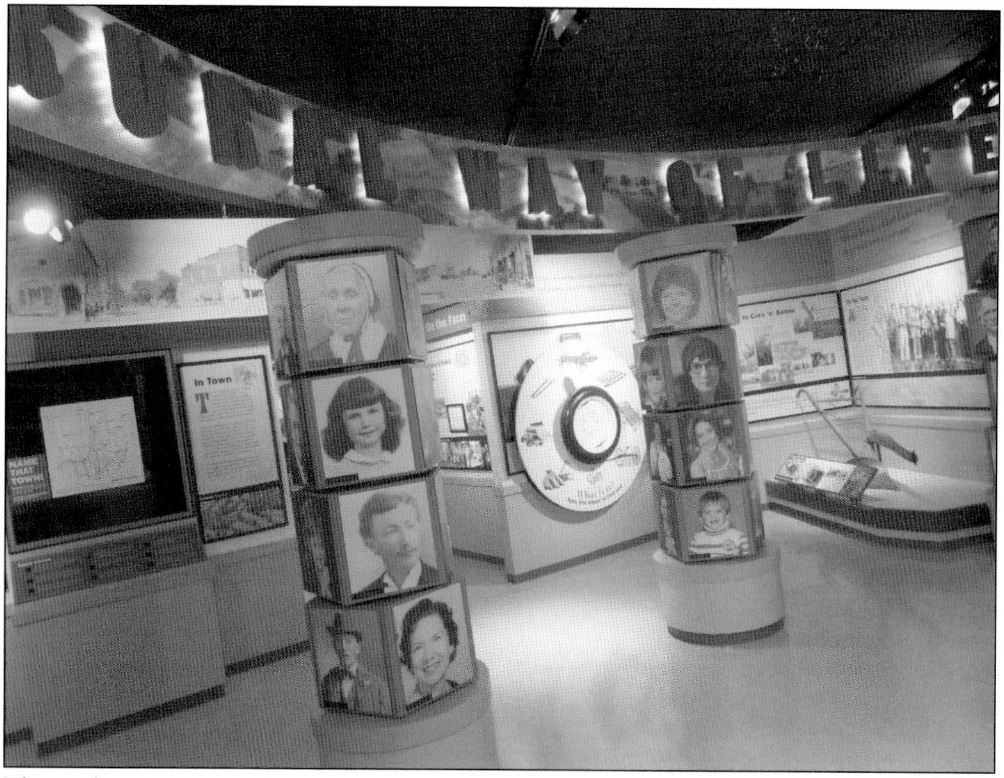

This is the entrance to the "Rural Way of Life" exhibit at the Andrew County Museum. The columns in the foreground display images of local people from the mid-19th into the 21st centuries. Their individual stories define the history of their county, as well as life on the "Middle Border." Exhibits are designed to appeal to the entire family. Visitors can enter a general store and see part of a silent film from the 1920s, and children can push a button and turn on a carousel displaying how country kitchens changed over more than a century or spin a tractor tire to identify different types of farm equipment. In short, visitors delight in learning about the rich heritage of life in town and on the farm. The museum is located at 202 East Duncan Drive in Savannah and is open Tuesdays through Saturdays from 10:00 a.m. to 4:00 p.m. To contact the museum, call (816) 324-4720. To learn about the full range of programs and research opportunities offered by the Andrew County Historical Society, visit www.andrewcountymuseum.org.